Critical Incidents

Ethical Issues in the Prevention and Treatment of Addiction

William L. White and Renée M. Popovits

Chestnut Health Systems
A Lighthouse Institute Publication

Published by the Lighthouse Institute
Bloomington, Illinois

Second Edition

Additional copies of this publication may be obtained by sending $17.95 plus $4 shipping and handling to:

Chestnut Health Systems, Inc.
Lighthouse Institute
720 West Chestnut Street
Bloomington, Illinois 61701
888-547-8271
Website: http://www.chestnut.org/li

Popovits and Robinson, P.C.
Attorneys at Law
Website: http://www.popovitslaw.com

White, William L., 1947-
    Critical incidents : ethical issues in the prevention and treatment of addiction / William L. White and Renée M. Popovits.
    p. cm.
    Includes bibliographical references and index.
    ISBN 0-938475-10-X (alk. paper)
    1. Substance abuse–Prevention–Moral and ethical aspects. 2. Drug abuse–Treatment–Moral and ethical aspects. 3. Alcoholism–Treatment–Moral and ethical aspects. I. Popovits, Renée M., 1964-   II. Title.
    HV4998 .W57 2001
    174'.2–dc21

                                                        00-065912

Dedication

This book is dedicated to the legions of workers who have carried the message of prevention and recovery without a clear set of ethical standards to guide their journey, and to those who fell by the wayside because the hazards were so poorly marked.

Acknowledgments

This book would not have been possible without the help of numerous persons. LeClair Bissel and James Royce's *Ethics for Addiction Professionals* has been a widely read resource within the field and laid an important foundation for this work. The prevention and treatment professionals who have participated in our workshops have been an important source of inspiration and encouragement. We want to acknowledge the endless hours of legal research conducted by Elizabeth Donohue, Kevin Morris, and James E. Long III. We appreciate their time, diligence and resourcefulness. We wish to thank the innumerable people who offered their comments on both editions of this work. We are also deeply appreciative of Jeanette H. Milgrom of the Walk-In Counseling Center in Minneapolis for permission to adapt some of her work on boundary issues in psychotherapy for inclusion here.

Joyce Thomas provided helpful assistance in the editing and formatting of the book.

We would also like to thank our families for making the sacrifices that allowed us the time to write this book which we believe is so important to the field.

Table of Contents

Preface

This is a book written for those who work in field of addiction treatment and allied fields. It is written for those who have dedicated their lives to the treatment of addictive disorders: the physicians, the nurses, the counselors, the outreach workers, the case managers, and other clinical support staff. It is written for the preventionists, the community organizers, the educators, the AIDS case managers, and the harm reduction specialists. It is written for those who are working with addicts in the criminal justice system, the child welfare system, the workplace and the schools. And it is written for all those whose labors support this service network: the administrators, the business office staff, the researchers, the trainers, and all the other support staff.

This book contains more than 200 "critical incidents"–ethical case studies–whose complexities will heighten your ethical sensitivities and sharpen your ethical decision-making. Each vignette is accompanied by a brief analysis and discussion of the ethical and legal issues in the situation. We don't expect readers to agree with all the points of view expressed in these analyses. The discussions are included as a way to stimulate discussion, not to define ethical standards for the field.

The greatest threat to our field comes not from changing drug trends, external regulation, or changing methods and levels of reimbursement, but from our own failure to define our work and ourselves. Ideological splits, competition, and a marked propensity for organizational isolation make it unlikely that the whole field will come together to fully back a single set of ethical standards and values. There is, however, a movement within local programs to more clearly define ethical standards and processes of ethical decision-making. This book is designed as an aid to speed the progress of this grassroots movement.

There are strong no-talk rules within the addictions field on many issues contained within this book. Such rules spring not from any orchestrated conspiracy but from the shameful sense that ethical breaches are idiosyncratic to person or organization rather than systemic. The silence is fueled by fear that open discussion of such events and issues would harm the organization and the professional field. However, these issues need sound and air and light. We hope the ethical vignettes and discussion formats set forth in this book will provide a safe vehicle for breaking this silence and heightening your level of ethical and professional practice.

The first edition of this book did not include legal annotations out of concern that the question "What is the ethical thing to do in this situation?" would be reduced to the question "What is legal?" In this latest edition, we continue to emphasize the distinction between the ethical and the legal, but we do include discussions of a wide variety of legal issues facing those who work in the prevention, intervention and treatment arenas. It is hoped these added discussions will enhance the book's usefulness.

This was a difficult book to write because the situations contained in it are our most difficult. It was difficult to write because the words depict the pain of real people. The composite vignettes —though fictional as presented—represent real situations and real clients and real workers. They represent ethical violations from the subtle to the horrific. They represent exploitations and injuries to already injured souls. They represent injuries to careers. They represent injuries to organizations and to our profession. They represent injuries to third parties and whole communities. No, they were not easy to think about nor write about. It was our belief in the importance of the subject, not the pleasure of the process that sustained our work on this project.

We welcome your comments, your criticisms, and your ideas. Correspondence can be sent to:

Bill White & Renée Popovits
Chestnut Health Systems
720 West Chestnut
Bloomington, Illinois 61701

Chapter
One

Introduction

Ethics for a New Century

An extensive network of inebriate homes, inebriate asylums, and proprietary addiction cures rose and then fell between the mid-19th and early 20th centuries. One of the significant factors in this demise was the damage to the field's professional and public credibility. That damage had resulted from ethical breaches in the field's clinical and business practices. Nearly a century later, an addiction treatment industry is again experiencing challenges that are threatening its character and its existence, and once again ethical breaches are playing a role in the field's vulnerability.

Daily reports of a crisis in the field of addiction treatment are most often framed in terms of two external threats: the restigmatization and recriminalization of addiction in America and an aggressive system of managed care that is compromising treatment accessability and quality, particularly for the growing number of disempowered, multiple-problem clients. Only the most deluded among us could deny that these ideological and financial backlashes have emerged in part out of the treatment industry's own excesses. Some of the field's leaders have begun to suggest that the field's crisis should be framed not in terms of economics but in terms of values. The field of addiction treatment is experiencing a crisis in values that calls for the field to once again find its clinical and ethical center.

Ethical and professional practice dilemmas are occurring with increasing frequency within the addictions field. Workers in a broad spectrum of roles are overwhelmed by their lack of preparation for the complex ethical issues they are facing. But as a field, ethical issues all to often fester in silence until they detonate into humiliating exposés of our personal and institutional shortcomings. Those of us on the sidelines of such explosions are prone to react with self-righteous indignation, seeing ourselves and our institutions as immune from such breaches and such falls. And yet the explosions continue, setting up the climate through which outside institutions paternalistically promulgate regulations to legislate our moral and professional conduct.

It has become painfully evident that the field has not developed a paradigm or process for ethical problem-solving nor has it developed a fully articulated set of ethical standards to guide professional practice. The field—as represented by the majority of its agencies—does not have a framework of ethical standards and ethical decision-making that can consistently protect our service consumers, our workers, our organizations and the public. This book is a call to action to fill this developmental void.

The primary goal of this text is to outline a medium through which those working within the arenas of addiction prevention, intervention, and treatment can be sensitized to recognize ethical dilemmas when they arise and to use a structured model of ethical problem-solving to respond to such situations. The book is designed to provide a safe format—a rehearsal—for the exploration of ethical dilemmas *before* workers encounter such situations in the practice of their professional roles. The stories of ethical dilemmas that make up the bulk of this book are intended to provide workers an engaging medium through which to explore their own values and enhance their own ethical decision-making abilities.

Another goal of this book is to outline a process through which standards of ethical conduct can be developed as a component of a healthy, service-oriented organizational culture. The following chapter outlines a process through which each organization can explicitly define the ethical and professional practice standards to which it and all of its members may be held accountable. The intent throughout the book will be to address ethics as both a personal-professional issue and as an organizational systems issue.

The reader will discover a work written not from the theoretical perspective of the ethicist but the practical perspective of a clinician and organizational consultant. The legal annotations are documented by the practical experience of an attorney who has represented institutional and individual addiction providers and who has served as an in-house attorney participating in agency management and business decisions. This book is predicated on the belief that ethical sensitivity and service effectiveness are inseparable and that well-defined ethics and values can empower organizations, the people who work in them, and the people served by them.

Ethical Issues in the Addictions Field: Special Concerns

There are special concerns related to ethical and professional practice issues in the addictions field that are qualitatively different than those encountered in other fields of health and human service. Such issues as the following add a special note of urgency to this book's call to action.

The Composition of the Field: Few fields can boast a work force as heterogenous as the addictions field. Few fields have ever brought within a professional umbrella individuals so diverse in terms of their age, race, culture, religion, sex, sexual orientation, education, professional training, and life experience. Such diversity is a source of vulnerability as well as a source of enrichment. The vulnerability of such diversity springs from the lack of a shared system of values guiding personal/professional decision-making and conduct. No health care field has ever existed in which so many service recipients have evolved into professional roles of service providers. This practice has raised complex ethical issues for which there are no precedents in the other helping professions.

The History and Transience of the Field: In the more traditional fields of psychiatry, psychology and social work, elaborate systems and rituals have evolved to define standards and values of professional practice and to internalize these values in new generations of professionals. The short history of the currently constituted addictions field and the high annual turnover of staff result in a daily depletion of the field's collective wisdom and expertise. High staff turnover is a wound from which bleeds all our informal systems of technology transfer, e.g., the professional values imbedded within oral history, professional etiquette transmitted through story telling, and the collective wisdom channeled through mentor relationships.

The Industrialization of the Field: While the genesis of professionalization in the field can be pinpointed with the founding of the American Association for the Study and Cure of Inebriety in 1870, the full industrialization of the field has occurred only within the last three decades. This period witnessed the legitimization of addictive disorders via their inclusion in public and private health care reimbursement systems, the rapid proliferation of addiction treatment programs, the emergence of addiction treatment services as popular and profitable business ventures, and the intensification of competition within the field. During the 1980s and 1990s, the addictions field experienced challenges to its character and its existence. Ethical abuses within the business practices of the field led to a virtual explosion of legal and regulatory controls and the emergence of system of managed behavioral health care that radically redefined who could be treated with what methods and for what length of time. For the first 100 years of our profession, ethical issues were defined primarily in terms of clinical issues. Events of the past twenty years have forced us to extend this definition to an examination of the ethical issues involved in the conduct of our business practices.

The Changing Context of Addiction: The culture of addiction in the United States changed dramatically in the closing decades of the 20th century. Increases in drug-related predatory crime and violence, the spread of HIV/AIDS and other contagious diseases among drug consumers, and the growing awareness of threats to public safety posed by drug-impaired workers all were part of the changing context of addiction in the United States. This changing context has brought infinitely complex legal and ethical issues into the prevention and treatment arenas.

Rethinking Our Assumptions about Personal and Professional Ethics

The failure to address ethical and professional practice standards rests on a foundation of unarticulated and unexamined assumptions that have long governed the practices of supervisors and managers of prevention and treatment organizations. Listed and critiqued below are nine such assumptions.

1. *Workers bring with them personal standards of morality and ethical conduct that can be relied upon to assure the ethical conduct of the agency.*

Traditional values are in great flux, due in part to the changes within the major institutions which have historically transmitted these values—the family, the extended family, the neighborhood, the church, the school and the workplace. Workers do bring standards of morality with them to the workplace, but we cannot assume what these values are. In the face of the growing heterogeneity of the culture and the workplace, organizations must take an active role in defining and reinforcing values congruent with their service missions.

2. *Workers have common sense.*

"Common" sense is the internalized wisdom that flows from cumulative experience. It springs from the discovery that lessons learned in past situations are applicable to new situations. To assume that all workers have common sense and can thus think their way through ethical dilemmas without guidance from the organization assumes that staff bring a shared body of life experience that would allow us to predict how they would respond to certain work situations. Few, if any, staff will bring life experience so broad in their diversity as to produce a body of "common sense" applicable to the range of situations presented within this book. Even where historical experience is rich, new ethical and clinical practice issues are arising for which there are no historical precedents. What is seemingly logical and "common sense" out of life experience can today be clinically inappropriate, unethical, and illegal. "Common sense" in the professional arena must be developed and nurtured rather than assumed.

3. *Workers have been trained in ethical issues and ethical standards as part of their academic and professional training.*

This assumption is particularly prevalent among persons whose own training in social work or psychology may have included a solid grounding in ethical standards and ethical decision-making. Scant attention is paid to ethical issues in the formal training of most individuals working in the addictions field. The training that does exist is often narrow in its definition of ethical issues, is prescriptive (Thou Shall Not...) rather than methodological (ethical problem-solving processes), and rarely addresses the subtlety and complexity of ethical issues currently encountered in professional practice. Persons working in non-clinical roles have usually had no orientation to the kinds of ethical issues that can be encountered in the addictions field.

4.   *There is no need for the agency to concern itself with ethical standards development because workers are bound by ethical codes tied to their professional certification/licensure.*

There are numerous problems with this assumption. Not all workers are certified or licensed or even hold positions or roles for which certification or licensure is available. Professional staff may be affiliated with numerous certification/licensure bodies, each of which has a separate code of ethical conduct. Many codes of ethics are abstract statements of aspirational values or principles which workers—without significant training and experience—may not be able to operationalize in complex, real life situations.

5.   *Ethical dilemmas are concerns for those staff in counseling roles.*
6.   *Ethical dilemmas are personal/professional issues, not an institutional issue.*

Discussions of ethical conduct in the addictions field have focused almost exclusively on clinical conduct. Ethical standards rarely address ethical issues involving other roles (administrative, fiscal, clerical, maintenance, prevention, transportation, education, consultation, research). Ethics must be extended beyond its application to a discipline or a role to the arena of organizational culture. Ethics is an institutional issue.

7.   *Workers who violate ethical principles are bad people. If we hire and retain good people, we will be assured of ethical conduct. Persons who violate ethical principles (since they are bad people) should be extruded from the agency/profession.*

This assumption is based on the belief that the etiology of all ethical breaches is psychopathy. There are predatory individuals who, in health and human service systems as with any system they are in, systematically exploit the environment and the people with whom they come into contact. There are persons who lack the knowledge, judgment and personal integrity to effectively work in a professional helping role. It is our institutional responsibility to keep such persons from working in our agencies and to exclude such individuals when they are identified. There are, however, numerous instances when ethical breaches are not made by bad people, but by good people who have historical patterns of both competence and personal integrity. Ethical breaches can reflect knowledge and skill deficiency, an ambiguity or conflict in agency policies, environmental stressors such as excessive overload, or the personal impairment of a worker. However, where systemic issues exist which compromise the ability of staff to act ethically, the extrusion of individual staff for ethical breaches constitutes a process of scapegoating that individualizes what is, in essence, a problem within the organizational environment.

8.   *A high caliber of professional and ethical conduct is assured because of the values and skills of our supervisors who place great emphasis in this area.*

The ability of supervisors to set (via role modeling) and monitor (via clinical and administrative supervision) high standards of ethical and professional conduct is a crucial aspect of assuring ethical conduct within the addiction treatment agency. The question is whether there are ingrained values and standards of conduct that transcend the presence of the unique individuals who hold supervisory roles within the agency. Are agency ethics merely a reflection of the personal/professional ethics of key supervisors? If key supervisors left the agency, would the nature of ethical conduct at the agency change as a result? There must be organizational values to guide professional practice that transcend the unique characteristics of persons occupying key organizational roles.

9.   *If workers get in trouble (encounter a difficult ethical or professional practice issue), they'll ask for help. If we as supervisors and managers don't hear about ethical conflicts, there must not be any.*

Workers may fail to bring ethical issues to supervision because they either fail to identify ethical dimensions of their work or they think that raising such issues would reflect negatively on their professional knowledge and competence. Unless there are permissions and procedures to address ethical issues within the framework of supervision, supervisors are left unaware of such issues until they detonate. What does it mean if no one is raising ethical issues within the day-to-day operation of the organization? No news is bad news.

Toward the Goal of Ethical Sensitivity

Ethics must be addressed as a personal-professional issue. This book calls for the development in the substance abuse field of what Biggs and Blocker (1987) have called "ethical sensitivity." Ethical sensitivity is the ability to step outside oneself and perceive the complexities of a situation through the needs and experiences of the client, the agency, allied institutions and the public. It is the ability to project the potential consequences of one's action or inaction on these various parties. It is the ability to recognize when one is in ethical terrain. It is the ability to identify and analyze the precise ethical issues involved in a particular situation and to isolate and articulate conflicting duties. It is the ability to weigh the advantages and disadvantages of various actions and to formulate ethically appropriate resolutions to complex situations.

Systemic Approaches to Professional Practice Issues

Ethics must be addressed as a systemic issue. A comprehensive approach to promoting high standards of ethical conduct within an organization requires interventions at multiple levels. Such interventions and levels are reflected in the following checklist that can serve as an inventory of strategies to promote an ethical organizational culture.

Knowledge & Skills

Yes No

_____ _____ Are education, experience and certification/licensure requirements for positions within the agency set at such a level as to increase the likelihood that staff have prior knowledge and skills in ethical decision-making?

_____ _____ Have ethical issues been addressed within the in-service training schedule, not just as a special topic, but integrated as a dimension to be addressed across all training topics?

_____ _____ Are there opportunities for staff at all levels to explore ethical issues with other professionals within and outside the organization?

_____ _____ Does the organization have access to outside technical expertise for consultation on complex ethical-legal issues?

Ethical Standards

Yes No

___ ___ Does the organization have a code of professional ethics integrated within its personnel policies or corporate compliance program?

___ ___ Have staff had the opportunity to participate in the development or episodic review of the professional practice standards?

___ ___ Are the ethical standards and values written with sufficient clarity and discussed sufficiently to allow their application in daily problem-solving?

___ ___ Are violations of ethical conduct addressed immediately and consistently?

___ ___ Could staff, if asked, define the core values of the agency?

Organizational Culture

Yes No

___ ___ Are ethical issues raised within the context of employee hiring and new employee orientation?

___ ___ Do organizational leaders talk about ethical issues in their communications with staff?

___ ___ Is adherence to ethical and professional practice standards a component of the performance evaluations of all staff?

___ ___ Does ethical conduct constitute a core value of the organization as reflected in agency history and mythology, the designation of heroes and heroines, agency literature, storytelling, symbols and slogans?

___ ___ Are rituals built into the cycle of organizational life that help identify practices that undermine or deviate from aspirational values and which provide opportunities to celebrate and recommit ourselves to those values, e.g., staff meetings, retreats, planning processes?

___ ___ Are there mechanisms in place through which organizational leaders can identify and rectify environmental stressors (role overload, role conflict, etc.) that can contribute to poor ethical decision-making?

    ___ ___ Does the organization have an active employee assistance program that addresses areas of personal impairment that could affect the ethical judgement and conduct of staff?

Ethical Decision-making

Yes No

    ___ ___ Have staff have been oriented to the multiple parties whose interests must be reviewed in ethical decision-making?

    ___ ___ Does the organization have a clear mechanism for reporting and investigating ethical violations?

    ___ ___ Are the forums clearly defined within which ethical issues can be explored, e.g., individual supervision, team meetings?

Ethical Violations

Yes No

    ___ ___ Are the potential consequences of breaches of ethical conduct clearly defined and communicated to staff?

    ___ ___ Does the organization have a clear mechanism for reporting and investigating ethical violations?

    ___ ___ Are the procedures through which ethical violations are addressed at the agency clearly defined and communicated to staff?

How to use this Book

As an introductory text, this book has been written for many distinct audiences within the addictions field.

If you perform professional, technical or supportive roles in an addiction treatment program, you will find in Chapters Three through Eight a large menu of critical incidents which can serve as a medium for the self-exploration and study of ethical issues in the field.

If you perform a specialty role within the addictions field, you will find in Chapter Nine a selection of critical incidents that relate to such specialty areas as prevention, early intervention (employee assistance, student assistance), outreach, training, consultation and research.

If you are a manager or supervisor, you will find in Chapter Two detailed instructions on how to develop and implement an agency Code of Professional Practice and Corporate Compliance Program. Additionally, Chapter Three provides a discussion of ethical issues related to business practices within the field, and Chapter Seven discusses ethical issues in supervision.

If you are a training specialist within the addictions field, we encourage you to incorporate the critical incident format of this book into the design of your workshops on ethical and professional practice issues within the field.

A Review of Ethical Values

The judgment of an act to be ethical or unethical depends upon the values and principles utilized to judge the act. In the analysis of critical incidents in this book, there are a number of values and principles that were used to explore the nature of ethical issues in various situations. These ethical values and principles, imbedded for centuries within ethical codes of conduct, include the following.

Autonomy (Enhance freedom of personal destiny.)
Obedience (Obey legal and ethically permissible directives.)
Conscientious Refusal (Disobey illegal or unethical directives.)
Beneficence (Help others.)
Gratitude (Pass good along to others.)
Competence (Be knowledgeable and skilled.)
Justice (Be fair, distribute by merit.)
Stewardship (Use resources judiciously.)
Honesty and Candor (Tell the truth.)
Fidelity (Don't break promises.)
Loyalty (Don't abandon.)
Diligence (Work hard.)
Discretion (Respect confidentiality and privacy.)
Self-improvement (Be the best that you can be.)
Nonmaleficence (Don't hurt anyone.)
Restitution (Make amends to persons injured.)
Self-interest (Protect yourself.)

There may also be cultural values of particular communities through which ethical decisions should be filtered. The forthcoming discussions will illustrate the application of such principles and how we should respond to situations where these values are in conflict, e.g., when telling the truth may hurt someone.

A Note on the Relationship Between Ethics and Law

There are important distinctions between the question of whether a particular course of action is ethical and whether that same course of action is legal. Thompson (1990) has identified six different relationships between ethics and law. A course of action could be:

1. Ethical and legal.
2. Ethical and illegal, in the case of breaking an unjust law.
3. Ethical and alegal, in a case where no law applies.
4. Unethical and legal, in the case of complying with an unjust law.
5. Unethical and illegal, in the case of breaking a just law.
6. Unethical and alegal, in the case of committing an unethical act that is not legally prohibited.

The primary purpose of this text is the exploration of ethical issues and professional practice values in the addictions field. Legal annotations have been added to this new edition to show the interface between ethical and legal issues.

A Note on Legal Annotations

The legal annotations are intended to provide a framework for analysis of certain key legal issues surfacing in the vignettes. Due to space constraints and readability of this text, not all of the vignettes will have a legal commentary and not all annotations will include a comprehensive analysis.

A legal analysis depends upon the specific facts and circumstances of each situation; laws, regulations and caselaw in existence at a particular point in time; and the applicable legal mandates of a specific jurisdiction. Because those laws change from time to time and vary from state to state, and because additional facts may alter a legal outcome, the legal annotations should not be construed as legal advice and only should be used for educational purposes. We recommend that you consult your legal counsel for advice on ethical/legal/clinical issues for which you believe legal consequences or implications may arise. In an effort to keep the legal research as current as possible, on an annual basis, the attorneys at Popovits & Robinson will update significant changes in the law impacting the analysis of the vignettes contained in this book. This update will be posted annually in February on the law firm's web site: www.popovitslaw.com.

In general, the legal commentary throughout the book is designed to assist the reader in:

1. Identifying certain legal issues intertwined in the ethical decision-making process;
2. Posing questions you should ask of your lawyer, if you consult one;
3. Recommending strategies to minimize liability (both personally and for your agency);
4. Addressing common questions related to legal structures and corporate practices;
5. Highlighting legal trends and hot enforcement issues; and
6. Raising issues of conflict, either within the law, between the law and ethics or among the parties (the potential winners and losers of the situation as further discussed in Chapter 2).

It is our hope that these legal annotations will provide a more comprehensive approach to the ethical decision-making process and facilitate additional guidance for clinicians and/or agencies to know when they are close to or have crossed that legal line.

Chapter
Two

The Code of Professional Practice

What is a Code of Professional Practice?

A Code of Professional Practice (CPP) is an explicitly defined set of beliefs, values and standards that guide organizational members in the conduct of activities in pursuit of the agency's mission. The code articulates values to which organizational members should aspire in the performance of their duties. The code defines boundaries of appropriate and inappropriate conduct. The code sets forth guidelines to be used by staff to guide them through difficult and complex situations encountered in the performance of their roles. The code provides a framework through which relationship boundaries can be defined and monitored. The code is a framework for day-to-day decision making within the organization.

What purposes are such codes designed to achieve?

1. The CPP is designed to protect the health and safety of, and promote the quality of services provided to, service consumers.

2. The CPP is designed to enhance public safety.

3. The CPP is designed to protect the integrity and reputation of individual agency staff members.

4. The CPP is designed to protect the integrity and reputation of the agency.

5. The CPP is designed to embed high standards of ethical and professional conduct within the culture of the organization.

Are all employees of the organization bound by the standards set forth in the code?

This question marks an important distinction between a professional code of ethics and an agency code of professional practice. A professional code of ethics is a set of standards that dictates who, when, where, how and under what conditions one can claim adherence to and practice a profession. Such codes are usually tied to licensure or certification by an independent body. Such codes transcend parochial concerns of a given agency and do not apply to any person outside the professional classification. In contrast, a Code of

Professional Practice is a set of standards to which all members of an organization are bound, regardless of the individual codes of ethics to which staff may be accountable via their professional specialties. Codes of ethics shape standards of practice within professional specialties; codes of professional practice shape values and standards of practice within organizations. The CPP flows out of the recognition of the ethical dimensions in the relationship between the client and the organization. Administrators, board members, clerical staff, maintenance staff, counseling staff, volunteers, and interns—all organizational members—are bound by the standards set forth in the CPP.

Why is there a need for a CPP? Shouldn't professional codes of ethics be sufficient in setting ethical standards of professional conduct?

Some of the conditions that have contributed to the desirability of Codes of Professional Practice include the following:

- The proliferation of academic and non-academic counselor training programs has resulted in a greater number of persons not professionally licensed and/or not bound by a code of ethics as a condition of their vocational role.
- There are many job functions in human service agencies that fall outside the realm of professional codes of ethics, such as administrators, planners, marketing and public relations specialists, clerical staff, billing clerks, outreach workers, case managers, aides, educators, preventionists, trainers, consultants, researchers, drivers, or maintenance personnel?
- Codes of ethics can guide the conduct of individual professionals, but they contribute little to the development of a strong organizational culture through which *all* members *share* values related to standards of professional practice.

Our agency is considering implementing a Corporate Compliance Program, how does this relate to the CPP?

A Corporate Compliance Program, in its simplest terms, is an ongoing comprehensive strategy to ensure an organization consistently complies with all applicable laws and regulations relating to its business activities. As such, the Compliance Program must:

- Evaluate the organization's business activities and any associated risks;
- Educate those persons in jobs having a material impact on processes

relating to compliance;

- Include auditing and reporting functions designed to measure program effectiveness and to implement problem solving actions as quickly and as efficiently as possible; and
- Contain enforcement and disciplinary components which ensure that employees understand and act upon their compliance responsibilities.

There are two basic components of a Compliance Program: structural and substantive. The structural component is the framework and essential elements of a program, including the components set forth in the Federal Sentencing Guidelines, United States Sentencing Commission, Guidelines Manual, Section 8A1.2, (Nov. 1998). The seven keys elements of those Guidelines are as follows:

1. **Written Policies and Procedures:** The organization must have established compliance standards and procedures to be followed by its employees and other agents that are reasonably capable of reducing the prospect of criminal conduct. (To satisfy this element, a comprehensive Code of Ethics is recommended.)

2. **High Level Responsibility:** A specific individual(s) within high-level personnel of the organization must have been assigned overall responsibility to oversee compliance with such standards and procedures.

3. **Due Diligence:** The organization must have used due care not to delegate substantial discretionary authority to individuals whom the organization knew, or should have known through the exercise of due diligence, had a propensity to engage in illegal activities.

4. **Educational Programs and Communication:** The organization must have taken steps to communicate effectively its standards and procedures to all employees and other agents, such as requiring participation in training programs or by disseminating publications that explain in a practical manner what is required.

5. **Employee Reporting Mechanism and Monitoring/Auditing:** The organization must have taken reasonable steps to achieve compliance with its standards, such as utilizing monitoring and auditing systems reasonably designed to detect criminal conduct by its employees and other agents and by having in place and publicizing a reporting system whereby employees and other agents could report criminal conduct by others within the

organization without fear of retribution.

6.   **Discipline and Enforcement:** The standards must have been consistently enforced through appropriate disciplinary mechanisms including, as appropriate, discipline of individuals responsible for the failure to detect an offense. Adequate discipline of individuals responsible for an offense is a necessary component of enforcement; however, the form of discipline that will be appropriate will be case specific.

7.   **Response and Correction:**   After an offense has been detected, the organization must have taken all reasonable steps to respond appropriately to the offense and to prevent further similar offenses – including any necessary modifications to its program to prevent and detect violations of law.

The Federal Sentencing Guidelines outlined above set forth the elements that are considered determinative of an effective Compliance Program and considered when an organization is sentenced in connection with a violation of federal law. It should be noted that violations resulting in criminal sentencing could also include exclusion of sentenced individuals/corporations from the Medicaid or Medicare programs.

The substantive component of a Compliance Program is the specific body of law (such as fraud and abuse associated with billing practices) with which the entity strives to comply. Therefore, a program must possess a sufficient framework on which to base its compliance goals, and these compliance goals must be thoroughly and consistently understood by the employees of the organization in order to be effectively implemented.

The Corporate Compliance Program and the CPP are related because both focus on a code of conduct for employees and reinforce guidelines for ethical and lawful behavior.

How can we integrate the CPP and a corporate compliance program?

A code of ethics, or better yet, a CPP could constitute one of the essential elements of a Corporate Compliance Program. Reducing the prospect of criminal conduct in an organization requires more than implementing a policy. An organization must articulate to all of its employees its expectations that employees will abide by applicable laws and provide guidance on the organization's definition of ethical conduct and behavior. Thus, the CPP in this case would not only provide the ethical framework within which employees would operate, but also place employees on notice that they will be held accountable for abiding by the CPP standards, including applicable laws. The CPP can be an integral part of a Corporate Compliance Program should your agency choose to implement such a program.

Why should we implement a compliance program and integrate the CPP?

In recent years the federal government, especially the Department of Justice (DOJ) and Department of Health and Human Services, Office of Inspector General (OIG), has increasingly scrutinized the Medicare and Medicaid billing practices of all types of healthcare organizations. Although the primary targets of these investigations have been hospitals, home health agencies and nursing homes, recent attention has been turned to community mental health centers (some of which provide addiction treatment services). The federal agencies have used the expanded definitions of healthcare fraud and related offenses as contained in the Health Insurance Portability and Accountability Act of 1996 (HIPAA), 42 U.S.C. §1320(a)-7(a). Moreover, Congress, through HIPAA, authorized increased funding for the Department of Justice, the FBI, and the OIG to audit, investigate and prosecute healthcare organizations suspected of fraud and related offenses, 42 U.S.C. §1320(a)-7(c).

In addition to the increased vigilance of federal agencies, private citizens have identified and reported more healthcare fraud due to incentives contained in the 1986 amendments to the False Claims Act, 31 U.S.C. §3729. These incentives encourage private citizens to file "whistleblower" suits against healthcare organizations. The individuals bringing suits are known as qui tam relators and they can collect a reward for their actions of as much as thirty percent (30%) of the value of any financial recovery made by the federal government, 31 U.S.C. §3730. Furthermore, federal prosecutors have increasingly demonstrated a willingness to hold corporations and their individual officers and employees, both financially and criminally responsible for their fraudulent actions. It is important to note that when fraud is discovered, both the DOJ and OIG look at the entity to see if reasonable efforts have been made by management to avoid and detect any misbehavior that occurs within their operations (i.e. a corporate compliance program). See OIG Criteria for Implementing Permissive Exclusion Authority, 62 Fed. Reg. 67392 (Dec. 24, 1997); The Office of Inspector General's Compliance Program Guidance for Hospitals (Feb. 1998); Department of Justice, United States Attorneys' Manual, Title 9, Sect. 162, Federal Prosecution of Corporations). The U.S. Attorneys' Offices will also consider, among a variety of factors: (1) whether the provider has a compliance plan in place and is adhering to the compliance plan; (2) the relationship between the compliance plan and the conduct at issue; and (3) if the provider has taken any other steps to comply with billing rules, Office of the Deputy Attorney General, Guidance on the Use of the False Claims Act in Civil Health Care Matters (June 3, 1998). The government will use this analysis to determine the level of sanctions, penalties and exclusions that will be imposed upon the provider. Since a Corporate Compliance Program will be an important mitigating factor if your agency faces an investigation and prosecution, we recommend that your agency explore the feasibility and associated costs, risks and benefits of such a program. In view of the law, federal enforcement policies, federal guidelines and potential liability, it seems logical that addiction providers seriously evaluate their need to implement a Corporate Compliance Program and integrate a CPP into such a program.

How is the CCP developed?

One of the authors has experimented with a variety of processes through which organizations can develop a CPP. The following steps offer a systematic process of CPP development that can be adapted for use in many organizations.

Step #1: Preliminary discussions related to the need for a Code of Professional Practice involve the chief executive officer, managers, supervisors, and the Executive and Personnel Committees of the Board.

This step is to assure that support for the development of a CPP is initiated and sustained at the highest levels within the organization. It is recommended that managers and board members review the steps outlined in this chapter to explore what refinements may be required to fit the unique characteristics of their organization. Such refinement can continue to evolve as more staff are involved in the CPP development process. Other key questions to be addressed at this time include the following:

- Are there sufficient internal resources to facilitate the CPP development process, or should the services of an outside consultant be acquired to assist with the process?
- Is there sufficient support for the benefits that can be derived from developing a CPP to warrant initiating the development and implementation process?
- Given other projects in various stages of development, when is the best time to initiate the CPP developmental process?
- What sources of resistance to the development of a CPP should be anticipated and how should such resistance be managed?
- Should a board-management-staff-consumer committee be created to guide the development of the CPP?

Step #2:   All agency staff are oriented to the purpose of the code and the steps that will be used to develop it.

This is an extremely important step in the CPP development process if staff involvement is to be maximized and staff paranoia is to be minimized. This can best be presented by the CEO at an all-staff meeting (for smaller organizations) or at divisional meetings (for larger organizations).   The questions and answers regarding the CPP summarized in this chapter should be touched on during the orientation session.

Step #3:   An ad hoc task force of organizational members is selected to guide the overall process of developing the code.

It is essential that a Code of Professional Practice emerge out of the process of the team, and not be an instrument arbitrarily foisted upon staff by one or more managers or by the agency board. The creation of an ad hoc task force to help facilitate the development of the code is one vehicle to assure continued staff involvement throughout the developmental process.

Task force members may be appointed by the CEO or may be selected by agency staff using a preset format (e.g., one staff member selected by their peers from each program area).   The most ideal task force size in my experience is 4 to 10 persons. Ideally, the task force should:

- include key representatives from the board and the management team
- reflect the demographic diversity of the agency, e.g., age, gender, culture, etc.
- represent a cross-section of the professional disciplines that make up the organization
- represent a cross-section of the units that make up the structure of the agency
- represent a mix of persons with short and long tenure at the agency
- reflect the selection of persons who exemplify and can articulate standards of service quality and professionalism
- include members with skills in group facilitation and writing, and
- include consumer representation.

The major responsibilities of the task force are to:

- review and refine the steps involved in the development of the CPP
- solicit feedback from staff on issues and recommended standards that

should be addressed or reflected in the CPP
- facilitate staff discussion groups about desired CPP standards
- write draft sections of the CPP
- play a leadership role in the review and redrafting process
- assist in the orientation of staff when the CPP is completed.

The responsibilities of the task force vary depending on whether or not the agency utilizes an outside consultant to facilitate the CPP development. If a consultant is not utilized, those tasks normally performed by the consultant are performed by agency managers and/or task force members.

Step #4: Sample codes of ethics of various health and human service professions are circulated to staff for the purpose of identifying those standards staff feel should be incorporated into the agency Code of Professional Practice.

The codes of ethics of those professional associations /disciplines to which agency staff are affiliated are circulated for review. Codes may also be included from professional associations whose standards address areas of service activity or job functions currently performed within the agency. One easy method of review is to have each staff person place their initials beside each standard which they feel should be incorporated into the agency CPP. There is a resource list included within the Appendix which lists professional organizations which may be contacted to obtain such codes of ethics.

Step #5: A series of small group meetings are held with organizational members in which critical incidents are presented to staff. Discussion of these vignettes of ethical dilemmas are used to elicit recommendations on standards to guide staff in responding to such situations.

The critical incidents presented in the remaining chapters of this book are designed to be used in conjunction with this step. Working with small groups of staff, the facilitator presents each small group with a critical incident and asks staff to: (1) identify the ethical/legal/clinical issues inherent within the incident, (2) identify how they would respond to the incident as presented, and (3) recommend a standard that could be included within the CPP that could guide staff who might find themselves in such a situation.

This step in the development of the CPP has an added benefit of sensitizing staff to a large range of ethical issues they are unlikely to have experienced or considered. Such critical incident training actually provides a safe and supportive environment through which staff can rehearse (or emotionally decompress from) their responses to very complex ethical/legal/clinical situations. Staff who complete this training often remark on their appreciation for the opportunity to explore such situations before being faced with them in real life.

The logistics of this training can best be handled by breaking staff into groups of 15-30 to participate in half- to full-day critical incident training. It is desirable to mix staff from different units and disciplines within each training group and to have a good mix by gender and culture. The goal is that every organizational member will have an opportunity to participate in at least one training session in which they share in generating recommended standards for the CPP.

During each training session, staff should be divided into groups of three-five members. The facilitator should assign each group a critical incident with all groups listening to all of the situations before they begin brainstorming. Each group should be given 20-30 minutes to address the three elements (issues, action, standards) with a recorder being selected from within each group to document the ideas and recommendations of the group. After the allotted time, each group reports the three elements of their critical incident. It is best to vary critical incidents with each training group. This assures the highest number of recommended standards generated within this step. It is also best if each training group receives critical incidents that cross a variety of areas of professional practice. Critical incidents within this book can be chosen by the task force to elicit recommendations on issues of greatest import to the agency. Critical incidents included in this text may also be supplemented with real incidents that have occurred in the life of the organization.

Task force members play important roles during this step. Where no consultant is utilized, they facilitate the small group discussions, and they have the very important role of recording the recommendations for standards that emerge from the small group discussions.

Step #6: The task force uses the recommendations for standards generated in steps 4 and 5 to develop a draft Code of Professional Practice for the agency.

It is particularly important that the task force not edit standards recommendations coming from step 5. The job at this stage is to present the recommendations as they came from the small groups as accurately as possible within the draft CPP.

Step #7: Copies of the draft code are circulated for review and comment to all staff members of the organization.

Mechanisms of review which can be incorporated into step 6 include:

- written comments providing reactions/recommendations related to the draft CPP
- verbal comments solicited on a one-on-one basis by task force members from peers within their program area
- a review and discussion of the draft code at divisional or program meetings with recorded minutes submitted to the task force, and
- open task force meetings in which staff/consumers can drop in and provide feedback and recommendations related to the draft CPP.

Step #8: Copies of the draft code are circulated to the Personnel Committee of the Board, the Board as a whole, the agency legal counsel, and any professional or consumer advisory committees for review and comment.

These reviews can occur concurrently with the staff reviews. The review by legal counsel is particularly important to assure that no standards inadvertently violate tenents of criminal or civil law or other regulatory standards governing the activities of the organization.

Step #9: The task force works with the Personnel Committee of the Board, the management team and the CEO to integrate recommendations from steps 7 and 8 into a final version of the CPP.

In this step, final decisions are made regarding standards and the language in which they are presented. Where consensus is not achieved, most organizations use the following procedure to achieve a decision on each standard in question. Recommendations for various options are set forth by the task force, discussed at the board level, and voted on, with majority vote ruling the final selection process.

Step #10: The recommended code is integrated into existing personnel policies and disciplinary procedures.

This step entails: (1) altering the personnel policies to acknowledge the existence of the CPP and to establish the CPP as the set of standards to which all staff members shall adhere, (2) clearly indicating that any member of the agency who fails to achieve such adherence shall be subject to disciplinary action, and (3) clarifying or creating appeal procedures regarding disciplinary action taken in response to violation of a CPP standard.

Step #11:   The Code of Professional Practice is approved by the agency Board with an effective implementation date.

The effective date of the CPP should be set with sufficient lead time to assure that all staff orientations can be completed prior to the date. The lead time also provides the opportunity for staff to complete any required activity set forth in the code. Several agencies in writing standards on staff representation of professional credentials have mandated in their CPP that all staff submit to the agency copies of all transcripts, diplomas, licenses, and certifications. The lead time of effective implementation provides staff an opportunity to complete such activity prior to the effective date.

Step #12:   All staff are oriented to the Board-approved Code of Professional Practice.

The use of the CEO, the Chairperson of the Personnel Committee of the Board, and staff/consumer representatives from the CPP task force to conduct the orientations symbolically places the full resources of the agency behind the implementation of the CPP.

Step #13:   All staff sign a statement for inclusion in their personnel file affirming that they have read the code, participated in an orientation session related to the code, and understand the standards set forth in the code.

This step reinforces the seriousness of the CCP and the expectation placed upon staff for adherence to the standards and values set forth in the code. The documentation eliminates the "Nobody ever told me about that" defense in response to serious breaches of the code.

Step #14:   A mechanism is established by the CEO and the Board for future review and refinement of the code.

A periodic review of the code by an ad hoc committee of board-staff-consumers is suggested to allow for the continuing evolution of the CPP. Step 14 sets the time frame of when revisions of the code will be entertained and the procedural steps that shall be used in such modification.

Step #15:   The Code of Professional Practice is included in all new staff
                 orientations.

The involvement of the CEO, Board members and key professional staff
to assist with this orientation is highly recommended. The CPP should be an
important tool of socialization for all new staff entering the organization. The
orientation to the code can include some of the same critical incident training
that was utilized in the code's development.

Step #16:   Decisions related to dissemination of the code beyond
                 organizational members are discussed and finalized.

Some programs may choose to use the CPP in ways that transcend its use
shaping the standards of quality and professional conduct to which staff will be
held accountable. Two such uses are recommended for consideration. The first
is the dissemination of the CPP to referral sources. This is a way of boldly
communicating the essence of one's organizational culture to outsiders. As one
director noted, "It's the best way we have of telling people who we are and how
we are different from all the other agencies out there."
    A second use involves the distribution of a copy of the code (or at least the
section of standards governing client relationships) to each client at admission.
This is a means of educating clients to the precise standards that will govern the
nature of staff relationships and decision-making. Retrospective studies of
clients who were sexually exploited by therapists, for example, reveal that a
number of such clients were particularly vulnerable due to their lack of
knowledge of what was appropriate and inappropriate in the therapy
relationship. Distribution of an agency CPP to all clients clearly defines such
boundaries of appropriateness and inappropriateness. Providing the CPP to
clients is a way of saying:

> "This is who we are. These are the standards of practice by which you can
> judge us. If we fail to meet these standards, we expect and ask that you
> bring this discrepancy to our attention immediately."

How long does it take to develop a CPP?

The development of an agency CPP should be done slowly and
deliberately. This, after all, will result in the single most important document
that communicates the professional values of the organization. A normal time
span for completing the above steps can be anywhere from 12 to 24 months
depending on the size of the agency and how many other major development

activities are occurring simultaneously.

How is the CPP updated?

One method of keeping track of new issues that may need to be addressed in the CPP is to refer all such issues for discussion and documentation to the agency's Quality Improvement Committee. This is a natural placement of responsibility since so many issues related to the CPP involve quality of care issues. The Quality Improvement Committee can make recommendations related to changes in the CPP that can be incorporated into the annual review of the CPP. Issues that cannot await such review can be handled by interim standards being issued by the CEO. Issues that arise over the year can then be formally reviewed using the review and modification provisions set forth in Step 14.

An Introduction to the Critical Incidents

The next seven chapters of this book catalogue critical incidents that raise potential ethical and professional practice issues related to:

- conduct of business
- personal conduct outside the work environment
- adherence to professional values
- relationships with clients/families
- professional peer relationships
- conduct in situations that pose a risk to public safety
- performance of specialty roles within the substance abuse field.

The critical incidents in each chapter can be selected for use in the staff focus groups described earlier in step 5 of the CPP development process.

The critical incidents that make up the heart of this book were constructed using the following procedures.

1. Situations were drawn from the authors' clinical and consulting experience and synthesized into representative composites with all names and identifying details altered. The composites constructed from the authors' experiences are fictional as written, although the ethical issues were drawn from real events. The names of all persons and organizations contained in the critical incidents are fictitious.

2.   Situations were solicited from professional colleagues. Similar situations were merged into fictional composites. Names and details of all incidents were altered, while maintaining an accurate depiction of the ethical dilemma involved in the real situations.

3.   Any uncanny similarity between a critical incident in this book and a real situation is purely coincidental and simply reflects the tendency for such events to be episodically recapitulated in organizations and communities across the United States. The number of readers who will know of incidents similar to those presented in this book adds further evidence that these problems are widespread and systemic rather than idiosyncratic to person or place.

4.   Where the authors had no direct or indirect experience from which to illustrate a particular ethical issue, a fictional vignette was created to facilitate discussion of the particular issue.

The critical incidents in these chapters are followed by discussion questions and a brief discussion and analysis of ethical issues raised by the critical incident. These discussions are not intended as in-depth analyses of the full range of ethical issues in each situation, but rather are intended as starting points of discussion for the facilitator who will be leading the small group discussions of these incidents. Each analysis identifies real or potential breaches of ethical conduct that could arise in the situation and notes the general response of the addictions field at this particular point in time. For those critical incidents that lack any such clear consensus, the analysis identifies and discusses various issues that must be weighed to plot an ethical course of action. The purpose of the analyses is merely to stimulate thinking about ethical complexity and ethical decision-making.

A Model for Ethical Decision-making

After experimenting with numerous models of ethical decision-making, the authors have settled on the following framework for the analysis of ethical dilemmas. The framework involves the application of three questions.

1.   Whose interests are involved and who can be harmed? Or put more simply: Who are the potential winners and losers?

While the situations in this book span the interests and vulnerabilities of many parties, most boil down to the following: service recipients (clients /

families), individual workers, the prevention or treatment organization, the addictions field, and the community. The analysis of interests and vulnerabilities is completed with the identification of areas of conflicting interest—where acting to benefit one party does harm to another party.

2.   What universal or cultural specific values apply to this situation and what course of action would be suggested by these values? Which of these values are in conflict in this situation?

This second step explores how widely-held ethical values (defined in Chapter One) could be applied to help formulate the best course of action in a particular situation. It is important in this discussion not only to isolate the values that apply to the situation but also to identify values that may be in conflict, e.g., the value of honesty conflicting with the value of loyalty. This opens the way to asking, "Which is the higher value in this situation?" The higher value is often determined by the degree of good to be achieved or the degree of harm to be avoided identified through the first question.

3.   What standards of law, professional propriety, organizational policy or historical practice apply to this situation?

This third step looks at established standards of professional conduct that dictate or prohibit certain actions relevant to the situation. These standards would include legal mandates, funding guidelines, accreditation or licensing standards, ethical standards of professional associations, codes of professional practice, personnel policies, or employment contracts.

The work sheet on the following page provides a format through which staff can individually or in small groups apply this three-step model of ethical decision-making to the critical incidents in the rest of the book. Multiple copies should be made so that a work sheet can be used for each incident analyzed.

Work Sheet For Critical Incident Discussion Groups

Critical Incident #_____

I.   Whose interests are involved; who can be harmed?

Interests and Vulnerabilities	Significant	Moderate	Minimal / None
Client / Family			
Staff Member			
Agency			
Professional Field			
Community / Public Safety			

Which interests, if any, are in conflict?

II. Application of Universal Values
        _____ Autonomy (Freedom over one's own destiny)
        _____ Obedience (Obey legal and ethically permissible directives)
        _____ Conscientious Refusal (Disobey illegal or unethical directives)
        _____ Beneficence (Do good; Help others)
        _____ Gratitude (Pass good along to others)
        _____ Competence (Be knowledgeable and skilled)
        _____ Justice (Be fair; distribute by merit)
        _____ Stewardship (Use resources wisely)
        _____ Honesty and Candor (Tell the truth)
        _____ Fidelity (Keep your promises)
        _____ Loyalty (Don't abandon)
        _____ Diligence (Work hard)
        _____ Discretion (Respect confidence and privacy)
        _____ Self-improvement (Be the best that you can be)
        _____ Nonmaleficence (Don't hurt anyone)
        _____ Restitution (Make amends to persons injured)
        _____ Self-interest (Protect yourself)
        _____ Other Culture-specific Values

III. What laws, standards, policies or historical practices should guide us in this situation?

IV. Discussion notes

Chapter
Three

Conduct Related to the Practice of Business

A number of forces have emerged that require that the addictions field extend its traditional concern with clinical ethics to encompass concerns related to our business practices:

- increased competition for limited resources
- emergence of Medicaid managed care
- conversion of grant and fee-for-service dollars to partial and full capitation models
- erosion of commercial benefit dollars allocated to behavioral health
- encroachment of for-profit entities upon the traditional non-profit community-based provider
- competition-spawned marketing wars between service providers
- continuing consolidations, joint venture frenzies and "merger mania" as a way to "diversify and survive"
- accelerating demands for and costs of technology
- demands for higher levels of education and training and the resulting salary wars among agencies
- pressures placed upon agency executives to produce excess revenues (no margin, no mission)
- escalating legal and regulatory standards governing substance abuse treatment
- increased scrutiny of treatment outcomes as well as regulatory compliance, enforcement and prosecution.

All of these trends have intensified the need to explore ethical dimensions related to the business conduct of our organizations. This chapter will explore a broad range of critical incidents in this area.

Critical Incidents
Macro-Planning
   Stewardship of Resources

♦♦ 1 ♦♦

An addiction prevention and treatment agency recently received a

$500,000 donation from the estate of a local philanthropist with no requirements as to how the money should be utilized by the agency. The management team of the agency has presented the following options for the potential use of this new money for consideration to the board:

- Launch a desperately needed specialized service program for addicted women and their children (the new money could fund this program for two years).
- Upgrade existing facilities and equipment.
- Provide salary increases to all staff (the goal is to bring salaries up to par with other health and human service agencies and reduce problems related to staff recruitment and retention).
- Add staff and material resources to do a better job (improve quality of care) with existing programming.
- Create the beginnings of a capital fund for the eventual construction of a new service facility.
- Maintain money as "rainy day fund" so the agency would have the ability to sustain services in the face of funding cuts or other financial crisis (interest made on money could be spent and the fund would reduce current interest paid by the agency on borrowed money used for operating expenses, due to delayed receipt of reimbursements).

Discussion Questions

How might you ethically weigh the various choices above?

Which is more ethical: provide the highest quality of service to a small number of clients or provide an adequate level of quality of services to a larger number of clients?

What standards or values should guide our stewardship of agency and community resources?

Policy makers and planners at federal, state, and local levels regularly confront the question of distributive justice—a kind of ethical arithmetic that determines how scarce resources are to be dispersed. Weighing alternative uses of resources from the above lists cannot be judged from an arbitrary designation of right or wrong choices. Given the particulars of a program's unique situation, each of the above options could arguably be the best or the worst option on the list. In real life, staff and board members would likely be making precisely such arguments.

What is important about considering ethical aspects of resource allocation is assurance that decisions related to the distribution of resources are filtered through and are congruent with the organization's stated mission and values. For a service organization to consistently utilize its resources in areas that do not enhance the accessibility and quality of services would represent a breach of honesty, fidelity and loyalty to the agency's clients and community constituents.

Typically, neither statutes nor regulations would govern the decision making for the expenditure of a $500,000 donation from an individual. However, it would be advisable to consult local counsel to determine whether there is a state charitable solicitation or charitable trust act that addresses this issue. These statutes will be of assistance in determining reporting require-ments for the donation in addition to any federal tax requirements in the 990 form if you have an exempt organization.

More importantly, an agency would be bound under contract principles to comply with conditions imposed by the grantor as acceptance of the gift. In this case, no such restrictions exist.

Planning

♦♦ 2 ♦♦

A community of 85,000 is served by two competing addiction treatment programs, one of which has operated a four bed detox and 20 bed residential rehabilitation unit for the past eight years. Since its initiation, the unit has gone from a 95% utilization rate to a 70% utilization rate, primarily due to changes in lengths of stay and the development of new substance abuse programs in other neighboring counties from which the unit once drew client referrals. The unit has maintained a good reputation and is clearly responding to a service need in the area. The competing program announces that it will be opening a 20-bed inpatient addiction treatment unit. The internal planning data upon which administrators based this decision suggested that the area could not fully utilize 40 beds for substance abuse treatment but that their program could pull 40-50% of the current substance abuse treatment admissions based on its geographical location and its links to local physicians. This program is opening a unit not in response to an unmet need, but to capture their market share of addiction treatment admissions from the other program. Within 18 months of service initiation, both programs are struggling with 25-30% utilization rates—rates that promise to further deteriorate when new state managed care guidelines go into effect.

Discussion Questions

Are there ethical issues raised by this scenario?

Are there ethical principles that should guide the initiation of new services by an agency, particularly when such services are already being provided by other service agencies?

What are our values related to competition and collaboration?

What values can help us resolve potential conflicts between institutional self-interest and community need?

Vignettes like the above are not uncommon. There are a number of potential ethical dimensions involved in the planning and initiation of addiction services in the above circumstances. The first issue is whether the short-term interests of an organization violate the long-term interests of the community. The ethical command to "first, do no harm" can be applied to communities as well as individual clients.

A service program supported by a community—by personal and industrial benefactors and by its consumers—takes on certain ethical mandates related to its stewardship of resources. Part of that mandate is to expend resources in ways that can support rather than weaken the network of local health care services available to local citizens. This mandate comes from a contract implicit in the support the community provides the program. Private and corporate benefactors support the program with the understanding that the program will use those resources to the long-term benefit of the community.

Maximizing short-term profits by moving into competition for a fixed number of clients already being served represents a misuse of the trust and the resources, which the community endowed to the program. The plummeting occupancy rates on both units in the above vignette will inevitably lead to an erosion of resources—e.g., staff, consultants, training, etc.—and a potentially poorer quality of addiction treatment services available within this community. Over time, the financial viability of both units may be threatened and could paradoxically result in both organizations being forced out of the provision of addiction treatment services.

There may also be ethical issues involved in the planning processes through which new chemical dependency services are initiated. These issues can include the blatant disregard of planning bodies or planning documents; the misrepresentation, manipulation, or outright fabrication of planning data to support a certificate of need (CON) application; and the misrepresenta-

tion/exaggeration of the extent of the local alcohol and other drug problems to garner support for the new unit.

This scenario is becoming more common as the addiction field integrates its services not only with other community-based mental health services but also with the primary care systems. A better way to approach this dilemma would be to explore a strategic alliance agreement between the two programs. These agreements do not require the level of integration or relinquishing of control that mergers or affiliations require. Rather, the premise is to build on the strengths and expertise of each party instead of creating or replicating services or infrastructure. This arrangement therefore results in a strategic aligning of the parties rather than competition for the same limited resources and clientele, ultimately achieving a coordinated and improved service delivery system for the communities the parties serve.

Lobbying
Misrepresentation of Information

♦♦ 3 ♦♦

In a hearing regarding a request for funding of detoxification services by a local city council, Rex, the Executive Director of the local addiction treatment agency, was asked by a council member how many clients were turned away or faced arrest because of an inadequate number of beds in the detox unit. The unit this last year averaged three persons per week turned away in the winter months and one person per week turned away in the other months. Last week (time of a spring festival noted for its heavy drinking) there were an unusually high number of people (16 persons) turned away because of the detox unit being full. In response to the council member's question, the Director responded; "We have routinely turned people away all this past year because of lack of capacity. Only this week, we turned away 16 persons who were in desperate need of detoxification simply because our unit was already filled to its current legal capacity." This statement conveys the impression that the service demand is much higher than the actual service demand data would indicate.

Discussion Questions

Is it ever justified to over-estimate or misrepresent information related to service need, quantity of services delivered, or the frequency and degree of service success?

How could the misrepresentation in the above vignette backfire, hurting the reputation of the director and the agency, as well as damaging the future accessibility of client services?

The above action stretches, if not punctures, the ethical principle of honesty. The concern with this action is both the wrongfulness of misrepresenting the scope and intensity of a problem and the potential harm that could be created through such misrepresentation. If the misrepresentation was suspected or discovered by the city council members, it could destroy the reputation and credibility of the agency to such an extent that future funding of services to clients could be jeopardized. The misrepresentation could also lead to a misallocation of resources—committing resources to underutilized detox beds while other more critical needs go unmet due to limited resources. It is through this spiral of unforeseen consequences that stretching or misrepresenting the truth poses potential harm to the agency, to clients, and to the community. The potential for inadvertent misrepresentation can occur particularly under the pressure for condensation of verbal testimony at legislative hearings or hearings reviewing requests for funding. To avoid the dangers inherent in creating such time-induced oversimplifications and misconceptions, it is helpful to always take along or submit afterwards a more detailed presentation of information.

Legally, we offer two items of caution. First, depending on the formality of the proceeding, one needs to be cognizant of committing perjury (misstating facts or lying under oath). Second, federal law makes it a civil, and in some cases, a criminal offense, to make false statements to governmental agencies. You should consult your local counsel to advise you of any similar state prohibitions. See the Civil False Claims Act, 31 U.S.C. §3729; Criminal False Claims relating to Medicare/Medicaid, 42 U.S.C. §1320a-7b(a).

Exploitation of Clients

♦♦ 4 ♦♦

A program, facing potential threats of having state funding cut for addiction services in their area, organizes community representatives and clients to lobby the state legislature to stop the proposed cuts. Clients are actively recruited, transported to this event, provided with placards and T-shirts that clearly identify them as clients of the agency, are coached for interviews with the media, and present testimony before a legislative committee considering the funding cuts.

Discussion Questions

Discuss the following issues and principles as they relate to the above vignette.

- discretion (protection of confidentiality and privacy)
- autonomy and freedom from coercion
- informed consent

Would the issues be different if the individuals in the above vignette were former clients not actively involved in services at the agency?

What standard should govern the involvement of clients in activities that transcend the service contract?

Would there be similar issues in soliciting parental (parents of active/former clients) involvement in such lobbying on behalf of funding for adolescent services?

The imbalance of power between a client in active treatment and his or her counselor or the program director diminishes the capacity for free choice and raises the potential for coercive involvement of clients in such marketing and fundraising activities. This is particularly true where refusal would be framed pejoratively as an indication of their denial, resistance, or some related psychobabble intended to escalate pressure on the client for participation.

Coercive involvement in such presentations violates client confidentiality and privacy. It is very helpful for programs to articulate standards that will govern the conditions under which clients or former clients will, or will not, be used in marketing or fundraising campaigns. The presentation of such programs is also a breach of honesty when they are represented to be educational programs but are in reality designed to generate referrals and contributions.

The above experience may be exploitive of clients or it may provide a very positive experience of empowerment to clients. The judgment we place on this activity can be based on an analysis of the following contextual elements of the activity:

- *Were clients briefed on the potential positive and negative effects of the activity, e.g., their public identification as addicts / clients?*
- *Was the staff's solicitation of client involvement manipulative or coercive?*
- *Were there untoward consequences to any client who chose not to*

participate in the activity, e.g., the alternative to not participating for a residential client is an unpleasant work detail?.

- Did the program avoid soliciting clients active in treatment whose autonomy of decision-making could be compromised by their dependence upon the program?
- Did the activity supplement rather than replace treatment services needed by the clients?
- Were there any aspects of staff-client relationships during the lobbying activity that would serve to undermine the capacity and quality of continued service to the client?

This vignette contains numerous legal issues. The first legal consideration is the obligation of drug and alcohol programs to comply with the confidentiality restrictions imposed under federal law and regulations, 42 U.S.C. §290dd and 42 C.F.R. Part 2, respectively. Under the federal confidentiality regulations, having clients wear T-shirts identifying the treatment program constitutes a disclosure. The federal regulations prohibit federally assisted substance abuse treatment programs from communicating patient identifying information unless the regulations expressly authorize such disclosures. Patient identifying information includes the name, address, social security number, fingerprints, voiceprints, photograph, or similar information by which the identity of a patient can be determined with reasonable accuracy and speed either directly or by reference to other publicly available information, 42 C.F.R. §2.11. For an in-depth discussion of the disclosures permitted by the federal regulations, consult Chapter 6. Obviously, appearing in person with a T-shirt identifying the person as a client of a treatment program is a disclosure. If clients willingly choose to lobby their legislators, the program should obtain a written consent for disclosure to cover the potential risk.

Informed consent, which is another issue in this vignette, differs from consent for disclosure. The principle of informed consent imposes an affirmative responsibility on the healthcare provider to give patients sufficient information to make an informed choice. Specifically, the patient should be told: (1) the nature and purpose of the procedure; (2) the risks and consequences; (3) the alternatives; and (4) the risks of no treatment. Failure to disclose risk is the most common source of liability.

To determine whether a professional practice standard for informed consent was breached in this case, courts would look to the standards of what a reasonably prudent addiction treatment counselor in the community would do in exercising reasonable care as well as any statutory or regulatory requirements to determine the "appropriate standard of care". Liability in *these cases is imposed under negligence theories. Thus, the plaintiff would be required to prove that the clinician had a duty, breached the duty, and that the client suffered injury as a result of the breach (meaning the clinician caused the client's injury). The key question in these cases is often whether the patient can prove that had the risk been disclosed, he or she would not have consented to the procedure or treatment (or in this case the public lobbying).*

Utilization of Staff Time for Political Lobbying

♦♦ 5 ♦♦

In the above vignette, staff members on paid work time accompanied clients and community representatives to participate in the lobbying effort.

Discussion Question

What ethical issues are raised by the use of paid staff time for lobbying particular issues or organizing support for or against particular political candidates?

The use of staff on paid time to participate in lobbying activities raises ethical issues and may also raise legal issues. Ethical issues raised by this practice include:

- *the involvement of staff in duties that far transcend the activities for which they were hired*
- *the potential use of coercion to involve staff in political activity*
- *the breach in the contractual commitment (with funding sources) to use staff only for specified service activities*
- *questionable to illegal billing practices in which third parties were billed for the staff time or bills for client services that encompass the time involved in lobbying.*

A more serious and enduring problem with political lobbying for some not-for-profit agencies would be the potential loss of their tax-exempt status (designation as a 501(c)(3) organization under Internal Revenue Service Code). The loss of this status as a result of political activity on paid staff time could threaten the future potential of the agency to sustain its role as a helping institution.

Federal law provides that no substantial part of the net earnings of a 501(c)(3) organization can be spent on lobbying. Generally, the safeguard is

5% or less of the organization's revenues. If a tax-exempt organization spends a "substantial part", it may lose its tax exemption. Despite the fact that tax exempt organizations may spend money on lobbying, strict rules exist on political campaign activities. Furthermore, there are federal and state laws and regulations limiting certain lobbying activities, requiring registration and disclosure of lobbying activities and prohibiting the use of public dollars for lobbying.

In general, lobbying expenditures are defined as expenditures for the purpose of influencing legislation through attempts to affect the opinions of any segment of the general public as a whole or through communicating with any member or employee of a legislative body who may participate in formulating legislation. Expenditures to make information available to lawmakers are not considered lobbying.

If your organization is interested in pursuing lobbying activities, you should consult your attorney on the following questions:

❐ *What are the types of activities that are considered "education" rather than lobbying?*

❐ *What are the types of activities that are not permitted by (1) IRS exemption rules; (2) federal contracting laws and regulations; (3) state contracting laws and regulations; and (4) municipal/county contracting laws and regulations?*

❐ *If your entity is a 501(c)(3) organization, should you file under Section 501(h) and 4911 of the IRS Code to elect to expend a certain percentage on lobbying activities?*

❐ *If you make a 501(h) election, what are the reporting requirements and related excise taxes that may be imposed?*

❐ *Should you engage in lobbying through a separate legal entity?*

❐ *What lobbying registration requirements exist under federal, state, county and municipal laws and regulations?*

❐ *What lobbying disclosure and reporting requirements are required under federal, state, county and municipal laws and regulations?*

❐ *Do you have any funding contracts that prohibit lobbying and how is lobbying defined under those agreements?*

Advocacy: Interest of Field Versus Agency Self-Interest

♦♦ 6 ♦♦

Alisha is a local program director and the Third-party Payment Committee chairperson of a professional association of addiction treatment agencies. She has just been called by a legislative committee staff member seeking her opinion on how criteria should be set for which agencies will be reimbursed through the state Medicaid program for the provision of treatment services to eligible clients. The legislative committee is considering using accreditation by the Council on Accreditation of Rehabilitation Facilities (CARF) as the primary eligibility criteria. The legislative committee is seeking Alisha's opinion based on her experience with the state association committee. Here is Alisha's dilemma: the CARF accreditation requirement would result in significant funding cuts to the large number of addiction agencies in the state who are not CARF accredited but who have been receiving Medicaid reimbursement for services. Alisha's own program is CARF accredited and would receive significant competitive advantage and a financial windfall if the legislature mandates the CARF requirement. The legislative committee staff person is asking for Alisha's off-the-record recommendation as to what action the legislative committee should take.

Discussion Questions

Identify the multiple constituents to whom Alisha is responsible in the above vignette.

What values might help Alisha sort out her conflicting role responsibilities in this situation?

If you were Alisha, how would you respond?

There is a clear role conflict depicted in this vignette in which the interests of Alisha as a program director are in conflict with her promise as professional association committee chairperson to represent the collective needs of treatment agencies throughout the state. To avoid exploiting the chairperson role for personal/agency gain, Alisha might consider one or more of the following actions:

1. *Seeking consultation—perhaps from the director of the association—before she responds to the request.*
2. *Declaring her potential conflict of interests to the legislative staff member*
3. *articulating both the short- and long-term advantages and disadvantages of the course of action being considered by the legislature.*
4. *Declaring her personal preference while at the same time acknowledging*

an alternative approach that would better serve the needs of the majority of agencies.

5.   *Suggesting that the staff member solicit opinions from a broader range of persons who reflect different interests within the field.*

The law does not dictate an obligation to disclose a conflict if interest, however it is always important when communicating with government agency or legislative representatives to clearly identify if you are representing a particular interest or agency, especially when you wear many hats.

Fundraising
Use of Professional Fundraisers

♦♦ 7 ♦♦

The Harambe Center—a local addiction treatment program—is considering entering into a contract with a professional fundraising organization to raise funds for the construction of a new treatment facility. Under terms of the contract, the fundraising organization will receive 50% of all funds raised as their fee for running the capital fund drive. In short, only $350,000 of the $700,000 target of the fund drive will actually go toward construction of the new facility. All promotional material distributed as part of the fund drive would reference the need for $700,000 to build the new facility. Nowhere would there be public disclosure of the amount of funds that are covering the administration of the fund drive itself.

Discussion Questions

How could the choice to use the professional fundraiser potentially help or hurt the profession, the agency, individual staff members, and current and potential agency clients?

What would be your position as a board member in response to this proposal?

Many addiction treatment agencies have struggled with the most appropriate means of raising funds to support special needs and some have sought the help of professional fundraisers. The ethical questions that emerge from the above vignette include the following:

1.   *Are there alternatives to the above fundraising strategy that will represent a better stewardship of agency and community resources? Is there a way*

in which the $350,000 going to support the administration of the fund campaign could be reduced so that these funds could be allocated to support needed community services?

2. *Does the failure to disclose the portion of funds raised that will actually go toward building construction constitute a breach in the principle of honesty, candor, and fidelity implicit in the relationship between the agency and the community?*

To determine whether such a compensation arrangement is legally appropriate you should ask your lawyer the following questions:

❏   *Are there any current IRS regulations restricting a percentage compensation arrangement to a fundraiser?*

❏   *Would such a compensation arrangement constitute prohibited private benefit jeopardizing our tax-exempt status?*

❏   *Does your state prohibit such percentage compensation arrangements under state charitable trust or charitable solicitation laws?*

❏   *Does your state attorney general require any registration before embarking upon such a fundraising campaign?*

❏   *If such registration exists, does the fundraising contract and corresponding compensation arrangement need to be disclosed to the state attorney general, to the potential donors and/or to the public at large?*

❏   *Is there any type of special reporting of this compensation arrangement on the organization's tax return (either federal or state)?*

❏   *Does your state have any consumer protection laws prohibiting such solicitation without disclosure of the 50% of funds raised going to non-charitable entity?*

❏   *Could the 50% split with a non-exempt fundraiser jeopardize the donors' tax deduction for the charitable contribution?*

Staff/Board Support

♦♦ 8 ♦♦

A fund drive by a local addiction agency has continually portrayed the importance of this drive to the continued access of critically needed treatment services to local citizens. The fund drive has been portrayed in crisis terms. A close examination of funds received to date would reveal almost no financial contributions by board members, staff, or volunteers of the agency.

Discussion Questions

Do the communications of the fund drive represent a breach of honesty if those most supportive of the agency's mission have not offered personal support of the fund drive?

If the funds are as critical as communicated, is it a violation of any ethical value for the board, staff, and volunteers to not contribute to the fund drive?

This is an ethically grey area that poses a rather provocative question: if the persons most closely associated with the project to be funded do not feel strongly enough to commit even token support, do their repeated admonitions on the importance and criticalness of the project to the community represent a misrepresentation of their beliefs? The issue of the degree to which professional staff and board members participate in community solicitation for funds is a question that should be explored by professional certification bodies, professional associations and within agencies.

There is no statutory legal obligation to contribute to the fund drive. However, you should review your corporate bylaws, board policies and personnel policies for specific mandates or prohibitions regarding solicitations and contributions. For example, some organizations have personnel policies that prohibit solicitation on company premises or on work-time. Additionally, some not-for-profit corporations have corporate bylaw provisions or board policies requiring a minimum annual contribution each year from directors.

Solicitation of Funds from Clients/Families

♦♦ 9 ♦♦

An adolescent treatment program launched its capital fund drive with a mass mailing to local businesses and private citizens appealing for contributions. Included within the many mailing lists used for this solicitation was a list of all clients/families who had received services through the agency, including those clients/families currently in treatment.

Discussion Questions

What are the ethical issues raised by agency solicitation of contributions from current or former clients and their families?

What standards could help define under what conditions, if any, such solicitation was ethically appropriate?

The concern raised by the above practice is the "targeting" of families in ways that manipulate and exploit their vulnerability as past or present service consumers. In this case, the agency's role as helper creates a power relationship that can be used to manipulate the gratitude, guilt or pain of former clients and their families. An important distinction may be the extent to which former or current clients are targeted to receive a solicitation for financial support. If, for example, a person received a fund drive mailing because he or she was the president of a local bank but also happened to be a parent of a child who went through treatment at the program, there was no targeting involved. In contrast, a solicitation sent from a mailing list of all former and current clients would in the view of many persons constitute exploitive targeting and could raise the risks of other ethical and legal breaches, e.g., inadvertent violation of confidentiality; violation of solicitation standards set forth in statutes, licensing regulations, or certification standards. The critical issue in assessing the ethical appropriateness of soliciting clients may differ depending on the nature of the service relationship and limitations defined within state statutes and regulations. The following two suggested principles may prove helpful:

1.   *The greater the intimacy of the service relationship—power of the service provider/vulnerability of the service consumer—the greater the potential for exploitation.*
2.   *The closer the solicitation is to the point in time of greatest service intensity, the greater the potential for exploitation (current clients are almost always more vulnerable for exploitation than former clients).*

(For a related discussion, see Chapter Six for a discussion of the ethical issues involved in the receipt of gifts from clients.)

Marketing
Misrepresentation of Scope or Intensity of Services

♦♦ 10 ♦♦

In an effort to increase admissions and rectify a chronically low utilization rate, an inpatient program announces two new specialized treatment tracks—one for methamphetamine users and one for chemically dependent women. The program promotional literature and media boldly proclaim the program's expertise and leadership in addressing the needs of these special populations of clients. In fact, these new tracks represent no substantive change in program design. The methamphetamine track consists of little more than a new lecture and recently purchased films and literature. The women's track includes assurance of assignment to a female counselor and a women's group held twice a week during a client's stay. No new staff have been recruited with special expertise to direct these tracks, and no new training has been provided to enhance staff expertise in these areas. Minor appendages have been added, but the basic treatment design has been neither reviewed nor revised for appropriateness to these new client populations.

Discussion Question

What ethical values are compromised by the misrepresentation of a program's service scope and intensity?

The marketing of specialty programs that represent exploitive experiments in superficial specialization to garner increased client admissions breaches a number of ethical principles. These practices first breach the principle of honesty through their failure to accurately represent the true scope and intensity of available services. Such practices also breach the principle of fidelity—the promises made to clients at admission that special services exist within the program to address their unique needs. Aggressive marketing of such specialty tracks of treatment that reflect only a superficial facelift of the existing program brings in clients whose needs will not only go unaddressed, but whose admission precludes their contact with more clinically appropriate treatment alternatives. Such superficial specialization also raises the danger of iatrogenic (treatment-caused) harm from such treatment.

When a treatment program holds itself out as providing specialized care, implying a clinically sound treatment service resulting in better outcomes than the treatment program down the street, many legal liability issues could arise. For example, because of the explosion of federal mandates and corresponding state legislation implementing welfare reform for families under TANF as well as permanency initiatives under the federal Adoption and Safe Families Act (Public Law 105-89) for children in the child welfare system, treatment agencies must be cautious of their "representations" to their clients. If clients receive treatment and fail, the failure could have severe consequences for the clients. This will be a hot area to monitor for class action suits especially against state agencies intervening to provide clinically appropriate services prior to terminating fundamental rights such as parentage or entitlements under the Medicaid programs. Other private attorneys may also be willing to pursue justice under theories of breach of contract, breach of implied promises, promissory estoppel and possibly third party beneficiary concepts of breach of contract.

Misrepresentation or Misallocation of Costs

♦♦ 11 ♦♦

The promotional materials emanating from a local treatment program highlight the fact that the program offers "free" assessments. The free assessment offer is, in fact, a marketing gimmick. The cost of assessment work is built into increased fees for all services provided by the agency.

Discussion Questions

Does the claim of "free" assessments constitute false advertising?

Does this arrangement bias an assessment process that technically can only be paid for if the person being assessed is determined to be in need of services?

If assessment fees are hidden within service fees, is it fair that persons requiring on-going services end up paying for the assessments of those clients deemed inappropriate for the agency's services?

While the marketing of "free assessments" or "free initial consultation" may help induce resistant clients to seek an initial discussion about treatment services, such marketing ploys do constitute a dishonest approach to soliciting client involvement. A more honest statement of fact would be that assessment charges are absorbed into fees for on-going services. While the client will not be billed for the initial consultation, costs for providing this service will be recouped through the fees paid by the client for any services that are provided after the assessment. Such an explanation places the service process on a more professional, contractual basis than on the stance of the client needing to be sold a bill of goods or otherwise manipulated into service involvement.

Exaggeration of Treatment Success

♦♦ 12 ♦♦

An addiction treatment program carried out an independent follow-up study of clients who they had treated. Based on a five year follow-up of treated clients, 25% revealed continuous sobriety since discharge, 31% revealed patterns of sobriety interrupted by one or more episodes of relapse, 15% who continued drinking problematically but with less severity than prior to treatment, and 29% whose drinking became more severe following treatment. Program personnel looked at the first three groups as all showing a positive effect of their treatment exposure, meaning that the program had "successfully impacted" 71% of clients who entered the program. This study and its interpretation were the basis for the 71% "success rate" regularly cited in program promotional materials and by program staff.

Discussion Questions

What makes the accurate presentation of likely treatment outcome an ethical issue?

What potential harm is created by program marketing efforts that create the illusion that recovery is easy—all you have to do is call?

The claim of a 71% success rate in the above vignette constitutes a misrepresentation because the communications:

- *failed to define "success," conveying the impression to the public and to other professionals that the 71% figure represented continuous, uninterrupted sobriety from the point of discharge from service*
- *failed to identify that the drinking patterns of 29% of clients who went through treatment actually worsened following their treatment experience, and*
- *failed to offer copies of the study to any who were interested so that the research methodology and overall integrity of the study could be assessed.*

A more accurate representation of "success rate" in the above situation would be to actually provide persons with the number of clients who fell into each of the four subgroups used in the study. The ethical concerns with the accurate representation of likely treatment outcome include the avoidance of exaggerated or fabricated claims of success intended to enhance a program's professional reputation and financial success and the avoidance of communications that oversimplify or exaggerate the ease with which one can move from addiction to recovery. Exaggerated claims of success and statements conveying the image that recovery is easily obtainable misrepresent the lethality of addiction—the number who will die or be severely disabled before they ever see a treatment program and those who will die or be disabled by their addiction following failed efforts at treatment.

Demonstrating outcomes is an issue that will continue to impact treatment providers not only in their marketing practices but more importantly in their funding negotiations and contracting processes. As the competition increases for the limited pool of resources in the field, providers must demonstrate quality, cost-effective services that produce outcomes. This trend is prevalent in both the private sector as managed care entities ration access and corresponding payment as well as in the public government-funded programs. Legislators and other government officials seek ratification of their decisions to invest tremendous resources into substance abuse treatment and prevention. As a result, providers have begun to see and will continue to experience outcome-related requirements in their contract conditions, accreditation standards and, in the future, their licensing requirements. When negotiating these outcomes, it is critical to have a common understanding of definitions and deliverables.

In addition to the contracting principles, federal and state laws govern research. It is important to identify whether your agency's outcome monitoring is a program evaluation or whether it constitutes research on human subjects requiring informed consent and institutional review board ("IRB") approval. See Chapter 9 for a discussion of research.

Exploitation of Family Members

♦♦ 13 ♦♦

The 30 second television spot for the newly opened treatment unit in the local hospital opens with a physician proclaiming that alcoholics and addicts are blinded by a disease of denial that makes it nearly impossible for them to initiate their recovery spontaneously. "It is the family," the physician exhorts, "not the addict that must initiate the change process. It is the family's responsibility." Panning through scenes of wrecked cars, then moving into a scene of a graveyard and finally a focused shot of one unnamed gravestone, the commercial ends with the words, "If you don't call us today, you may have no reason to tomorrow!"

Discussion Questions

Is this an effective tool to penetrate family denial or exploitive sensationalism?

Is this good advertising or poor taste?

Do such aggressive media campaigns unduly exploit and manipulate family guilt and emotional pain?

What standards should govern the design of such marketing devices?

A growing number of programs are attempting to define standards of good taste and standards of ethics that can be utilized to ethically critique potential marketing strategies. Some of the questions being used to evaluate and eliminate marketing pieces that breach standards of good taste and ethics include the following:

- *Does the spot manipulate and exploit the guilt and emotional pain of family members?*
- *Could the spot have unintended and harmful consequences to some viewers, e.g., a viewer of the above ad whose alcoholic family member recently died of disease, accident or suicide?*
- *Does the style (aggressiveness, inappropriate use of humor) of the spot demean the profession?*
- *Does the spot inadvertently contribute to stereotypes or myths about the nature of addiction or recovery?*
- *Do the images or words in the script of the spot contribute to demeaning ethnic or sexual stereotypes?*
- *Does the message of the spot oversimplify or create unrealistic expectations about the recovery process?*

You should check your state licensing, certification and code of conduct statutes and regulations for any advertising restrictions.

Financial Management

♦♦ 14 ♦♦

Ellen found herself increasingly frustrated in her role of Executive Director of a county-run treatment agency. Of particular note was the escalating layers of red tape it took to implement any decision, no matter how minuscule the issue. Lacking any petty cash mechanism that did not require weeks of time to successfully process, Ellen found herself taking money out of her own pocket to pay for minor needs rather than to confess to her staff that it would take three weeks to get the three dollars to buy felt tip markers for tomorrow's seminar. After months of frustration, Ellen found the following solution to her red tape nightmare. The agency was sponsoring quarterly workshops for human service professionals that were beginning to generate a substantial amount of income from registration fees. Ellen began to withhold the cash paid for workshop registrations to create a special "off the books" fund to deal with emergency needs and to make purchases unlikely to be approved by the county, e.g., food for an annual staff retreat.

Discussion Questions

What are your views on Ellen's solution to this problem?

What future problems might be anticipated with this secret fund?

While Ellen's intent in the above vignette may be benign, her actions have thrust her into an area of ethical and legal vulnerability. First, the practice of using her own money for agency expenditures could easily lead to a lack of clear boundary definition between Ellen's personal money and agency money. Secondly, her failure to turn over income through the normal agency procedure for the receipt of cash could leave Ellen open to charges of theft or embezzlement, particularly with no records as to how the cash was expended. Further, accounting practices which do not adhere to state or local requirements governing the accounting or auditing of the funds could result in claims of fraud, breach of contract or failure to comply with applicable laws and regulations. Additionally, these purchasing practices may circumvent a state or local law governing procurement practices. This error in judgment and the eventual disclosure of this practice could damage Ellen's professional reputation and the reputation of the agency and lead to a crisis in confidence through which the county board decreases funds or terminates the contract and community members decreases their contributions to support critically needed services.

♦♦ 15 ♦♦

A local not-for-profit treatment agency set up a sister corporation with overlapping boards. The purpose of the new corporation was to hold capital assets for the agency and to initiate a new set of counseling, training, and consultation services on a fee for service basis. The long range idea was that the new corporation would generate profit that could be pumped back into the agency as a means to offset recent decreases in the levels of federal and state funding available to the agency.

Discussion Question

Are the following smart business practices or breaches in ethical business practice?

- Funds from the agency are used to seed the private corporation.
- The private corporation leases space from the agency at far below market value.
- The private corporation routinely utilizes equipment and supplies of the agency.
- Agency staff supported by public grants perform clerical, accounting, and administrative functions on behalf of the private corporation.
- Staff who work at the private corporation are able to be paid salaries considerably above the market because of the overhead costs absorbed by the agency.
- The Executive Director of the agency also draws a salary from the private corporation.

The development of linked corporate structures has proved very beneficial to some not-for-profit service agencies while for others such experiments have resulted in a disastrous drain on agency resources. The overriding ethical concern in these situations is the question of who benefits from the arrangement. Additional concerns relate to compromises in ethical standards in the evolving relationship between the two related organizations. The dangers in this experiment include:

- *The private corporation diminishes rather than enhances the agency's service capacity by exerting a drain on agency resources. The relationship progressively compromises the agency's stated mission and values.*
- *The agency-private corporation relationship is structured to the personal financial advantage of a single individual or a small group of individuals.*
- *The misappropriation of resources from the agency to the private corporation breaches the principles of honesty and fidelity governing the relationship between the agency and its funding sources.*
- *The agency-private corporation relationship is used for purposes of deception, e.g., hiding the true extent of financial rewards being accrued by key individuals.*
- *The misappropriation of agency resources to the private corporation extends to the corporation an unfair advantage not available to its competitors.*

Several legal issues exist in this vignette. First, the vignette raises concerns relating to overlapping boards along with shared staff, utilization of equipment and supplies, leasing at below fair market value and services provided by staff paid under other grants. These commonalties between the two corporations could raise liability by "piercing the corporate veil." Generally, two corporations are considered separate and distinct legal entities, each liable for their own acts and debts. If the corporations fail to observe corporate formalities, one corporation could be held responsible for the liability of the other. To pierce the corporate veil, courts typically consider the following factors, (although no one factor is determinative):

- *Common directors, officers and employees exist.*
- *Parent corporation finances the subsidiary, pays salaries and other expenses.*
- *Subsidiary has inadequate capital to meets its reasonably foreseeable needs.*
- *Subsidiary has substantially no business except with the parent.*
- *Subsidiary has no assets except those conveyed by the parent.*
- *Parent corporation owns the property used by the subsidiary.*
- *Directors and executives of the subsidiary take their orders from the parent.*
- *Formal legal requirements of the subsidiary are not observed.*
- *Intra-corporate transactions are not at arm's length.*
- *The two operations are integrated through the commingling of funds, activities, common direction and supervision.*

As detailed above, it appears a court could find that the corporate veil is pierced, thus questioning the efficacy of establishing a separate corporation. A fallacy exists that not-for-profit organizations cannot generate a profit. That is simply not true. Engaging in for-profit purposes versus generating excess revenues are two different issues. If a not-for-profit company also has tax-exemption under Section 501(c)(3), the key question is whether the purposes and activities of that organization continue to further the charitable, religious, scientific or educational exempt purposes. So, if the subsidiary corporation was established because it was intended to engage in non-exempt purposes, the private benefit issues could jeopardize the parent corporation. Similarly, if the separate corporation was created to shield the parent from liability, it is likely that a plaintiff could pierce through the corporate veil. If the parent corporation was created to line the pockets of the individuals in control, there would be serious questions of fraud, misappropriation of charitable assets as well as misrepresentation and potential false claims allegations under the funding contracts for a diversion or misallocation of resources charged to that contract.

Treatment agencies should consult with legal counsel to explore creative legal structures to address a variety of concerns including liability issues, shielding assets, licensure or certification restrictions, enhanced reimbursement and focused organizational mission.

Fee Structure and Billing

◆◆ **16** ◆◆

In an effort to improve its collection of unpaid service fees, a treatment agency contracts with a bill collection agency.

Discussion Questions

Does providing the names of clients with unpaid bills to a collection agency constitute a violation of client confidentiality?

What about providing the names of past clients with unpaid bills to whom no communication was made at the time of service entry that the failure to pay bills would result in the involvement of a collection agency?

What are the ethical concerns inherent within the issue of fee collection?

*Helping professions differ from other businesses in the recourse available to collect unpaid bills in that the act of turning over the name of a client to a collection agency could constitute a breach of confidentiality if the agency does not execute a Qualified Service Organization ("QSO") Agreement or include a QSO provision in the contract with the collection agency. Under the federal confidentiality regulations, 42 C.F.R. §2.12(c)(4), communications between a program and a QSO are permissible even without patient consent. The regulations state that a QSO provides services to a program such a data processing, **bill collecting** (emphasis added), dosage preparation, laboratory analysis or legal, medical, accounting or other professional services. QSOs are required to state in writing that they will follow the regulations and will resist to the full extent of the law any efforts by unauthorized individuals and entities to access patient records. This promise includes maintaining the security requirements (42 C.F.R. §2.16) and complying with the prohibition against redisclosure of the information (42 C.F.R. §2.32). It is important to note that if the collection agency needs to file information in court to pursue legal remedies relating to the debt collection, specific court proceedings would* *need to occur under the federal confidentiality regulations (See 42 C.F.R. §2.64). To facilitate optimal communication, it is important that fee collection procedures be discussed with clients at the beginning of treatment and that the agency's fee collection policies be explained. Before contracting with a bill collection agency, you need to consult your attorney to determine whether any state consumer protection laws exist governing the behavior of the collection agency and whether any of your funding sources (such as Medicare or Medicaid) have specific statutes or regulations governing the assignment of payments to debt collection agencies or contingent percentage compensation arrangements. The helping agency's methods of fee collection should, to the greatest extent possible, be congruent with its service mission and not place undue strain on the agency-client relationship. Talking openly and candidly about fee payment problems and maintaining an openness to arrange for extended payment plans usually results in the agency being paid for its services without so alienating the client that they would refuse to seek future services from the agency.*

♦♦ 17 ♦♦

A family, following months of concern, has their son assessed at a local addiction treatment program. The assessment recommendation is that the youth participate in a 45-day program of inpatient treatment. The parents are told that the "daily rate" is $295 per day (or $13,275 for the 45 days) which with their 80% insurance coverage they estimate would leave them about $2,650 to pay out of pocket. Following their son's treatment, they are shocked to receive a total bill of more than $20,000. It appears that the physician's services are not covered in the "daily rate" and that numerous other billable services are provided daily which are also not included within this rate.

Discussion Questions

What ethical values were compromised in this situation?

What guidelines or standards should be used in discussing service fees, billing, and payment policies with clients?

If the same services a client was seeking are available from another community agency at half the price, is there an ethical duty to inform the client of this alternative to lower cost services?

Communication to the parents in the above situation constitutes a breach of the informed consent process by failing to adequately apprise the parents of the full financial burden they would have to assume related to their son's treatment. This breach involved the failure to inform the parents that there were fees for many services not included in the daily inpatient charge, the nature of those services and related fees, and a reasonable estimate of what the parents' portion of the total treatment costs was likely to be. While there is some variation from client to client based on the precise menu of services each receives, use of a regularly updated average of total treatment costs is a more honest representation of costs than the "daily rate" used in the above vignette. The ethical demand is that clients have as full and accurate a picture as possible of service costs with which they can make the decision to pursue or not pursue service involvement

This is a newer area that will continue to generate potential activity for court decisions and future legislation – the issue of economic informed consent. As discussed in vignette #4 above, informed consent requires the disclosure of the proposed course of treatment by balancing the probable risks against the probable benefits. Economic informed consent suggests that the treatment provider discuss with client limitations on services available to the client resulting from provisions in the client's insurance or managed care plan as well as the corresponding costs for which the client will be responsible. For a detailed discussion on this issue see Managed Care Technical Assistance Series Volume Five: "Ethical Issues for Behavioral Health Care Practitioners and Organizations in a Managed Care Environment" (DHHS Publication No 98-3241) produced for SAMSHA.

◆◆ 18 ◆◆

An addiction treatment program following several years of problems in collecting co-payments (that portion of client fees not reimbursable via private insurance or other third party) implemented the following procedure: Services fees were raised approximately 30%, insurance companies were billed for the 50-80% of the costs of client service, and client co-payments were routinely written off as uncollectible.

Discussion Questions

Comment on the potential ethical issues raised by this practice.

What is your response to a justification of this practice which says writing off co-payments increases client access to services and decreases the financial burden on the client?

Many health and human service organizations have utilized some variation of the above procedure and justified it as a service to its clients. For an agency to reduce the co-payment portion or waive the co-payment fee to be paid by the client in cases of extreme hardship would be beneficial. In such cases the agency absorbs the loss of all or a portion of the co-payment and there would be no problem of fraud or deception of the insurance company. In the above case, however, agency fees are artificially raised so that what the agency is alleging to be 80% of their fee to the insurance company is actually 100% of their fee. This practice would constitute a breach of honesty and fidelity in the relationship between the agency and the insurance company. This practice would leave the agency open to potential charges of deception or fraud.

Organizations must be careful about waiver of co-pays. Depending on the health insurance policy or managed care agreement, the treatment provider may be bound by contract to collect the co-pay. In certain contracting and regulatory situations, co-pays are prohibited. You should carefully review your contracts, provider manuals and other payment policies of the third party payors with whom you conduct business to determine whether you have a legal obligation regarding collection and/or waiver of co-pays.

Additionally, certain Medicare/Medicaid fraud and abuse laws prohibit these practices. Federal law prohibits a person from offering or transferring payment to any individual that is likely to influence such individual to order or receive any item or service paid by Medicare or Medicaid. This prohibition would include the waiver of coinsurance amounts, except in certain narrowly defined circumstances, such as copayment waivers that are not advertised, not routine, and made after a good faith financial determination. Have your attorney check the Safe Harbor regulations to see if the waiver of co-pay falls into an exception. See 42 C.F.R. §1001.952.

♦♦ 19 ♦♦

A hospital recently integrated its psychiatric and addiction treatment services into a single unit, partially to bypass increasingly restrictive inpatient admission and length of stay criteria imposed by third party payers on alcohol-drug treatment admissions. Under the new unit structure, those addicted clients who appear to need extended care are given a primary psychiatric diagnosis, e.g., depression, and a secondary substance abuse diagnosis. This use of a "billable diagnosis" is rationalized by the view that the practice opens up avenues of service for clients that would otherwise be unattainable. Some of these patients (due to their financial status) would be denied access to services if it were not for this "billable diagnosis" practice.

Discussion Questions

Who are the good guys and the bad guys in this story?

Discuss the short- and long-term effects of this practice on the profession, the agency, individual staff members and current or potential clients?

This practice of "billable diagnosis" or "administrative diagnosis" violates the ethical principles of honesty and fairness upon which the relationship between the service provider and the insurance company is based. In spite of the rejoinder that such misrepresentation is the only way to get clients needed services, such misrepresentation violates the integrity upon which diagnosis and treatment is based and opens the practitioner to charges of deception and fraud—charges that could damage the reputation of the individual practitioner, damage the reputation of the program, and threaten the future accessibility of client services.   The diagnosis should reflect an objective and accurate assessment of the client's clinical condition, not the status of the client's income or scope of insurance coverage. When accurate client diagnosis falls outside the boundary of insurance coverage, efforts can be made to assure access to services by:

- *providing plans for long-term payment by the client/family*
- *soliciting public support to subsidize services to the uninsured or underinsured*
- *providing services on a pro-bono basis*
- *referring clients to lower cost or publicly funded treatment alternatives.*

"Upcoding" is a taboo in today's legal environment that can result in enhanced reimbursement but also a free trip to the federal penitentiary. As previously discussed in Chapter 2, a trend is occurring in the health care industry, as a whole, to vigorously investigate, prosecute and punish corporations, including its officers and employees who engage in fraudulent billing practices. Your organization should implement a corporate compliance program to detect questionable billing practices, train employees, systematically communicate the legal restrictions and company policy, institute a code of ethics, implement an employee reporting mechanism to alert management to improper practices and draft detailed procedures for investigating, responding

to, correcting or halting improper or illegal practices as well as enforcing discipline as appropriate. Violations of the statutes and regulations in this area could put your agency out of business and you in jail.

Referrals

◆◆ 20 ◆◆

Over the past two years an informal arrangement has been made between a private practice therapist and your inpatient program. The private therapist refers a large number of clients to inpatient addiction treatment. The inpatient program refers a large number of its clients to the therapist for on-going outpatient counseling following inpatient treatment.

Discussion Questions

Does this practice simply reflect a good utilization of community resources both by the program and the private therapist?

What ethical issues or problems, if any, could arise from this arrangement?

If, in the vignette above, the inpatient program paid the therapist a fee of $250 for each inpatient referral, most persons would readily raise ethical concerns about this practice of what has come to be called "fee splitting." And yet there is a thin line between the exchange of dollars for referrals and the practice of referring other clients (in addition to those referred by the therapist) for outpatient counseling with the therapist. The concern is that the best interests of particular clients may be compromised by the institutional self-interests inherent within such informal arrangements. Exceptionally close scrutiny must be maintained to assure the clinical integrity of the referral process—an assurance that referrals are being made to a particular therapist because it is judged that the therapist will provide the best possible services for this particular client, not because of the financial self-interests of the institution.

The issue of referrals is another hot issue in the health care legal arena. Multi-billions of dollars have been invested to audit, investigate and prosecute healthcare organizations suspected of "fraud and abuse." This is a very complex area and what may appear to be a simple favor or creative business structure may now be grounds for civil fines of $10,000 each, criminal penalties, including imprisonment and exclusion from government funded *programs such as Medicare and Medicaid.*

When structuring any business relationship that may involve a referral fee or reciprocal referrals, have your attorney review the transaction for any fraud and abuse implications. Generally, the fraud and abuse laws prohibit: (1) direct, indirect or disguised payments in exchange for the referral of patients; (2) the submission of false, fraudulent or misleading claims which characterize the service differently than the service actually rendered, or claims which otherwise do not comply with applicable program or contractual requirements; and (3) making false representations to any person or entity in order to gain or retain participation in a program or to obtain payment for any service. There are also anti-referral laws commonly known as the Stark laws, however, many of these laws apply to physicians or health care providers with investment interests in the entity to which they seek to refer. Because these laws, court decisions, administrative opinions and HHS, Office of Inspector General (OIG) guidance are an evolving area and the consequences for non-compliance so severe, you should consult a health care attorney who is familiar with these federal laws, the safe harbor regulations, OIG opinions and any applicable state law self-referral prohibitions.

Dual Relationships
Conflict of Interests

♦♦ 21 ♦♦

Agency vehicles for the last four years have all been purchased from an auto dealership owned by the President of the Board of the agency. All of the cars have been bought at or below market value, but without competitive bidding.

Discussion Questions

What ethical issues could be raised about these transactions?

What standard or process could facilitate decision-making in situations where staff, volunteers or board members might have, or might be perceived to have, a conflict of interest?

The concern raised by the above vignette is the potential for someone to exploit their role within the agency to receive undue advantage and financial gain. Although a superficial investigation would lead to the view that the President is selling cars to the agency at cost as a personal favor, a closer analysis may be warranted. Since the wholesale price a dealer pays for his or her merchandise is often prorated according to volume, the President of the Board reaps an indirect benefit from these transactions even though the agency gets the cars at cost. By influencing the agency's choice of makes and models of cars desired, the President could also use this mechanism as a way to move cars he could not otherwise sell. Another concern is whether the local community's perception of potential impropriety in such transactions damages the professional integrity of the agency. Opening up the process for competitive bidding reduces both real and perceived problems.

Anytime a transaction is entered into with a Board member, the agency must adhere to its conflict of interest policies. For a tax-exempt organization, a recent law was enacted in 1996 as part of the Taxpayer Bill of Rights 2. This Act imposes a two-tiered excise tax penalty on "disqualified persons" who receive "excess benefits" in a business transaction with a 501(c)(3) or 501(c)(4) organization. This excise tax of $10,000 may also be levied against each organization manager/director who knowingly participated in an excess benefit transaction. The Act was intended to provide the IRS with an intermediate tax enforcement tool, short of revocation, to improve enforcement (hence, this law is commonly referred to as the intermediate sanctions law). This is significant because of this penalty that can be imposed not only on the disqualified person but on your volunteer board members as well. Specific IRS concerns are unreasonable salaries and other benefits paid to charitable organization executives, various types of non-fair market value transactions involving insiders, sales and conversions of nonprofit healthcare organizations at less than fair market value and other transactions that divert charitable assets into private hands. Some key issues to consider include:

- *Identify disqualified persons (check the regulations and statute for definitions relating to relatives and 35% of the control or beneficial interest in an entity).*
- *Examine potential excess benefits transactions with Board members; the President, CEO, COO, CFO, treasurer, the founder of the organization, a substantial contributor and those with key managerial authority.*
- *Examine who will benefit from these transactions.*
- *Examine revenue sharing arrangements.*
- *Have the board or a committee comprised of non-interested persons approve the transaction.*
- *Prohibit members from voting on conflict situations.*
- *Obtain comparability data in determining the reasonableness of the compensation or the fair market value.*
- *Document the reasonableness of transactions in board minutes.*

- *Implement a conflict of interest policy.*
- *Institute procedures requiring the interested person to leave the meeting during the discussion and vote.*
- *Require an annual conflict of interest disclosure signed by Board members.*

♦♦ 22 ♦♦

Horace and Mary have been close friends and professional colleagues for more than ten years. During these years, Mary served as Director of a large treatment agency and Horace served as Director of a statewide professional advocacy group. They shared many professional battles and through the years developed a close relationship between their respective families. Horace has just been appointed by the Governor to direct the state agency responsible for the licensing, funding, and monitoring addiction services. More than 80% of the funding of Mary's agency comes from the agency Horace now directs.

Discussion Questions

What ethical issues might arise for both Horace and Mary given the nature of their past personal and professional relationship?

Will Mary inevitably have special access to Horace, not available to Directors from other agencies?

What would be examples of how Mary could try to take undue advantage of this relationship?

The challenge in the above situation is to assure that the pre-existing personal and professional relationships do not interfere with the judgment and actions of either Horace or Mary. Mary must be careful not to exploit the prior relationship for special favors, while Horace must guard against loss of objectivity through granting special favors due to the nature and duration of their relationship or withholding normal favor to Mary out of fear of perceived favoritism.

Typically, having a professional business relationship will not trigger a legal conflict of interest unless you (or a relative) have an investment or other financial interest in the transaction. When faced with the dilemma, you should check your state laws and administrative codes governing conflict of interest, purchasing and procurement. Due to the increased public scrutiny during recent years over government spending and political patronage, your state may have adopted a more stringent procurement code prohibiting certain transactions or state business with relatives and other business partners. That issue should be thoroughly researched to determine the impact on the agency's existing funding. In clearer cases of legal conflicts of interest, Horace may wish to address the matter with the Governor's and the State agency's legal counsel to formally recuse himself from decisions impacting Mary's agency. The recusal letter and substitute decision-making process should be carefully documented at the onset of Horace's appointment. Notwithstanding adherence to the law and recusal procedures, when a perceived conflict exists, in reality a conflict exists and action may need to taken to address and remove the perceived conflict.

Management of Facilities, Property and Supplies

♦♦ 23 ♦♦

Your agency receives donations of a whole range of goods and services from individuals and businesses throughout the service catchment area. In recent months, donations of non-durable food items have far exceeded the quantities needed for your residential programs. The Director, rather than turning such donations down, has begun to disperse non-durable food items which are not needed to the staff. The thinking of the Director is that staff are underpaid and any extra perks such as the food items are well-deserved.

Discussion Questions

Do you agree or disagree with this practice? What unforeseen problems and issues could arise related to this practice?

What alternative solution might exist to such surpluses in non-durable food items?

The ethical principal of fidelity commits us quite simply to keep our promises. In the above situation, the agency made an implicit promise when it solicited food items that these goods would be used to help feed clients involved in residential substance abuse rehabilitation. The dispersal of these items to staff—no matter how underpaid and deserving they may be—constitutes a breach of this promise. The actions, if revealed publicly, could jeopardize the willingness of other local businesses to provide donated goods and services and could lead to an overall deterioration in community support for the program. The potential damage to the reputation of the program resulting from disclosure of such practices would also have to be measured in reduced willingness of clients, families and other agencies to seek out the program's services. Many agencies handle this situation by reciprocal agreements to share such expendable supplies with other helping organizations and inform their donors of this practice.

◆◆ 24 ◆◆

One of the largest budget items for your residential program is the contract for food service which for the past two years has been awarded to Food Services, Inc. The President of Food Services, Inc. stops by today to drop off a "token of appreciation" for your business. Knowing your passionate and masochistic support for the Chicago Cubs, the president provides you (and your spouse) with a packaged free trip, hotel, and box seat tickets for an upcoming series with the St. Louis Cardinals.

Discussion Questions

As the Director of your agency, would you accept this offer?

What ethical issues, if any, could be involved in accepting this "token?"

What standards should govern agency—contractor/supplier relationships?

There are a number of issues and problems raised by this vignette. The first is that acceptance of the gift may create a sense of obligation to continue contracting with Food Services, Inc., which may or may not be in the best interests of the agency. The concern is that social or financial relationships (including receipt of gifts) with contractors might unduly influence contracting decisions at the expense of the organization. Any gift or special benefit received as a result of the contract should accrue to the agency. It was agency resources through which the contract was executed and any secondary benefits derived from the contract should go to the agency, not the personal benefit of one or more of its staff persons. The other concern with accepting the gift is that such acceptance creates a special relationship that could alter the equity of access to contracts by other community vendors.

The issue of acceptance of gifts from vendors, except in cases of government and funding agencies, is not prohibited by law. These issues are more commonly addressed in personnel policies, codes of ethics, codes of conduct and corporate compliance program guidelines. However, be aware that if you are a director, officer or key management person (i.e. CEO or CFO) who has made a decision not in the best interests of your agency, you could face potential liability under theories of breach of fiduciary duty. In evaluating a director's or officer's duty of care, courts will look to: (1) whether the director's action reflected honesty and faithfulness to the director's duty and obligations; (2) whether there was any intention to take advantage of the corporation; and (3) whether the director in fact believed the action was in the best interests of the corporation.

Sale of Non-Profit

♦♦ 25 ♦♦

Your agency, Treatment Techniques, is a non-profit, community-based provider founded in 1980. Over the past two decades you have built this agency from a $100,000 budget to a $20 million organization. Approximately 90% of your funding is derived from state contracts, state grants and Medicaid. The remaining 10% comes from private pay and private insurance. For the past 10 years, you have successfully generated excess revenues ranging from $200,000 to $1.2 million each year. A major, national for-profit company called Behavioral Health Solutions wants to expand services in your state. Behavioral Health Solutions is impressed with your financials, clinical programs and staff so they approach you to sell Treatment Techniques.

Discussion Questions

When you respond to this situation ask yourself:

Who benefits from the sale?

What ethical/legal dilemmas arise from a non-profit community-based agency "selling out" to an out-of-state for-profit company?

This vignette raises a number of troubling ethical questions. The first question is: who owns and to whom is a non-profit service agency accountable? In most cases, the accumulated resources of such agencies have come from the community itself with the understanding that the agency will endure to provide the services that it has promised the community. Values of loyalty and fidelity would dictate that no agency can precipitously abandon its commitment and promise without just cause and without the larger community's involvement in that decision. The essential question here is whether the long range impact of this decision upon the community will be one of benefit or harm. The second question is whose needs will be served by the decision to sell the non-profit agency to the for-profit company. The concern here is that the needs and interests of the agency staff (e.g., promises of financial incentives to the CEO and/or staff) might lead them to put their own needs above those of the community. This vignette raises the rather troubling question: Is the soul (mission) of a non-profit service agency for sale to the highest bidder?

The sale of not-for-profit companies or assets to a for-profit is being scrutinized across the country by a number of state attorney generals, as well as the IRS. Should a board of directors determine that such a sale is truly in the best interests of the community, numerous legal barriers pertaining to funding contract assignments and restrictions would need to be addressed and thorough due diligence conducted.

Merger Mania

♦♦ 26 ♦♦

You have been told in order to survive these tight financial times, your agency should diversify and combine forces with like or complimentary organizations. The competitors around you have or are intending on merging or affiliating. You and your Board of Directors decide to actively pursue a merger where your agency would be merged into a larger agency and no longer have independent existence. To seal the deal, the larger agency promises you a nice title, retention of existing responsibility, and $10,000 more in salary per year.

Discussion Questions

What kinds of questions should you and the Board address before making a merger decision?

Should you disclose the employment offer to anyone and how does that affect your decision-making, negotiating strategy and bargaining position for the company as a whole?

This increasingly common scenario poses three ethical issues. The first is the merger decision itself and whether the best interests of the agency's clients and the larger community will be served or disserved by this decision. If the needs of these constituents would be best served by the merger, then it might even constitute a breach of ethics not to pursue a merger. The second ethical question is the extent to which the financial and other incentives offered the CEO might influence his or her decision-making process. Given what could emerge as a conflict between the CEO's own financial interests and the best long term interests of the agency and its clients, it would be best if the CEO was recused from direct involvement in the final decision of the agency to enter into this particular merger.

The final question involves the issue of disclosure of the financial and other rewards that might have come to the CEO through the merger. No information pertinent to the final merger decision should be withheld from the community. The agency, as a non-profit, community-based organization, has promised its constituent community that it would use the resources provided it to serve the needs of that community. The community has a right to know all information pertinent to such an important decision so that it can assess the quality of stewardship of the resources it has provided the organization.

Due Diligence Discovery

♦♦ 27 ♦♦

Your agency is proceeding with a corporate affiliation with another agency. During a due diligence process, you disclose that an external audit is pending with Medicaid. The day of the closing, your facility receives the results of the audit indicating that your agency owes Medicaid $400,000 in recoupment for erroneous billings.

Discussion Questions

What should you do and what could be the consequences of disclosing or not disclosing prior to the Closing of the transaction?

Would your answer differ if the recoupment amount was $30,000 rather then $400,000?

The value of honesty would dictate that this disclosure be made, even if it postponed or derailed the merger. Failure to disclose this information would breach the good faith, no surprise, all-information-on-the-table stance essential to a successful merger. While refusal to disclose this information might produce short-term benefits, it would likely harm the merger process and create a subsequent climate of distrust and conflict that could harm the staff and clients of both participating agencies. Failure to disclose could also constitute a material breach of the merger agreement or a false representation made. If discovered, later civil as well as criminal liability could result, not to mention unwind the transaction.

Fraud & Abuse

♦♦ 28 ♦♦

Your CEO has been impressing upon your program directors "no margin-no mission" and giving them regular pep talks to "keep those beds full, increase census, keep up those counseling hours, you must meet budgeted revenue projections!" A data entry clerk at your facility approaches you today and says "I know Counselor Jones was not here last night, yet he signed the billing statement saying he ran two group last night. I would have gone to my program director but she says we need to do whatever it takes to meet budget projections."

Discussion Questions

How would you respond to the data entry clerk?

How would you approach the program director?

Assuming the facts are true, do you have an obligation to tell anyone about the billing "error"?

There are many potential targets of harm that could unfold in this situation: the data entry clerk, the program director, the agency as a whole and its clients and to you--the individual to whom this information has just been disclosed. Having heard this information, you now bear a responsibility to correct this ethical/legal breach. It might be best to simultaneously disclose the information you've just heard to the program director and to the CEO and to place such disclosure in writing to protect yourself. If such communication does not result in correction of the practice of false billing, then you need to consider disclosure of this information to an outside authority. (See later discussion on whistle-blowing.) See also discussion in Chapter 2 on Corporate Compliance.

E-mailing Price Information

♦♦ 29 ♦♦

One of the staff in the accounts receivable department received an e-mail from a local competitor in the community. This competitor, Counseling Centers of Cocomo, wrote, "Please forward to me your current price list. If you do so, we promise to match your prices and make sure we do not exceed prices of Alternatives Counseling Center (another local competitor)." In an effort to help the agency, your staff person e-mailed the price list with an informal message stating "here's the info, please send me a copy of your price list to verify that we have the same agreed upon prices which are lower than Alternatives Counseling Center." Now, two months later, you as the Executive Director found out that Alternatives filed an antitrust lawsuit against Counseling Centers of Cocomo. You approach the A/R staff person and ask to review all her e-mails for the last 6 months. She nervously refuses claiming some are personal and you have no right to monitor her e-mail.

Discussion Questions

What are the ethical/legal issues raised by this vignette?

What policies/procedures should you have in place to avoid this ethical/legal dilemma in the future?

There are two ethical issues here: First, we have a form of collusion between agencies ("price fixing") that while enhancing the interests of the agencies, does potential harm to the community by artificially inflating prices for services that would normally be contained as a result of competition. Second, we have the issue of the degree of needed discretion regarding e-mail communications. Because of their informality, e-mails may include information potentially harmful to many parties that their creators would never consider putting in a memo or letter. The value of discretion dictates that great care be taken in such communications that can come back later to harm the individual who wrote the e-mail and potentially many other parties. Your personnel policies and code of ethics need to clearly address confidentiality of pricing information to avoid federal antitrust and other state law restraint of trade prohibitions. Additionally, your policies should indicate that e-mails are company property and may be monitored at any time.

Telecommuting

♦♦ 30 ♦♦

With the emphasis on outreach and case coordination, several of your clinical staff perform much of their documentation on laptops or home computers. These "telecommuters" are only required to come into the office twice a month. They e-mail the clinical documentation once a week to the facility. Even after e-mailing the information, the counselor maintains a copy of the confidential case notes on the computer. The counselor also allows her high school age son to use the computer for his English papers.

Discussion Questions

Under this vignette, has the counselor compromised confidentiality for her clients?

How does this arrangement affect the integrity of the clinical record system?

What if someone in the business office approached you and says, "I want to work from home too. I can input the accounts payable checks at home." What ethical/legal issues arise in this era of telecommuting?

The increased use of laptop computers for service documentation in the field raises a host of new ethical issues, most involving potential breaches of confidentiality. In the vignette above, the worker is using agency resources for non-agency business (her son's homework) and is doing so in ways that could provide others access to confidential information. A laptop with such information must be thought of as a file cabinet containing confidential client information and great care must be taken regarding its security. (Imagine the potential repercussions of such a laptop stolen from an automobile during the worker's daily rounds.)

To safeguard the confidential information on your laptop:

- *Make sure your password is unique. Try not to use birth dates, addresses, your name or a family member's name, or social security numbers. Try to make the password at least six, or more preferably eight characters long. Keep your password separate from your computer.*
- *Make sure your laptop is marked or labeled with a control number and, if possible, a clearly visible organization logo (if it belongs to the company).*
- *Keep your laptop in a secure place. Keep your laptop in a locked cabinet in your office, or in a secured place at home.*
- *When traveling, don't advertise that your are carrying a laptop. Keep it in a nondescript bag. Keep alert when putting your luggage through the x-ray equipment. If necessary, wait until the person in front of you is completely through before putting your laptop on the conveyor belt.*

- *If you use your laptop in a public area, consider obtaining a filter screen to prevent individuals on either side of you from reading what is on the computer screen.*
- *Use only authorized software. Bootleg software or software downloaded from unfamiliar sources can contain viruses or other problem that can corrupt the information stored in your laptop.*
- *Back-up the information on your laptop periodically.*

♦♦ 31 ♦♦

Staff/Managerial/Executive Compensation

What do the following two situations share in common? Agency A pays its counselors nearly 40% below the average paid to counselors in the geographical area. Agency B pays its CEO and two other key executives three times the average for such roles in the state and more than five times the level of compensation provided for counselor positions within the agency.

Discussion Questions

What are the ethical issues raised by these situations?

How should a non-profit, tax-exempt organization determine the level of compensation for all of its employees?

The practices of Agencies A and B both involve potential harm to one or more parties. The over- and under-compensation of those who work in addiction treatment agencies moves into the ethical arena when the level of a salary, level in relationship to other salaries, level in relationship to community norms, speed at which a salary is raised, the process through which a salary is raised, or the structure of the salary increase (e.g,, hidden compensation) threaten direct or indirect harm to service consumers, individual employees, the agency, or the community.

Under-compensation of staff undermines the principle of justice, but also poses potential threats to service consumers by compromising the ability of the agency to recruit and retain staff with adequate levels of education, training and experience. The resulting deterioration in levels of competence and morale and high levels of staff turnover create a climate in which harm to clients is possible and probable.

Excessive compensation of staff could violate several ethical principles: stewardship (of community resources), fidelity (the promise that resources give to the agency would address community needs), and honesty(where the level or process by which salaries were determined was hidden from the community.)

At a legal level, the primary issue for a tax exempt provider is whether the compensation is reasonable and complies with the IRS statutes and regulations pertaining to "intermediate sanctions." For a discussion on intermediate sanctions, see Vignette #21 in Chapter 3. In determining the reasonableness of compensation paid to Executives, the IRS requires: (1) a disinterested Board of Directors to approve the compensation; (2) the Board or committee to obtain appropriate comparability data; and (3) the Board to adequately document the basis for determining the compensation was reasonable. For comparability purposes, the Board should look at: (1) compensation levels paid by similarly situated organizations (both taxable and tax exempt, for profit and not-for profit agencies for functionally comparable positions); (2) the location of the organization, including the availability of similar specialties in the geographic area; (3) independent compensation surveys by nationally recognized independent firms; and (4) actual written offers from similar institutions competing for the person's services. The relationship or disparity in salaries between employees paid by the organization is not a legal factor but an ethical consideration.

Our best advice on the issues of staff compensation is that any such compensation (no matter how low or how high) should be able to pass what we call "The Mike Wallace Test": Would full public disclosure of this level of compensation to a local, state or national audience bring embarrassment or harm to the agency? Would it alter local citizen support for the agency and their degree of willingness to seek services from the agency?

Chapter
Four

Personal Conduct

Nearly every profession in the course of its birth and evolution must address the boundary line between personal and professional conduct, between the individual's right to privacy and autonomy and the ethical and moral conduct that constitutes an implicit duty of the profession. Where and how this line is drawn is likely to differ from profession to profession, from organization to organization, across programs within the same service organization, and across different cultural contexts.

If there is a general rule on this issue it might be summarized as follows: behavior of those working in the addictions field during non-work time is a matter of personal privacy until there is an inextricable linkage, or *nexus*, between this private behavior and their public, professional performance. But as we shall see, defining where to draw this point of nexus can be most difficult. The following vignettes will help the reader explore his or her own thoughts about this question of nexus.

Critical Incidents

Use of Alcohol/Drugs

♦♦ 32 ♦♦

You are a supervisor at a community social service agency that provides mental health and addiction treatment services. Your emergency crisis calls are handled by alternating staff from the mental health and addictions units. You have just received a formal complaint from the Medical Director of a local hospital regarding the following situation: the hospital emergency room called your agency to assess an adolescent who had been brought to the hospital by his family in a state of alcohol and drug intoxication. When the emergency on-call staff person from the agency arrived, the ER charge nurse noted the strong smell of alcohol on the worker's breath. The non-drinking parents, also smelling alcohol on the worker's breath, took their child and left the hospital after voicing their strong condemnation of the hospital. When asked about the situation, the worker, who to the best of your knowledge has no history of alcohol-related problems, responds that he had one beer before his beeper went off, and that he was neither intoxicated nor impaired.

Discussion Questions

How would you respond to this situation?

Identify the ethical or performance issues that would be of concern to you.

Is "on-call time" personal time or professional time? If you feel it is professional time, what is the implication for key supervisory staff who may technically always be "on-call?"

What standards would be appropriate to address the issues raised in the above situation?

Many agencies have found it necessary to define explicit standards of professional conduct related to on-call duty. These standards include such issues as accessibility, response time, professional appearance in situations involving face-to-face contact with clients or allied professionals, and drinking/drug use. The primary concern is that smelling alcohol on the breath of a service provider assessing the needs of alcohol and drug dependent persons would very likely do injury to the professional credibility of the helping person. Most of the agencies that explore this issue define on-call time as professional time and prohibit drinking while on-call. The application of professional standards to on-call time assumes that there is a clear schedule or other delineation of when these standards do and do not apply. It is best if such scheduling also applies to supervisory or administrative staff. This structuring of on-call assures that the issue of alcohol-impairment in the chain of staff-supervisory decision-making in an emergency situation should never have to arise. It also assures that the line between on and off call is clear enough that the private lives of staff members are not totally consumed by their professional responsibilities.

From a legal perspective, agencies can clearly impose conditions of employment during on-call time. The key legal issue is paying the employee for the on-call time consistent with the wage and hours laws in the Fair Labor Standards Act, 29 U.S.C. §207. If an employee is "waiting to be engaged", then the time that he is waiting is non-compensable and any hours worked will start when the employee is actually engaged to do a particular job. If an employee is "engaged to be waiting" then all hours that the employee is waiting will be compensable hours of work. There is no hard and fast rule. The primary analysis focuses on the restrictive nature of the conditions of employment and whether the employee has freedom to move about and pursue private interests while "on-call." In this case, the imposition of no drinking of alcohol/use of drugs alone is not restrictive enough to suggest the employee is "engaged to be waiting." Therefore, the on-call time does not need to be compensated. In addition to the federal wage and hour laws, you should consult your state labor and employment laws and regulations for additional guidance.

♦♦ 33 ♦♦

You are an employee of a local addictions prevention and treatment agency. You are at a social gathering of 15 persons and observe a stranger in a state of extreme intoxication leaving the party by himself to drive home.

Discussion Questions

What, if anything, would you do?

Would your action differ if you were hosting the party?

Is there any increased duty to act or increased liability in such situations given the nature of our profession? Would failure to act in the above situation be comparable to a physician, who while dining at a restaurant, failed to intervene and assist a fellow patron who was having a heart attack?

The question in this vignette is not what should anyone do in response to a person intending to drive in a state of extreme intoxication, but whether there is any special ethical duty for action in such a situation that emanates directly from one's professional training and role within the addictions field. It is very helpful for agencies to explore staff responsibilities in such situations and articulate values or standards to guide staff who find themselves in such circumstances. Most such discussions conclude that addiction workers do have a special duty to model assertive intervention with the intoxicated person who poses a threat to public safety. This duty springs from multiple sources: the worker's training to recognize alcohol-drug impairment, the worker's advocacy of such intervention to the public through his or her professional role, the imminent harm posed by the impaired driver, and the damage to the reputation of the worker and the agency that could result from failure to intervene.
    As a guest, you would have no legal duty to intervene. In fact, if you tried to detain someone they could potentially bring a false imprisonment claim against you, although this cause of action would be rare. The legal responsibil-

ity under this vignette would differ if you were the host. Some states impose a legal duty upon social hosts to refuse to furnish alcoholic beverages to an obviously intoxicated person, if under the circumstances, such person will constitute a reasonably foreseeable danger or risk of injury to a third person. See Manning v. Nobile, 411 Mass. 382, 391 (1991). The basis for imposing liability upon social hosts is the proposition that between the social host and the public in general, the social host is in a better position than third parties to prevent harm to others resulting from a guest's intoxication. Public policy supports the imposition of a duty only in cases where the host can control and regulate the supply of alcohol. State laws vary on the nature of their "dram shop laws" that would be potentially applied to the situation in this vignette.

◆◆ 34 ◆◆

Many addiction treatment agencies are addressing the issue of smoking among their staff and clients. There are many indicators of this trend: the emergence of restrictive smoking policies, the growing number of smoke-free treatment facilities, and the definition of nicotine addiction as part of a client's total pattern of drug addiction requiring assessment and treatment. A growing number of addiction agencies are taking the position that only non-smokers will be hired to work in direct service roles with clients.

Discussion Questions

Given the unique nature of addiction counseling, are there special standards of personal conduct to which staff can and should be held accountable?

If staff are to be held to a professional standard related to smoking, what about obesity, gambling, workaholism or other patterns of behavior that are viewed by some as excessive or potentially addictive behaviors?

Are these important ethical and/or professional practice issues or signs of growing over-intrusiveness of organizations into the personal lives of their employees?

The misuse of drugs by an addictions counselor would be an ethical breach in no less measure than the immoral conduct of a minister. In the addictions field, one's relationship with drugs and beliefs about drugs are work-related issues (Bissell and Royce, 1987). The only thing that has prevented the experience of this ethical duty related to smoking is the historical failure of the culture (and the professional field) to define nicotine as a drug and define the continued use of nicotine as an addiction. As this changes, the issue of smoking will be posed as an ethical issue for workers in the addiction treatment field. This suggests that ethical sensitivities and ethical standards can evolve over time as knowledge and perspectives change.

Private behavior is a professional issue to the extent that private behavior affects professional performance. What some might consider private behavior is an issue of professional conduct to the extent that smoking or other excessive behaviors compromise the reputation and ability of a person to work with addicted persons or carry the prevention message – in short, to perform his or her job duties. Each organization must draw this line in a way that is consistent with and supportive of its mission and philosophy. Professional standards related to other excessive and compulsive behaviors are likely to evolve as the understanding of the etiology, prevention and treatment of these conditions evolves. Defining the nexus between private behavior and professional duty and obligation in these areas is likely to be an uncomfortable but important issue for staff to explore. There are twin dangers here: one, that we ignore this issue completely and two, that we succumb to the field's own propensity for excessiveness by creating inordinately narrow and intrusive standards for private conduct.

Almost half of the states have statutes limiting smoking in private work sites. Of these states, only California meets the nation's Healthy People 2000 objective to eliminate exposure to smoke by either banning indoor smoking or limiting it to separately ventilated areas. Over 80% of the states have laws restricting smoke in state government worksites. According to a recent CDC Morbidity and Mortality Report (June 25, 1999), little progress has been made in protecting citizens from secondhand smoke. As for the trend of some employers seeking to hire non-smokers (primarily because of health insurance costs), this will be an area of future legal activity (especially if persons are successful in demonstrating an addiction). It is conceivable that smokers could bring lawsuits under the Americans with Disabilities Act, 42 U.S.C. §12101, and the Rehabilitation Act, 29 U.S.C. §793-794, alleging a disability. On the other hand, treatment centers may try to argue non-smoking is an essential function of the job. The legal answer to this dilemma will be addressed through the evolving case law.

For a discussion of these issues as they relate more specifically to prevention workers, see Chapter Nine.

♦♦ 35 ♦♦

Ben, one of the staff members who conducts remedial education classes for impaired driving offenders at your agency was arrested last Saturday night for impaired driving. The arrest occurred at a time Ben was not on duty, and there was no agency vehicle involved in the incident. To the best of your knowledge, Ben has no prior history of alcohol or other drug-related problems and did not self-identify himself as recovering when he was hired. The same weekend, Fred, another staff member who works in the maintenance department at your facility, also was arrested for impaired driving.

Discussion Questions

Could Ben and Fred be subject to disciplinary action to include firing for such behavior or does such behavior on non-work time constitute private behavior that is none of the agency's business?

Should our response to Ben and Fred be different given their different roles? Could nexus exist for Ben but not for Fred?

Discussion of this vignette with workers in the addictions field usually focuses on the following points:

- *The innocence of the worker should be assumed until the facts of the case prove otherwise. If facts confirm the act of driving while intoxicated by the worker, the following points would be relevant.*
- *For Ben, driving under the influence of alcohol violates the ethical mandate of honesty because the behavior so contradicts the most basic tenents of DUI education presented by Ben in his professional role.*
- *Ben's behavior violated the principle of nonmaleficence not only in threatening the safety of others but in harming, via damage to reputation, his own capacity and that of his agency for continued service.*
- *While Ben could be subject to disciplinary action on the grounds of a direct link between his private behavior and his ability to perform his professional role, the case of Fred is a bit more complicated.*
- *The response to Fred's DUI would depend on the personnel standards and ethical or professional practice codes which have been defined by the agency and communicated to its staff. Lacking any explicitly relevant standards, there may not be a link between Fred's private conduct and the performance of his maintenance functions. On the other hand, if Fred was required to drive as part of his job, the point of nexus might be his lack of*

a valid drivers license rather than the behavior that led to the loss of his license. Some agencies try to heighten staff awareness of this issue by including in their personnel policies or CPP sentiments like the following: "Agency staff shall remain aware of the prevailing moral and legal standards in the community and the effect of their private behavior on their professional reputation and the reputation of the agency."

Most addiction treatment centers are bound by the federal Drug Free Workplace Act, 41 U.S.C. §701, as well as a corresponding state Drug-Free Workplace Act. Your state drug-free workplace laws should be checked as well as your licensure laws and regulations to determine the legal requirements, if any, pertaining to alcohol/drug usage by employees. Your agency may choose to have a more stringent personnel policy governing drug testing as well as prohibiting certain activities impacting the reputation of the agency. If you choose to implement a more stringent standard, make sure it is uniformly applied to all employees. Based upon the facts in this case, there would be no drug-free workplace violation. Among other mandates, the federal Act requires employees to notify the employer of any criminal drug statute conviction for a violation occurring in the workplace no later than 5 days after such conviction. Since neither of these violations occurred in the workplace, no violation of the Act occurred. However, as stated above, there could be a violation of agency personnel policies or other state laws.

Relapse

♦♦ 36 ♦♦

Ray is a recovering alcoholic working as a counselor in your agency. He is both a trusted friend and valued colleague. Ray has two years of addiction counseling experience and up until a month ago had seven years of uninterrupted sobriety. A month ago, Ray experienced a short relapse (two days) following the sudden death of his spouse. He immediately re-engaged himself in his recovery program and is receiving grief counseling. Your agency has a policy that recovering counselors must have two years of continuous sobriety to work in the counseling program. No one knows about Ray's relapse at the agency, and Ray fears that disclosure of this event will cause him to lose his job. Ray seeks your advice and counsel as a friend and trusted co-worker at the agency.

Discussion Questions

How would you respond to Ray's request for advice?

What standard could guide staff when presented with a situation or condition in their personal life that could potentially influence the quality of their clinical practice?

Would you be under any ethical obligation to report Ray's relapse to a supervisor at the agency?

There are ethical issues for you and for Ray in the above vignette. Ray feels his rapid return to an active recovery program and his current emotional stability will allow him to continue to be effective in a counselor role but many would question whether he can independently make this judgment. There are additional concerns that withholding the information about his relapse is a breach of honesty–a misrepresentation of his recovery status–in the relationship with his employer, his professional peers and his clients. There is concern of whether maintaining the secrecy of his relapse will not pose an obstacle to his continued recovery. For you, the trust and confidence of a good friend and colleague must be weighed against loyalty to the agency and the profession as well as against the potential threats to clients and public safety posed by a worker whose addiction recovery and mental status is of uncertain stability. The struggle to sort the conflicting interests in this vignette are eased if the agency has discussed and formulated its values related to such eventualities. Nearly all of the appropriate intervention strategies are contingent upon breaking the secrecy of the relapse either through Ray's self-revelation to his supervisor or through your judgment that such disclosure must be made to the agency. Strategies that address different interests and needs in the above vignette could include:

- *removing Ray from his active counseling duties*
- *offering agency EAP services to assist Ray in re-establishing his recovery program and dealing with the loss of his wife*
- *exploring Ray's need for a medical leave of absence*
- *developing with Ray a strategy of communication to other staff and to Ray's clients*
- *developing a structure of increased supervisory review and support of Ray's clinical work (if a decision was made to not remove Ray from his current role)*
- *developing an individualized process of client termination and transfer of*

clinical responsibilities

• *exploring alternative professional role responsibilities for Ray within the agency*

• *providing continuing support for Ray and the re-activation of his recovery program.*

There are recent trends suggesting that treatment centers that require minimum sobriety standards for hiring could face challenges under the Americans with Disabilities Act (ADA), 42 U.S.C. §12101. Imposing sobriety requirements certainly seems to be justified for counselors and supervisors. Conversely, positions not directly involved with clients may not support minimum sobriety requirements. However, agencies may legitimately require all employees to comply with drug-free workplace and related personnel policies.

To minimize exposure to liability, employers should base hiring and firing decisions on the particular employee, his/her history of substance abuse (rather than a blanket generalization) and the specific nature of the job. If you choose to set a minimum sobriety requirement, a shorter period (such as six months to one year) is more likely to he held as valid rather than five years. This is an area counselors and centers should monitor for both federal and state cases and Equal Employment Opportunity Commission (EEOC) guidance. See Vignette #140 for an indepth discussion on sobriety requirements. (For discussions of potential responses to an impaired counselor, see Anderson and Blankman, 1986a; Anderson and Blankman, 1986b; Kinney, 1983; Lisnow, 1989; Moyer and Moyer, 1989; Wein, 1989; Wilson, 1984)

Moral and Legal Standards

♦♦ 37 ♦♦

Robert, a counselor you supervise at your agency, was recently arrested for solicitation of prostitution in a highly publicized, local undercover sting. (The event did not occur on work time, but did occur in the local community served by the agency. Robert's affiliation with the agency was repeatedly noted in media coverage of the arrest.)

Discussion Questions

What would your response, if any, be to this counselor?

Would the response differ if your agency was in a remote rural area compared to a large metropolitan area?

Would your response be any different if the charges involved theft, statutory rape, assault, or illegal possession or sale of drugs?

A review of the codes of ethics governing a wide spectrum of helping professionals reveals the consistent inclusion of an ethical duty for professional helpers to be sensitive to prevailing legal and moral standards in their communities and to the adverse effects the violation of such standards can have on their and the agency's professional reputation and their service relationships with clients and families. The ethical command in this area may be even more intense on the addictions worker given the nature of our clients. Given the high prevalence of alcohol- and drug-related criminal activity of clients entering addiction treatment, the addictions counselor has an even greater duty than in other human service settings to exemplify and model appropriate legal and moral conduct. In a similar manner, personal involvement with prostitutes may have implications that are particularly important within the addictions field. The fact that a high percentage of male and female prostitutes are alcohol/drug dependent makes such persons likely candidates for agency services. Personal conduct with such vulnerable populations should enhance their receptiveness to treatment rather than posing obstacles to such treatment. It is doubtful that the addicted prostitute in crisis would feel comfortable with the discovery that the agency which he or she has chosen to get help from is staffed with "tricks" known from his or her life in the culture of addiction.

To determine legal responsibility for the agency in cases like this, you should check:

- *personnel policies to ascertain any violation*
- *funding contracts to determine restrictions on employment of individuals convicted of certain offenses*
- *funding contracts to see if the agency has an obligation to disclose certain offenses, even arrests (this may be especially important for treatment programs operating in prisons and jails)*
- *facility licensing regulations to determine whether continued employment upon conviction could present a problem (typically licensure regulations will have requirements pertaining to felony convictions)*
- *counselor licensing/certification codes of ethics to ascertain reportability for potential discipline/suspension and/or revocation of the license.*

Financial Investments

♦♦ 38 ♦♦

Shana, the business manager for a large addictions agency, has a partner who is part-owner of FutureTech, a company that specializes in computer sales and service. All of the computer hardware and almost all of the computer software purchased by the agency in the last five years have been purchased from FutureTech.

Discussion Questions

What ethical issues could arise in this convergence between Shana's personal interests and professional responsibilities?

What problems could this arrangement potentially create for Shana and the agency?

The personal financial interests of an employee are none of the organization's business until their existence alters how the employee performs in his or her professional role. The fact that the agency has purchased equipment from the company in which Shana has a vested interest may be a coincidence and may have involved decisions over which Shana had little input or control. The ethical concern in situations like the above is the extent to which personal financial interests create conflicts of interests in professional decision-making. To the extent that Shana's personal financial interests influence her decision-making within the agency and at the expense of the agency, Shana's actions would represent a breach of her promise to serve the best interests of the organization. It is appropriate for a worker to declare any outside financial interests that might bias his or her objectivity in a particular situation (or might be perceived as a source of bias).
(See Vignettes 22 and 23 for a legal analysis on conflict of interest, the intermediate sanctions laws and procurement procedures. For a discussion of the ethical issues raised by addiction professionals having financial interests in alcohol, tobacco and pharmaceutical industries, see Chapter Nine).

♦♦ 39 ♦♦

Your agency has been providing counseling services through a contract with a local EAP/behavioral health care company. One of the clients you have seen under this contract arrives today extremely distraught. The client, who is a senior official in a company served by the EAP contractor, explains his emotional condition by reporting to you that several senior executives are about to be served with federal warrants for their arrest in a major price-fixing scheme. The investigation of this scheme will break public within the next two weeks and your client fears that the company's stock and long term financial health could be devastated by this announcement. What your client is not aware of is that you recently inherited a substantial quantity of this company's stock from your grandmother and that you were relying on these stocks to put your children through college.

Discussion Questions

What parties could potentially be injured in this situation?

Would you call your stockbroker and sell the stock before the public announcement and potential fall of the stock prices?

Would selling this stock now constitute a breach of confidentiality or violate any other ethical principles of addiction counseling?

While anyone confronted with this situation would be tempted to take action to prevent their own financial losses, there are a number of difficulties with this action. The most obvious has to do with the issue of confidentiality. The promise made to this client that only narrowly prescribed types of shared information could ever be disclosed by the counselor without the client's consent would be clearly violated if the counselor acted upon the information disclosed in the counseling session. Another question raised by this situation is whether a professional helper can use information gained in a professional role for personal gain in his or her private role. Such use would likely violate the counselor's fiduciary pledge that the focus of the relationship and the interests that would drive decision-making would be those of the client. Subsequent discovery of the counselor's use of this information could damage the counselor-client relationship, the reputation of the counselor and the agency, and potentially lead to the agency's loss of the contract to provide these types of services. Guidelines outlined in Vignette #191 can help protect the agency, the counselor and the client under such circumstances.

In this case, both the client and counselor could face liability as a result of insider trading laws, prohibited by the federal Securities and Exchange Act of 1934. "Insider trading" generally refers to buying or selling stock, in breach of a fiduciary duty or other relationship of trust and confidence, while in possession of material, nonpublic information about the stock. For example, insider trading violations occur when friends, business associates, family members, and other persons receive insider information from a corporation's officers, employees and trade the securities after receiving such information. The civil penalties can be severe (up to three times the profit gained or loss avoided as a result of insider trading). Section 21A(e) of the Securities Exchange Act of 1934, 15 U.S.C. §78u-l(e).

Discrimination

♦♦ 40 ♦♦

Mariam works in a small addictions agency in which she performs both administrative-supervisory responsibilities and provides some direct client services. Mariam is also a member of a local social organization which has never had any members who were men or non-white.

Discussion Question

Under what conditions, if any, would Mariam's membership in this organization raise issues of inappropriate ethical and professional conduct?

Mariam's membership in the above organization would not necessarily mean that she has participated in any personal acts of discrimination. The fact that an organization has no men nor people of color does not in and of itself prove the existence of discriminatory practices that would support an accusation that Mariam belongs to an organization that is blatantly sexist or racist in its orientation. But are these questions even appropriate to be raised? As long as Mariam does not commit overt acts of discrimination on the job, is her personal conduct away from work her own business even if that business might involve discriminatory behavior? Does Mariam stop representing the addictions profession and her agency when she leaves the work environment? As these questions have been raised within state associations of addictions counselors, a growing number of such organizations are saying that one's duty to the values implicit in the service profession do not stop when one leaves the job site each day. More and more of these agencies are stating that the professional must conduct his or her private life in a manner that does not compromise the reputation and integrity of the profession or otherwise decrease the willingness of clients to seek service within these organizations. Given the increased number of people of color, women and gays and lesbians receiving prevention and treatment services, sensitivity and competent responses to the needs of these individuals is an absolutely essential ingredient for all workers. In fact, all government funded contracts and most licensing rules have anti-discrimination provisions relating not only to hiring and employment practices but also admission of and service to clients. Discriminatory acts –even in one's private life–would reflect a lack of such sensitivity and competence and pose threats to the profession and the agency's capacity to serve these populations of clients.

Personal and Agency Reputation

♦♦ 41 ♦♦

You have just relocated to a new community and taken a position with a local addiction treatment and prevention agency. You have been invited to a party by a casual acquaintance and after your arrival find that illicit drugs are being openly used by many of the persons there.

Discussion Questions

How would you respond to this situation?

What situations or ethical dilemmas could arise from such a situation?

Is there any collective wisdom about how to handle incidents that could potentially damage our professional reputation as well as the agency's reputation?

One does not cease wearing the mantle of identification with the profession or with the agency simply because it is Saturday night. The ethical admonition to "first, do no harm" can be extended beyond our service procedures with clients to include managing our personal conduct in ways that avoid harm to our personal and institutional reputations. There are any number of unforeseen consequences potentially arising within the above vignette. Helping persons have been present and publicly identified in raids of such parties. Persistent and potentially damaging allegations or rumors about use of drugs have been traced to one's presence in such situations. Persons (potential clients) who know of your agency affiliation could, based on your presence at the party, eschew agency services on the assumption that staff are "dirty." Many workers have learned the painful lesson that it is best to avoid situations involving illegal activity in which one's physical presence could be interpreted as participation or approval. Such interpretation could even lead to criminal charges.

♦♦ 42 ♦♦

Tim has worked as a therapist at your agency for the past four years, splitting his time between the adult and adolescent outpatient programs. Tim is gay, a fact that he has kept well-hidden from the community and the agency. Tim is considering "coming out of the closet." There is a forthcoming public hearing on the special needs of gay and lesbian clients in treatment at which he would like to speak. Tim feels that acknowledging his own homosexuality would add weight to his testimony. He has also felt himself moving closer to this decision for his own personal feelings of sanity and self-respect. Tim's one concern is the potential repercussions this decision could have on his job. He fears that his disclosure could trigger public reaction in this rural community that could jeopardize his professional reputation and the reputation of the agency. Tim seeks your advice as a trusted friend and co-worker.

Discussion Questions

What advice might you offer Tim?

What ethical or professional practice issues are involved in this situation?

Is there any collective wisdom or standard that could guide staff facing such a situation?

If, in response to Tim's public disclosure of his homosexuality, a number of parents withdraw their children from treatment at the agency, the schools stop referrals to the adolescent program under community pressure, and a community group proposes that funds for the adolescent program be cut and transferred to another agency–an obvious effort to scapegoat Tim–how should the agency respond to these events?

Tim must explore how his personal needs can be reconciled with the needs of his agency and the needs of his clients. The decision to publicly disclose his homosexuality involves weighing the risks and benefits of such disclosure to himself and others along with the benefits and harm of continued secrecy. It involves exploring the potential short and long term effects such disclosure will have on the agency and the immediate effects such disclosure may have on the clients and families with whom he is working. It also involves weighing the harmful effect his silence has in perpetuating homophobic attitudes and discriminatory practices against gays and lesbians. While the decision of whether to disclose is a personal one, how such disclosure should be handled, if that is desired, would be very appropriate to bring into the process of supervision. This allows the agency some time to prepare for any potential public reactions and allows some structured time for Tim and his supervisor to talk about how the knowledge of this disclosure should be handled clinically with clients/families.

A related issue that is likely to arise in the future involves the issues of "outing." The process of disclosing the homosexuality of public figures without their consent raises a number of ethical issues. The issue could arise where a gay addictions professional publicly identifies one or more other health or human service professionals as being gay without the consent of these persons. The question will be: is such disclosure a breach of professional ethics, particularly where the knowledge of the other person's sexual orientation was learned in the professional context.

The issue of sexual orientation has been an area of the law attracting the interest of many legislators on the national and local levels (more recently because of domestic partner rights to property and health insurance participation). In 1986, the U.S. Supreme Court addressed the issue of homosexuality for the first time in the renowned case of Bowers v. Hardwick, 106 S.Ct. 2841 (1986). The Court held that a Georgia statute criminalizing sodomy was constitutional and did not violate any fundamental rights, including the right of privacy. Since that landmark case, some states and local jurisdictions have amended their human rights acts to include prohibited discrimination for sexual orientation. You should check your local statutes and regulations as well as your funding contracts and licensure regulations regarding this issue. At least one case has held an individual's sexual orientation or preference is not protected by the federal Rehabilitation Act. (Blackwell v. Dept. of Treasury, 830 F.2d 1183 (CA CD 1987). Similarly, a few states have held transsexualism is not a physical or mental impairment or a handicap under state human relations/anti-discrimination statutes. See Dobre v. National Railroad Passenger, 2 AD Case 1567 (DCE Pa. 1993) and Doe v. Boeing Company, 2 AD Cases 548 (Wash. Sup. Ct. 1993).

Personal Replenishment

♦♦ 43 ♦♦

Gary is by everyone's agreement one of the best workers at your agency. In some ways, he is too good. Gary works an excessive number of hours every week. He is clearly "married to his job." Some staff have expressed personal concern about Gary's health, his excessive smoking, his weight, and his lack of exercise. Periodic admonitions about his excessive hours and poor habits of self-care have done little to effect Gary's pattern of work/living.

Discussion Questions

Is this a performance problem?

Are there any ethical issues related to care of oneself in the helping professions?

Is there a standard of personal care or replenishment to which staff should aspire?

Is there an organizational value related to this area that you would want reflected in an agency Code of Professional Practice?

Would these values only apply to staff in direct services roles with clients or in roles in which they represent the agency to the public? Would these values apply to clerical staff, maintenance staff, and administrative staff?

There are at least two values that could be raised in response to the above vignette—the value of self-replenishment and the value of self-care.

The value of self-replenishment is based on the supposition that sustained service to others is only possible if the helping person has and utilizes resources for personal replenishment outside the professional role. By participating in nourishing activities and relationships outside of the work setting, the helping professional is able to enter the service setting without his or her unmet needs contaminating the service relationship. In a similar manner, acts of self-care model the legitimacy of one's own needs and establish a foundation of health from which the service process is initiated. The failure of a helping professional to adequately mirror values of self-replenishment and self-care is an ethical issue to the extent that:

- *the individual models poor standards of physical and emotional health to his or her clients*
- *the unmet needs of the caregiver interfere with effective service delivery to clients or otherwise prevent the performance of one's professional duties*
- *the lifestyle of the worker contradicts and undermines the values the agency represents to its clients and to the community.*

As noted in our discussion of an earlier vignette, the line between personal and professional life should be drawn by the agency at the point one's personal behavior negatively effects work performance: (e.g., service relationships with clients, team relationships with professional peers, and service relationships within the community). Agencies can affirm this value of self-care by articulating it as an aspirational value within the Code of Professional Practice. One agency's standard reads as follows:

> *"Working with individuals and families in emotional crisis can be both physically and emotionally depleting for staff. The health of both clients and staff hinge on the ability of each worker to seek physical and emotional replenishment outside the work setting. Center staff are encouraged to develop a network of replenishing relationships and activities that support their overall health and increase their ability to enter into nurturing relationships with clients."*

Issues relating to health and even weight have been the subject of ADA claims under various theories of perceived disabilities and handicaps relating to obesity. Agencies should be careful not to cross this line of discrimination in their personnel policies and employment practices.

Chapter
Five

Professional Conduct

There are many areas of professional conduct within the addictions field that do not involve issues related to our business practices or our relationships with service recipients. Issues of ethics, etiquette, and questions of appropriate protocol often arise that fall outside these areas. This chapter will explore such issues as professional self-development, personal appearance, competence, representation of credentials, use of agency resources, use of information, secondary employment, and public statements. Clear standards of ethical conduct and etiquette have not been defined in all of these areas within the addictions field. The critical incidents presented within this chapter can assist the individual worker or the addictions treatment and prevention agency in defining values and standards applicable to these areas.

Critical Incidents

Self-development

♦♦ 44 ♦♦

Jeremy, a case manager at your agency, consistently resists exposure to in-service training and avoids participation in outside workshops and seminars. His rationale for this resistance ranges from being overwhelmed with seeing clients to a dislike of travel. As a result, Jeremy has not attended any significant training activity within the past year.

Discussion Questions

Are there ethical issues inherent in the pursuit, or failure to pursue, new knowledge within one's profession?

What standard do you feel should guide staff conduct in this area?

competence

The principle of self-development permeates nearly all defined professions. This principle establishes the professional duty to stay abreast of new knowledge and to acquire new skills throughout the development of one's career. While the idea of self-development is admirable and consistent with the ethical value of competence, an even greater ethical duty emanates from the potential harm that could be created through the lack of self-development. Prevention and treatment professionals have a duty to incorporate the latest information and service technology into their interventions with individuals, institutions, and communities. The failure to pursue self-development denies service consumers the benefits that could accrue from new knowledge. Continued education and training are more than optional perks; they are professional, ethical and legal mandates under various facility and licensure and certification codes.

Personal Appearance

♦♦ 45 ♦♦

A publicly funded addiction treatment agency launches an aggressive marketing campaign designed to increase the percentage of insured and self-pay clients seeking services at the agency. Following several weeks of this campaign, the following incident occurs. A very well-dressed client arrives at the agency at 7:30 A.M. and nervously announces that he has an 8:00 appointment and that this is his first appointment. The receptionist greets him politely and offers him a seat in the reception room. The receptionist views this client fidgeting impatiently, his eyes darting to the door each time it opens, perhaps wondering if he might be recognized or possibly concerned about what other "clients" look like who come here. It is clear to the receptionist that sitting in the waiting area of a public service agency is quite a new and discomforting experience for this obviously well-to-do client. The entry door of the agency opens and a man walks in discarding a cigarette as he enters. He is wearing a badly wrinkled shirt and slacks, his eyes are bleary, and his hair is disheveled. The man mumbles something about coffee as he walks past the client into a hallway off the reception area. The impeccably dressed client who has watched this transaction somewhat wide-eyed, looks at the receptionist and says: "Some of the people who come here must be in pretty bad shape." The receptionist is speechless because the person who triggered this statement is the therapist scheduled to see this client in five minutes.

Discussion Questions

Provide any comments you might have on ethical or professional practice issues in this situation.

If you were the receptionist, how would you respond to this situation?

There are two issues raised in the above vignette: 1) the desired response of staff who observe any condition potentially compromising the safety, health, or comfort of a client, and 2) the ethics and etiquette of professional appearance.

The receptionist could take the position that it was not her responsibility to get in the middle of this situation—the "it's not in my job description" position—or she could take some action to address the impending discomfort of the client. Which action she takes will depend not only on her personal characteristics and values but also on expectations of staff set by the organization. When the event portrayed above really happened, it occurred in an agency with a strongly instilled value that the care and comfort of clients was everyone's concern. The receptionist walked into the Clinical Director's office and briefly described the morning's events as portrayed above and expressed her concern about the likely discomfort of the client when he discovered that who he thought was a severely impaired client was to be his therapist. The supervisor proceeded to observe the therapist, informed the therapist that the supervisor would be seeing the therapist's 8:00 appointment, conducted the intake himself, and then met with the therapist to discuss standards related to professional appearance at the agency. This expectation for action to address client comfort and safety—which the receptionist acted upon in the above vignette—is an important component of a strong, service-oriented organizational culture.

There are many interests that influence appropriate professional dress of persons working in prevention and treatment agencies. The value of respect for clients (and professional peers) dictates standards of cleanliness. Disregard for appearance reflects a lack of respect or importance attributed to the client—a kind of "professional slumming." The service provider's professional appearance should signal to the client that the work they are to do together is important and serious. Respect dictates that dress not be sexually provocative. Other interests that influence how workers in the field present themselves is the reputation of the individual worker, the reputation of the agency and the reputation of the field. There is an implicit expectation that one's personal appearance will enhance and not detract from such reputations.

The issue of professional dress is difficult to define in many organizations due to the differences in program activities and roles for which different standards of comfort and appropriateness apply. The appropriate professional dress for an EAP counselor working with predominantly white collar companies would be different from a recreational therapist in an adolescent inpatient program or an outreach worker serving homeless alcoholics. Many

*agencies seeking to define professional standards of appearance do so by
stating the expectation that workers will follow the standards of appearance
that are appropriate for their program, their role, and the nature of their
scheduled daily activities. This allows for standards to be set at the program
or unit level and modified by the supervisor for appropriateness to daily
activities.*

Recognition of Limitations

♦♦ 46 ♦♦

Sarah, a counselor recently hired at your agency, administers the
Minnesota Multiphasic Personality Inventory (MMPI) to all of the clients
assigned to her. Sarah is quite taken with the MMPI as an assessment
instrument and has read everything she can get her hands on related to the
MMPI and addiction. Although the MMPIs she's administering are not being
placed in her clients' clinical records, indirect references to MMPI findings are
being made in client progress notes and are frequently referenced by Sarah
during clinical staffings of clients. The issue of concern is that Sarah has no
formal training in psychological testing. She is a certified addictions counselor
but there is nothing in her professional history that validates her ability to
administer or interpret the MMPI.

Discussion Questions

What are your thoughts about this practice?

As a new supervisor assigned to Sarah's unit, how would you respond to
this situation?

See discussion following Vignette 47.

♦♦ 47 ♦♦

Randy is a parole agent whose caseload includes large numbers of
individuals in need of addiction treatment services. Randy also serves an area
in which there are few such treatment resources, particularly for people coming
out of the criminal justice system. Randy has attended many workshops on
addiction counseling and the supervision of drug-involved offenders and has
an extensive personal background to sensitize him to the needs of addicts.
Randy came from an alcoholic family, is himself in long term alcoholism

recovery, and has a great interest in helping those addicted to alcohol and other drugs. Randy does not have formal academic training in addiction counseling, has not been certified as an addictions counselor, nor does Randy work for an organization that has been licensed to provide addiction counseling services.

Discussion Questions

What are the ethical issues in Randy performing any or all of the following:

* performing alcohol and other drug evaluations for the court
* providing addiction counseling to parolees
* recommending early discharge of parolees based on the counseling he has provided to particular inmates.   Competence

Haas and Malouf (1989) have defined three components of professional competence: 1) the knowledge to fully understand a particular issue, 2) the skill to effectively apply this knowledge, and 3) the judgement to know when, where and under what conditions to use, or not use, this skill. The ethical demand is to practice within the boundaries of one's own competence. That boundary is defined primarily by one's professional training and professional experience as well as applicable facility and counselor licensure codes. In the case of Sarah, her administration, scoring and interpretation of the MMPI involve areas of professional practice for which she has not been trained, lacks supervised experience, and for which she possesses no external credential to validate her competence in this area. While she may have some technical knowledge of the MMPI, her lack of formal training exposes her to potential errors in technical skill and judgement that could result in potential harm to her clients. Sarah's use of information derived from the MMPI would constitute a breach of the ethical principle of competence. In a similar manner, Randy must be very careful not to move beyond the boundaries of his education, training, and experience and licensure codes in his role of parole officer. The agency Randy works for must be particularly careful in not mistaking Randy's passionate desire to help addicts with the technical knowledge and skill that is required to provide addiction counseling.

Competence to perform may be defined by educational training, licensure or certification, or in some cases, through an actual demonstration of knowledge or skill. A growing number of addiction treatment programs, particularly those involved in the JCAHO accreditation process, have implemented and have begun to refine a process of clinical privileging to address this ethical principle of competence. Like the hospital setting in which each doctor is granted privileges to perform certain medical procedures within the scope of his or her training and experience, the privileging process involves the delineation of the specific tasks each substance abuse worker may perform based on his or her academic and experiential preparation and his or her role in the agency. Within this system, workers may not perform activities for which they do not have clinical privileges. In the cases above, Sarah would have been prohibited from administering or interpreting psychological tests because she would not have privileges to conduct this activity, just as Randy would have been extremely limited in what he could provide in the name of addiction counseling.

♦♦ 48 ♦♦

Bill, a therapist in an outpatient addiction treatment agency, was raised in a family that took in numerous foster children who had been severely abused. Having seen the physical and emotional ravages of such abuse in his foster siblings, Bill has always viewed the perpetrators of such abuse with great hostility. In his few years in the counseling field, he has not been involved in assessing or treating any child abusers. Today, Bill recognizes the name of a court referred intake assessment as a person who has appeared prominently in the local newspapers due to his arrest for a particularly brutal beating of his five year old son. Bill's evaluation could have a significant influence on whether this client gets probation and treatment or incarceration.

Discussion Questions

What should Bill do regarding this evaluation?

What should any staff member do in response to any unique mismatch between themselves and a particular client that would potentially contaminate their objectivity and clinical effectiveness?

How should a situation like the above be handled when one works alone or is in a similar situation in which there are no options for transferring a client to another worker?

The vignette above illustrates a situation in which an otherwise competent worker could have that competence compromised because of the unique characteristics or circumstances of a particular client. All helping professionals experience problems of countertransference with some clients that can impede the relationship-building and service delivery process. Many of these problems can be resolved through self-awareness of potential bias and supervisory consultation. There may, however, be areas of bias so strong as to make such resolution impossible. Under such circumstances the worker has a responsibility to identify this problem with his or her supervisor and seek a reassignment of the client to a person who can more objectively and more adequately assess and respond to their needs. While many workers may hesitate to acknowledge such a problem to their supervisor for fear it will reflect on their competence or motivation, such notification reflects a high level of ethical sensitivity and professionalism. This issue should be addressed in the agency code of ethics or personnel policies. The JCAHO has recognized a staff's right to refuse to treat patients based upon certain conflicts of interest or other ethical issues as long as such refusal is not the result of illegal discrimination.

♦♦ 49 ♦♦

Counselors and other non-medical interdisciplinary team members in addiction treatment programs can often be heard giving advice to clients about the dangers of mood-altering medications. Such dialogue inevitably triggers a give-and-take about specific medications—which are "safe" and which are "risky" for the alcoholic or addict in recovery. These questions usually elicit a professional opinion or recommendation.

Discussion Questions

Are addictions counselors clinically bound to address issues of prescription drug use with their clients, or does this role for non-medically trained members of the team constitute a gross breach of ethical conduct–practicing beyond one's training and competence?

How would you draw the boundary between appropriate and inappropriate professional conduct in this area?

What are the responsibilities of the addictions counselor who works in an area where no addiction-specific medical expertise is available for consultation with clients?

The line defining the boundaries of knowledge and appropriate role behavior has not been clearly defined for the above vignette within the addictions field. However, states have addressed professional boundaries in terms of medication prescription, dispensing and administration issues in medical practice/physician licensure acts, nursing licensure statutes, pharmacist licensure codes and other controlled substances laws. For addiction counselors, however, it may be possible to define at least the ends of the continuum from appropriate to inappropriate conduct. It is within the province of the addictions counselor to speak of the potential addictiveness of certain prescribed psychoactive drugs and the potential risks such drugs may pose to the recovering alcoholic or addict. It is not within the boundaries of competence of most addictions counselors, unless they are also trained in medicine or psychopharmacology, to speak authoritatively about:

- *the appropriateness or inappropriateness of a particular medication for a particular client or for a particular condition*
- *drug dosages that would be safe or unsafe for a particular client*
- *the contraindications or potential side-effects of various prescribed medications.*

While the counselor may have acquired considerable knowledge over the years about various prescribed drugs, he or she lacks the specific training to pronounce judgment about the risks/benefits of a particular drug on a particular client. The counselor should defer to his or her medical director/consultant when queried about such issues. Consultants with expertise in addiction medicine can answer such questions based on both their knowledge of the drugs and the unique medical and addiction history of the particular client. Where such medical expertise is not available for consultation with clients, the counselor can refer the client to a growing number of books written by physicians who address the issues related to prescribed medications for persons in addiction recovery. The danger is that the counselor, by overstepping the boundaries of competence will, through oversimplification or misinformation, threaten the health or safety of the client. The counselor making pronouncements about prescribed medications should be very explicit about the basis and limits of knowledge from which he or she speaks. See also the discussion in Vignettes #4, 71, 73 regarding informed consent and issues regarding psychotropic medications.)

◆◆ 50 ◆◆

Marybeth, an addictions counselor in a remote rural area, has a client that needs special counseling related to childhood sexual abuse. There are no local mental health services and no geographically accessible persons who have been trained or have prior experience counseling client's around sexual abuse issues.

Discussion Questions

Given the client's current emotional pain, would it be unethical for Marybeth to fail to counsel the client regarding these experiences?

Given Marybeth's lack of training and experience in this area, would it be unethical for her to attempt such counseling outside the boundaries of her current expertise? If you were Marybeth, what would you do?

While the ethical command to practice within the boundaries of one's own competence is a noble one, there are numerous instances, like the one above, where this command conflicts with the desire and duty to address a client's immediate needs. In an ideal world, Marybeth would have alternative resources who were trained and experienced in addressing sexual abuse issues. However, in the real world, she is in an area where no such services exist that are both geographically accessible and affordable to her client. Under such circumstances, Marybeth might seek a solution that represents the best effort to address the client's needs while minimizing the potential for harm resulting from Marybeth's lack of prior training and experience. She might agree to counsel her client on these issues while seeking technical support through:

- *reading books and journal articles on the counseling of persons sexually abused as children*
- *finding and attending one or more workshops that would increase her knowledge of how best to assist this client*
- *identifying and seeking an outside clinical consultant to help supervise (even by phone if such expertise was not geographically accessible) her work with the client.*

Representation of Credentials

♦♦ 51 ♦♦

Your agency just received a contract to provide managed behavioral health care for a local hospital. You have agreed to provide this care through three of the senior therapists at the agency. After signing the contract, the hospital requests verification of the credentials of the therapists who will work under the contract. Two of the therapists immediately comply, while the third begins what will be a long string of delays and excuses as to why the educational credentials cannot be supplied, e.g., diplomas were lost, there are delays getting transcripts sent. Getting somewhat concerned, you review this employee's personnel file and discover that the employee came with glowing recommendations from former employers but that no verification was made of the employee's education and training. Before you investigate further, the employee in question resigns, reporting that he has taken a position at another agency with a substantial raise in salary.

Discussion Questions

As a supervisor in this situation, what, if anything, would you do?

Is the verification of employee credentials an ethical issue, and should such verification be maintained on all employees?

Should the supervisor in the above situation contact the director of the agency to which the staff person is going to express his or her suspicions about the worker's lack of credentials?

Is there an ethical mandate for the supervisor to continue some action related to documentation of the worker's credentials as a protection of public safety or would such action constitute an invasion of privacy of the staff person who has now left the agency?

The protection of the health and safety of clients and the protection of the reputation of the agency demand that the credentials of all staff be verified and accurately represented to clients and the community. In the historical development of many addiction treatment organizations, there were periods in which credentials of staff were never verified. Emerging fields, due to their lack of such rigorous scrutiny, are vulnerable for deception by persons who bring great exploitive proclivities along with their fabricated educational and/or work histories. Verification of credentials should be submitted and validated BEFORE a worker begins the performance of his or her professional duties with clients.

Under most accreditation processes such as JCAHO and NCQA, addiction agencies are required to credential their providers. As part of that process, applications elicit information on education, licenses, certifications, experience, areas of specialty insurance, malpractice history and references. The credentialing process must include primary source verification (i.e. copies of school transcripts, copies of licenses, interviews with former employers, references and background checks). Depending on the health care workers' specialty, many also check national data banks (regarding malpractice claims or other adverse credentialing activities).

There is an emerging trend to hold employers liable for "negligent hiring" as well as "negligent retention." Under both of these theories, an employer can be held liable for an employee's conduct even if it is outside the scope of employment. These cases are increasingly common in "workplace violence" situations. In this case, the agency could face potential claims of negligent hiring if the worker has, for example, engaged in a sexual act with an adolescent client and the worker had previously been convicted of child abuse. Generally, employers are not liable for every act of their employees, but only those acts which could have been avoided through a reasonable background investigation. Thus, negligent hiring occurs when prior to the time the employee is actually hired, the employer knew or should have known of the employee's unfitness, and the issue of liability primarily focuses on the adequacy of the employer's pre-employment background investigation.

The principle distinction between negligent hiring and negligent retention is the time at which the employer is charged with knowledge of the employee's fitness. Had the staff member not resigned and the agency retained him without verification of credentials, liability could have resulted.

♦♦ 52 ♦♦

It has come to your attention that a new detox counselor who you supervise is grossly misrepresenting his length of time working in the addictions field in his self-introduction to other professionals within the community. This counselor has apparently divided his "experience in the field" into three phases—the number of years he drank, the number of years in early recovery, and the number of years he has actually worked as a counselor—and decided to simply report the total number of years represented in all the phases. According to this formula, he has "16 years experience in the field" versus the one year he has worked as a detox counselor.

Discussion Questions

How would you respond to this situation?

What ethical issues are involved in the representation of work experience?

The misrepresentation of the length of work experience is no different than the misrepresentation of an academic credential—particularly in the addiction treatment field which has often valued depth of experience on an equal par with academic preparation. The counselor should be confronted and told that no matter how benign his intentions, his current references to "16 years experience in the field" constitute a misrepresentation of his professional credentials and that such references should stop immediately.

Use of Agency Resources

♦♦ 53 ♦♦

Ginny frequently takes pens and legal pads from the office home with her in case she decides to work on a particular project in the evening. The problem is that these office supplies never seem to find their way back to the office.

Discussion Question

What ethical issues are involved in the use or misuse of agency resources?

The ethical principles of honesty, fidelity and stewardship are potentially all involved in the above vignette. There is a breach of fidelity when resources are given and received with the understanding that they will be utilized for agency business but are subsequently taken for personal use outside the work environment. When agency resources are diverted to personal use, additional resources that could have gone to support service delivery must now be re-allocated to make up the deficit. This often represents an area more characterized by "moral drift" than malicious intent. The homes of staff for whom the thought of stealing from the agency would be reprehensible can be filled with an assortment of supplies from the agency without the staff having any awareness that the continued presence of these items in their homes constitutes, by consequence if not intent, a theft of agency resources. There are similar ethical concerns related to the use of other agency resources: misuse of staff time, use of phones for personal calls, misrepresentation of travel expenses, use of agency vehicles for personal activity. The appropriate stewardship of agency resources must be a value raised to a high level of professional consciousness to avoid the problems of "moral drift" described above.

Secondary Employment
♦♦ 54 ♦♦

Lana, a full time counselor at your agency, is also involved in providing counseling services through a private practice in the same community served by the agency.

Discussion Questions

Which of the following behaviors would be of concern to the agency as professional conduct issues? What standards within a Code of Professional Practice could address the ethical and conflict of interest issues that can arise in the area of secondary employment?

1. Lana is providing the same services through the private practice that she is providing through the agency. In short, she is both an employee and a professional competitor of the agency.
2. Lana visibly identifies her affiliation with the agency in the advertising materials used to promote her private practice.
3. Lana responds to crisis calls from private practice clients during working hours at the agency.
4. Lana receives calls to schedule, cancel and change private practice appointments at the agency.
5. Lana refers/channels agency clients into her private practice.
6. There are some clients that Lana sees both at the agency and at her private practice.
7. Lana uses agency time (e.g., attendance at inter-agency meetings) to market her private practice.
8. Lana uses her agency office to see private practice clients on a routine or emergency basis.
9. Lana uses proprietary products or information from the agency for her financial benefit in the private practice.
10. Lana consistently requests attendance at workshops (to be paid for by the agency) which include knowledge and skills more applicable to her private practice work than her agency role.

What potential problems could arise if the secondary employment involved working part-time for a competitor of the agency or a primary funding source of the agency in which the staff person is employed full-time?

The potential range and complexity of ethical issues that can arise from secondary employment are illustrated in the above list. The dual roles of employee and competitor raise potential conflicts of interests and conflicts of loyalties. The use of the agency name in the promotion of the employee's private practice exploits the name and reputation of the center and may deceptively imply agency involvement or endorsement of the services provided through the private practice. The use of agency time and resources (telephones, office) to support one's private practice without formal negotiation with the agency constitutes a misuse of such resources. Channeling agency clients into one's private practice, by diverting paying clients, reduces the total resources available to the agency for service delivery. This practice may inject financial self-interest as a source of bias in the client assessment and service delivery process. Seeing clients both at the agency and in private practice creates a dual relationship with the client that can result in both role confusion and role conflict.

The nature and conduct of secondary employment, particularly the conduct of similar services on a private basis, can, in addition to the issues raised above, damage the reputation of the individual practitioners involved, damage the reputation of the agency and provide a source for disruption of team relationships within the agency. Due to the scope of such effects, each agency should establish clear guidelines governing the ethical and professional conduct related to secondary employment.

The following legal issues should be considered when a counselor has secondary employment providing virtually the same services:

- *Misappropriation of agency property or resources.*
- *Misappropriation of proprietary information.*
- *Conflict of interest.*
- *Personnel policy/code of ethics compliance.*
- *Insurance coverages for property (general liability claims).*
- *Malpractice/professional liability insurance coverage.*
- *Worker's Compensation coverage.*
- *Agency funding contract conditions/prohibitions.*
- *Federal and State law anti-referral prohibitions.*
- *Medical records documentation (especially if Lana sees clients both at the agency and her private practice).*
- *Potential confidentiality breaches.*
- *Continuity of care/issues exposing the agency to potential professional liability issues.*

Publishing

♦♦ 55 ♦♦

Robert, a supervisor at a community-based addiction treatment agency, assigned several staff to research and write papers on various issues related to the assessment and treatment of clients who presented concurrent patterns of addiction and psychiatric illness. The alleged purpose for this research was to help the agency develop a dual diagnosis treatment track. Robert was so impressed with these materials when they were completed that he wrote an introductory chapter, edited the staff-prepared materials, and published the manual through the agency. Robert listed himself as the sole author of the manual, with other staff who contributed neither listed as co-authors nor acknowledged for their contributing role. His rationale for this was that the work of the staff had to be rewritten for consistency of style and that he in fact did write the manual.

Discussion Questions

Discuss the ethical issues in this situation.

What suggested guidelines or standards might be considered to prevent this kind of situation?

The principles of honesty demands that authorship of documents presented to the public be accurately represented. The principle of justice demands that credit for work should be proportionate to one's contribution. Both ethical principles were violated in the above case. Many hard feelings and misunderstandings can be avoided if agencies clearly delineate policies governing authorship of professional products prepared at the agency. Recommended etiquette for the appropriate acknowledgment of contributions for a written product would be the following: the principal author (name listed first) should be that person who had the most direct responsibility for the design, conduct of the research, interpretation and writing of the material in the manual. Co-authorship should be shared by all persons who shared leadership in these same functions. Persons who provided significant supporting roles should be acknowledged in a preface or in a footnote to the manual. Institutional contributors to the work—whether through funding of the project or support of staff time—should also be acknowledged.

Although claims of plagiarism, false representation or misrepresentation could be alleged under this vignette, the key legal issue that would arise would involve the copyright of the manual. In general, the author of a work is the party who actually creates the work (i.e. the person who translates an idea into a fixed, tangible expression entitled to copyright protection). When two or more authors have prepared a work with the intention that their contributions be merged into inseparable or interdependent parts of a unitary whole, the work is a joint work. A joint work may result from the efforts of authors working at different times and in different places. The contributions need not be equal. Rather, each contribution must be more than "trivial or de minimis."

To determine whether joint authorship exists here, (1) the parties must have intended to be joint authors when the work was created; and (2) each party's contribution must be independently copyrightable. For additional information on copyrights, compilations and derivative works, consult Nimmer on Copyrights. §1.01 et. seq; Matthew Bender & Co., New York, NY, 2000. Additional discussions on plagiarism and research integrity guidelines can be found in Chapter 9.

♦♦ 56 ♦♦

You have written a program manual which is being published by your agency for sale to other agencies. In preparing a direct mail flyer on the manual, you have solicited reviews from four nationally known professionals in the field whose words you would like to appear on the brochure supporting the quality of the material. One of these individuals, who has known you for quite some time, suggests that she has no time to review the manuscript or prepare comments but that you are welcome to write your own suitable comments and attribute them to her when they appear on the brochure.

Discussion Question

What do you do?

The misrepresentation of your own words as those of the recognized expert constitutes a breach of honesty even if the expert has given you permission for such action. While the inclusion of the fourth expert's name on the brochure would be attractive from a marketing perspective, an ethical response would be to decline the offer and use the three remaining reviews in the promotion of the manual.

Respect for Proprietary Products

♦♦ 57 ♦♦

Randy was the lead therapist for four years in an innovative project designed to work with chemically dependent men who presented with histories of physical violence toward their family members. During this period, the team developed a number of assessment instruments, program designs, roughly drafted descriptions of the intervention and treatment process and client educational materials. At the end of four years, Randy left the agency and spent considerable time updating and expanding the above materials which he then was able to get published. Although the agency and other team members were acknowledged in the introduction to the book, the materials were published without consultation with the agency, and copyrighted under Randy's name, with all potential royalties being paid to Randy.

Discussion Questions

Comment on any ethical issues inherent within this situation.

Who do you think "owns" these materials?

What if these were materials that Randy had himself brought to the agency and it was the agency who had copyrighted and published the materials?

Many hard feelings and misunderstandings can spring from the failure to clarify issues of ownership in situations like the above. The general rule is that products developed on work time belong to the agency. In the case above, the original materials –instruments, written treatment designs, and all other written products –clearly represent proprietary products owned by the agency. It would have been advisable for Randy to approach the agency and request formal permission to use and expand the original materials. Arrangements for co-authorship or acknowledgment of the agency's contribution in the original work upon which the book was based could have been negotiated at this time. Discussion of any portion of the royalties due to the agency from sale of the book could also have been discussed at this early point in the process. If Randy had brought much of the original material with him to the agency and the agency had asked him to continue development of the material for use by the agency, Randy should have clarified the status of ownership of the materials before proceeding with the development work

The key legal questions to ask are: (a) was this a "work made for hire" entitling the agency to the copyright and royalties, and (b) did the materials change enough so the work is not considered a derivative work but an original copyrightable work. Copyright issues can be very complex and in these cases, you should consult an intellectual property attorney. General legal principles governing work made for hire are as follows:

- *Copyright in a work protected under the copyright laws,17 U.S.C. §201(a), vests title in the author of the work.*
- *In the case of a work made for hire, the employer is considered the author not the employee unless the parties have expressly agreed otherwise in a written instruments signed by them.*

- *Works made for hire by persons who are independent contractors and not employees are owned by the author unless the work falls into a special category listed in the statute, AND there is a written agreement specifying that the agency is paying for the work,17 U.S.C. §101.*
- *People can also assign copyrights or license copyrights for a royalty.*

♦♦ 58 ♦♦

In a highly competitive addiction treatment environment, Troy left one program to take a position with its primary competitor. In the earliest weeks at the new program, he is asked many questions about the program which he just left. The questions solicit details of his former program's financial and clinical operations that Troy would not have disclosed to outsiders while he worked for the program.

Discussion Questions

Does Troy's ethical responsibility for confidentiality of proprietary information stop with his exit from the program?

Should Troy, out of loyalty to his new employer, disclose information that would help strengthen the program position in the market and improve the quality of their clinical operations?

If you were Troy, how would you respond to such questions?

Troy is being asked information, not with the intent of improving the quality of services to clients, but to improve the competitive positioning of his new agency in the addiction treatment marketplace. As an employee at his former agency, there was an implicit agreement that confidential program information would not be disclosed to persons outside the program. Just as the ethical demand for client confidentiality does not end with the termination of counseling services, the demand to hold confidential proprietary program information does not end with one's termination of employment unless there are other overriding commands, e.g., imminent threat to health and safety of clients, threats to public safety, etc. Troy is free to share his knowledge and skill but the disclosure of proprietary information that could harm the competitive position of his old employer would be a breach of his promises of loyalty and discretion. For the protection of the agency, it is important to address the confidentiality and ownership of proprietary information in your code of ethics or personnel policies.

This policy should address confidentiality of business documents and information of the treatment agency, information relating to proposed and existing relationships with other organizations, information relating to organizational structures, company policies, procedures and protocols, business methods, business plans, pricing and rate structures, corporate systems, employee information, training materials as well as computer systems and data.

Use of Name and Professional Judgment

♦♦ 59 ♦♦

Raymond, a counselor that you once worked with, is calling to request that you write a letter of reference in support of his application to work in an adolescent treatment center. During the time you worked with Raymond, you had serious concerns about both his clinical competence and his ethical judgment.

Discussion Question

What do you say in response to his request?

This is a difficult situation in which the potential to hurt the feelings of an acquaintance must be weighed against the potential harm this person could do if misplaced in a helping role. The ethical command is to avoid becoming an accomplice in the placement of someone in a caretaking role who could through breaches of competence or judgment harm clients, the treatment agency, the professional field, or the public. In practice, managing this command differs widely from person to person, to include the following responses:

- *telling the individual quite candidly that you would not feel comfortable writing such a letter of recommendation because of concerns you have about his or her knowledge or skills*
- *telling the individual you would be uncomfortable writing the letter of recommendation because of the length of time since you had worked with him or her*
- *telling the individual you are overwhelmed with work and will not have time to prepare such a letter*
- *agreeing to write the letter but never getting around to it*
- *writing a letter that is so lukewarm in its praise that any potential employer*

would be able to intuit your reservations about the person.

From a legal perspective, employers are hesitant to respond to reference requests for fear of exposure to potential defamation claims. Typically, employers limit their responses to job title, dates of employment and last compensation amount. Some states have enacted laws providing immunity from civil liability if an employer provides a reference in good faith. Recommendations to limit exposure to liability to reference requests include the following:

- *Designate one person to oversee the company's response to all reference requests.*
- *Prohibit others, including the former employee's supervisor from responding independently.*
- *Do not respond to telephonic requests (require that reference checks from the new employer be sent in writing on official company letterhead).*
- *Provide only factual information about the employee's job performance and qualifications.*
- *Do not include comments reflecting emotions, personal feelings, rumors, non-work-related comments or exaggerations.*
- *Make sure the documentation is supported by evidence in the personnel file.*
- *Retain a copy of your written response and document the contents of any oral response (although a verbal response is riskier).*
- *Require a former employee seeking a job reference to sign and return a release (holding the company harmless from any liability associated with providing reference information) prior to responding.*

♦♦ 60 ♦♦

Roary, a tenured and well-respected addictions counselor, received a call today asking if he would endorse a film that Roary has long used in the intensive outpatient program in which he works. The company that produced the film was going to prepare a brochure and do a national mailing to addiction treatment programs and wanted Roary's endorsement to appear in the brochure.

Discussion Questions

What ethical issue could arise in this situation?

How might Roary protect himself and the field in this situation?

What if Roary was offered a fee as part of this request?

The concern here is that Roary not lend his name to the promotion of a product or service in a manner that could do injury to potential consumers of the service or product, to Roary's professional reputation, or to the reputation of Roary's agency. Let's consider that Roary views this film as one of the most effective tools of client education he has ever seen. One option is that Roary could say that his provision of a statement about the film would be contingent upon his ability to review the entire brochure and then provide a final decision regarding the use of his statement. This would assure his ability to help support a clinically useful product while linking his name to a promotional campaign that misstated the range and degree of effectiveness of the film. The NAADAC Code of Ethics discourages counselors from lending their name to any service or product in a way that is either incorrect or misleading. Endorsing a service or product in exchange for a fee is not appropriate as the acceptance of such monetary reward is likely to color one's evaluation of the service or product. The judgments of professional addictions counselors should not be for sale. What more subtle influences might be brought to bear on the addictions counselor being asked for such an endorsement?

Public Statements

♦♦ 61 ♦♦

You have become active in supporting a political issue that is very unpopular in your local community. To date, there has been no conflict between your role as a supervisor in a local addiction treatment program and your outside political activities. You have now been asked to serve as spokesperson for the grassroots political organization which will involve frequent interaction with the public and the press.

Discussion Questions

What ethical issues might arise in these dual roles?

What standards could assure the separation of these roles?

The challenge in this vignette is to avoid harming your professional reputation and the reputation of the agency without compromising your rights of free speech and political participation. Perhaps the most important strategy in this situation is to rigorously separate one's professional role from one's personal/political role. This separation would entail the following actions:

- *not utilizing your agency affiliation to add support or credibility to your political position*
- *avoiding the conduct of political activity, e.g., phone interviews, on professional work time*
- *making explicit that you are speaking in your role as a private citizen and not in your professional role as an addictions counselor or as a representative of your agency.*

See the legal discussions in Vignettes #5, 6, 21 and 24 regarding lobbying activities and conflict of interest issues.

♦♦ 62 ♦♦

A local television station has approached your agency with the following idea. The station would like to begin a local talk show in which callers could call the station and seek information and personal advice regarding alcohol- and other drug-related problems. The format will be a ten minute opening between the television host and your agency "expert" followed by 20 minutes of calls from the public. Calls will be screened by the station for appropriateness and public interest and each call-response will be limited to two to five minutes to maximize the number and variety of calls.

Discussion Questions

How would you respond to their proposal?

What ethical issues and problems can arise from the many formats in which prevention and treatment professionals are called upon to make public statements through the major entertainment media?

Ethical issues raised in one's involvement with the information media have increased dramatically for the helping professions as the press, radio and television vehicles have explored, and at times exploited, the information and entertainment value of human problems. Ethical concerns raised by the structure of the media format in the above vignette would include the following:

- *Will potential callers be screened out by the station if their problems lack audience appeal and, if so, what would be the effect of such refusal?*
- *What happens to the calls –persons waiting on the line to seek the advice of*

the expert –for which there is not time within the structure of the 20 minute call-in period to handle?

- *What potential to do harm is inherent in the program's time limitations of two to five minutes per call, e.g., misunderstandings due to time-induced oversimplifications, misinterpretations?*
- *How could the problems posed by lack of continuity of contact and lack of follow-up be overcome?*

Haas and Malouf (1989), after discussing the way in which ethical principles could be positively served through media appearances, define and discuss the following five prescriptions to guide the human service practitioner involved in media appearances:

1) *Take full and personal responsibility for public statements.*
2) *Speak within, and only within, the limits of your competence.*
3) *Recognize and actively manage potential conflicts of interests (e.g., needs of caller versus entertainment concerns of the show's host).*
4) *Do not demean or otherwise exploit callers for purposes of entertainment.*
5) *Seek consultation from the growing body of knowledge on media psychology.*

Addiction prevention and treatment professionals concerned about ethical issues in media work are encouraged to investigate the growing body of literature being produced by members of the media psychology division of the American Psychological Association. This will be a new emerging area for case law as well as potential legislative action. Because of the trends in the health care field towards telemedicine and as a result of the new technologies available via teleconferencing and the Internet to address client needs, you should consult your attorney for guidance on the legal implications and restrictions for counseling in media other than face to face.

♦♦ 63 ♦♦

In conducting an interview with a client (in early recovery) and his wife, it is clear that there are serious long-standing problems in the couple's sexual relationship that are presented as a central issue within their marriage. Since the treatment of such disorders is beyond your area of expertise, you make an appointment for the couple later in the week at a nationally-recognized center that specializes in treatment of sexual disorders that is only a few hours from your community. You re-schedule the couple for another appointment to continue to focus on addiction recovery in the family. You receive a message a week later that the couple has canceled this appointment and on the following Sunday morning awake to the following: your client's spouse has written a letter to the editor in your local paper stating that two dear friends of hers who were having marital problems sought services at your agency (mentions you as the counselor by name) and that you recommended that the husband seek the services of a prostitute. The letter charges the agency and you with gross immorality, demands that the county stop funding the agency, and suggests that an investigation of the agency would reveal practices that would shock everyone in the county. The letter is signed by the client's spouse. The second you walk into the agency on Monday morning, a reporter is on the phone wanting to do a follow-up story on the letter to the editor.

Discussion Questions

Identify the multiple clinical and ethical issues inherent within this situation.

How would you respond to the overall situation?

What, if anything, would you say to the reporter?

What standards should guide staff interactions with the news media? Who can speak for the agency?

May a client's affiliation with the agency and comments on his or her problems or progress be discussed with the media if the client has signed a release of information for such disclosure?

Could disclosure under certain circumstances be fully legal but still represent a breach of ethical conduct?

Unbeknownst to the counselor, what actually occurred in the above story is the following: the couple kept their appointment at the clinic but while waiting in the reception room to be called into an office for their initial interview, the wife looked through a variety of informational brochures on the clinic and picked out a brochure on sexual surrogates. Having read little more than a paragraph, she grabbed her husband and demanded that they leave immediately. Her outrage that her husband might have sex with another woman in the name of therapy propelled the letter to the editor about her "two dear friends" which she composed in the car on the way home from the clinic. There are any number of clinical and ethical issues raised in the above vignette. Questions to be reviewed in clinical and administrative supervision would include the following:

- *Was it an appropriate time to make sexuality a focal issue in the counseling process or to refer the couple to a specialty clinic that focused on problems of sexual dysfunction?*
- *Was the couple adequately prepared for the referral?*
- *Within the agency procedures established to maximize client rights, the couple has the right to file a formal complaint with the agency. Who should contact the couple to express the concern about the letter and inform them of their grievance rights?*
- *What continuing responsibility does the agency have to serve the couple and who would be the best person to contact the family to re-initiate the service relationship or refer them to alternative resources?*

The letter to the editor poses threats to the reputation of the individual worker and to the reputation of the agency. The agency's response to the media must address these threats without violating the rights of, or otherwise harming, the couple involved as clients at the agency. Ethical responses to media inquiries involve two fundamental questions: 1) who within the agency can speak on behalf of the agency? and 2) what are the scope and limits of what, if anything, may be shared with the media?

Defining who may speak for the agency is critically important. It serves as protection for both the agency and individual staff persons. It also protects clients from inadvertent breaches of confidentiality that could be made by the direct service provider who might be defensive over what he or she did or did not do in a particular situation.

The spokesperson for the agency must represent the interests of the worker and the agency without harming the client. In the case above, the spokesperson can and should talk about any number of agency policies relevant to the inquiry. The spokesperson can respond to and solicit questions related to:

- *the agency's client grievance procedures*
- *the agency's use of outside referral sources*
- *the relationship between the agency and the clinic identified in the letter to the editor*
- *the agency's policies governing client confidentiality.*

Under no circumstances can the author of the letter be identified as an agency client or the details of the couple's particular case be disclosed to the media. Questions can be answered in terms of agency policy, not in terms of detailed transactions involving individual clients.

Other guidance for releasing information to the media include:

- *Have the designated spokesperson give information from a prepared fact sheet.*
- *Have your legal counsel approve the statement if the situation could result in litigation.*
- *Stick to the facts - never speculate.*
- *If a reporter wants information that cannot be released, do not evade. Tell him or her that you cannot release the information and why.*
- *Even if a reporter says "tell me something off the record", remember, nothing is "off the record."*
- *If you do not know the answer, say so and offer to find out.*
- *Be brief. Get your message out as succinctly and clearly as possible. The less you speak, the less likely it is you will be misquoted.*
- *Identify friends and allies from outside the company who can speak well of you or who can be quoted when there is a need for positive statements about your company. Such statements appear more credible if made by someone who is not an employee of the company.*
- *Remain calm. If you appear rushed or defensive, it will hurt your message, no matter how truthful or earnest you really are.*
- *Remain dignified. No matter how aggressive, rude or emotionally charged an individual's questioning may be, if you reply in a dignified way you can defuse the situation and use it to your advantage.*

♦♦ 64 ♦♦

The Code of Ethical Standards of the National Association of Alcoholism and Drug Abuse Counselors calls upon the counselor to "respect the limits of present knowledge in public statements concerning alcoholism and other forms of drug addiction."

Discussion Questions

To illustrate how difficult complying with such a standard can be, describe how you might respond to the following questions following a presentation to a local community group, e.g, PTA, church group, etc.. In reviewing your responses, do you feel your answers accurately reflect "the limits of present knowledge" within the field?

"Is alcoholism really a disease?"

"Can you inherit alcoholism?"

"Does AA work?"

"Is treatment effective?"

"Can alcoholics ever return to non-problematic drinking?"

"What do we know about the effectiveness of methadone? Isn't that just substituting one drug for another?"

"Would legalization of drugs reduce drug-related problems in the U.S.?"

"Is D.A.R.E. an effective primary alcohol and other drug abuse prevention program?"

The ethical mandates for the addictions counselor facing what may be quite controversial questions are to:

- *State as clearly and objectively as you can the state of knowledge on a particular issue.*
- *State the sources that you have used to draw that conclusion.*
- *Declare, "I don't know" to a request for information beyond the scope of your knowledge (and suggest alternative sources where such answers can be found).*
- *Present as objectively as you can multiple sides of complex issues.*
- *Acknowledge that people of good faith with high levels of technical expertise disagree about how to interpret the evidence on some issues.*
- *Separate and distinguish between personal opinion and professional information.*

Social Obligations

♦♦ 65 ♦♦

John maintains a rigid separation between what he views as his job and the world outside his agency. He works full time as a counselor, feels he does a good job with his clients, but sees no need to involve himself in the broader professional and social worlds that impact addiction treatment. John has never been involved in outside professional activities and turns down every request to speak to professional and community groups or to participate in broader political advocacy issues relevant to addiction treatment.

Discussion Question

While some would simply describe the above as John's unique professional style, are there any broader professional and social obligations that John is failing to fulfill?

While John's clinical work may be exemplary, many addiction professionals would take the position that John's definition of the role of the addictions counselor is much too narrow and that the addictions counselor has a broader social obligation to confront societal factors that contribute to addiction and to confront forces that undermine client access to addiction treatment services. NAADAC's Code of Ethics is quite explicit on this point, suggesting that "the NAADAC member shall to the best of his/her ability actively engage the legislative processes, educational institutions, and the general public to change public policy and legislation to make possible opportunities and choice of service for all human beings of any ethnic or social background whose lives are impaired by alcoholism and drug abuse."

Chapter
Six

Conduct in Client/Family Relationships

Exploration of the ethical issues governing relationships between helping professionals and their service recipients (clients) is predicated upon an understanding of the special nature of these relationships. To understand what distinguishes these relationships from all others, we will first introduce three words into our discussion: *fiduciary, iatrogenic* and *boundary.*

The professional service relationship between the addictions counselor and his or her client is a fiduciary relationship. This means that the caregiver has a special legal and ethical obligation to care for the welfare of the client in contractually prescribed ways. Fiduciary relationships are not characterized by an equality of power; one party enters the relationship with greater vulnerability and the other enters the relationship with greater power. Fiduciary relationships are also not expected to be reciprocal as that of a friendship. In a fiduciary relationship, the professional pledges that he or she will serve the best interests of the client and base decisions in the relationship on the client's best interests and needs. This fiduciary duty to the client requires an inordinately high commitment of the professional helper by way of loyalty, personal advocacy, objectivity, fairness, integrity and honesty. Ethical concerns encompass the broad range of conditions under which this duty and commitment to protect and serve the interests of the client can be compromised or abdicated.

Iatrogenic is a term drawn from medicine that means physician-caused or treatment-caused harm. The term implies that the most well intended of interventions conducted in the name of helping a client can, and sometimes do, have unforeseen harmful consequences. There is a long history of addiction treatment interventions that have had iatrogenic effects: bleeding, blistering, purging, and dosing alcoholics with toxic drugs in the 18th century; treating alcoholism and morphine addiction with cocaine and bromides in the 19th century that resulted in further addiction or death; and mandatory sterilization, psychosurgery, and the indiscriminate application of convulsive and harmful drug therapies in the 20th century. (See White, 1998) To acknowledge the potential iatrogenic effects of addiction treatment interventions is simply a way to acknowledge that implicit within the power of the professional to do good is the power to also do harm.

Fiduciary responsibilities and containment of potential iatrogenic effects of treatment interventions take place within the context of the boundaries that mark the degree of intimacy and vulnerability within helping relationships. A *boundary* is a line of demarcation that defines what is and is not appropriate in the helping relationship. The boundaries of appropriate and inappropriate behavior within professional helping relationships can be portrayed across a continuum of intimacy. (See Figure 6-A) Boundary management involves monitoring decisions that dictate the pace and degree of intimacy and vulnerability in the relationship between the professional helper and the client.

Figure 6-A

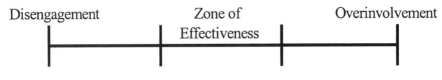

Disengagement   Zone of   Overinvolvement
                                 Effectiveness

The Intimacy Continuum

A professional relationship on the extreme far left of this continuum would reflect physical and emotional disengagement of the professional helper from the helping relationship. Ethical breaches at this end of the continuum reflect abandonment of the client and a failure to fulfill one's commitment to loyalty and service. They include: inappropriate exclusion from services, a disregard of informed consent, breaches in confidentiality, depersonalization of the client, demeaning and disrespectful communications, neglectful and abusive behavior, and precipitous termination of services. A professional relationship on the extreme right end of the continuum would reflect a violation of intimacy barriers through over-involvement with the client. Ethical breaches at this end of the continuum include: cultivation of client dependency, paternalistic decision-making, violations of privacy, invasive service interventions, and the social, financial and sexual exploitation of the client. The task for each agency and each worker is to define the zone of effectiveness that represents a level of appropriate and effective involvement based on the nature of the service contract.

If the intimacy continuum is bent (Figure 6-B), a more complex portrayal of ethical dimensions in the helper-helpee relationship emerges. This figure shows that both ends of the continuum represent zones of abuse and exploitation, suggesting that the extremes of disengagement and over-involvement may be more dynamically related than would be superficially apparent. In both cases, the primary force shaping the helper-helpee relationship is something other than the needs of the person seeking help. It should not be surprising then to find that professional helpers who have sexually exploited one or more clients were during this period simultaneously disengaged from most of their other clients.

The Zone of Effectiveness has now been marked Zone of Safety. A new zone, the zone of marginality, has been added that marks an area of increased vulnerability for the client and/or the professional helper. The zone of marginality represents areas of heightened or decreased intimacy that may be clinically appropriate but that heighten the vulnerability of both the client and the professional helper. This zone also reflects an area of professional and "moral drift" that can often precede the more blatant and visible violation of ethical and professional conduct in our relationships with service consumers.

Figure 6-B

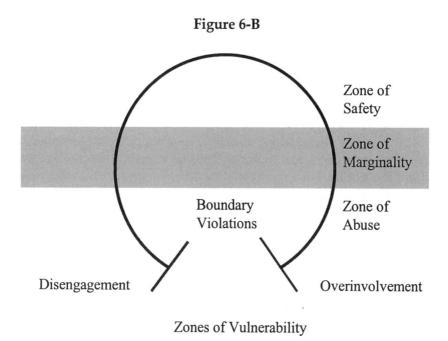

Zones of Vulnerability

Defining these zones of effectiveness, marginality and abuse are complicated by recent research suggesting that recovery from addiction is characterized by different developmental stages and that interventions that may prove quite therapeutic in one stage may be ineffective or even harmful at another stage. Actions that promote client autonomy at a late stage in treatment might constitute clinical abandonment at an early stage of treatment. This is a way of saying that while there are some things that we may want to define as never okay, other interventions can be measured only within the clinical and cultural contexts in which they occur.

It is our belief that many breaches of ethical conduct in professional helping relationships are not isolated incidents but are, in fact, the consequence of a progressive disengagement or progressive over-involvement in the helper-helpee relationship. To see such breaches as processes rather than events has important implications for the elimination or minimization of breaches in ethical conduct within the helping professions. If sexual exploitation of clients, for example, is an event that happens without context or history, little prevention or early intervention measures would be accessible to stop such incidents before they occur. If, on the other hand, sexual exploitation often reveals itself through a progressive violation of intimacy barriers in the helper-helpee relationship, then a broad range of educational and supervisory strategies become available to stem this progressive over-involvement prior to sexual exploitation.

The zone of marginality represents behaviors to which increased supervisory surveillance and education must be directed. If an adult survivor of sexual abuse in the addiction treatment setting begins to clinically deteriorate during his/her early period of sobriety, it may be clinically appropriate to increase the frequency of sessions. But increased frequency of sessions moves the relationship toward heightened intimacy and this increases the potential vulnerability of both the client and the counselor. Likewise, we know that terminations are always a period of heightened vulnerability, particularly for clients with developmental issues of abandonment. If it is clinically appropriate for workers to move into this zone of increased involvement or disengagement, then they should not be there alone, but rather should be there strategically under the guidance and support of peers, supervisors, and clinical consultants.

The critical incidents described below will help each worker and each agency clarify and define the boundaries of the zones of effectiveness, marginality and abuse. Such boundaries will differ based on the organizational setting, staff characteristics (style and professional training), client characteristics, service provider role, stage of service delivery, and cultural context. While such boundaries may vary across agencies, they should be clearly defined and articulated *within* each agency. While such boundaries may vary across persons and roles within a service agency, it is crucial for each worker to define their own zone of effectiveness and for each agency to define those boundaries of effectiveness to which *all* organizational members will be held accountable. While such boundaries may vary somewhat from client to client, it is essential that they be defined *within* each staff client relationship.

Critical Incidents

Definition of Client

All expectations and standards shaping the relationships between professional helpers and clients are based on an assumed definition of "client." The critical incidents below will help the reader explore the following three dimensions of this definition.

1. Of the large number of persons the agency interacts with, e.g., individuals, family members, friends, employers, and personnel from other agencies; which are encompassed within the term "client?"
2. How and when does one achieve the status of client?
3. Once attained, when, if ever, does one lose the status of client? Does a client stay a client forever even if service delivery has ceased?

If prevention and treatment agencies are going to promulgate standards of behavior defining what actions are and are not appropriate with clients, it is crucial that this status of "client" be defined. The definition of client/patient may technically differ from state to state under various facility and professional licensure codes. However, when establishing a code of conduct/ethics, you need to consider whether clients should be defined as persons involved in some form of treatment or counseling or whether it extends to institutional relationships resulting in funding contracts or referrals.

One definition of client consistently interpreted across all states is the meaning of "patient" as defined by the federal confidentiality laws. Those regulations define a patient as "any individual who has applied for or been given diagnosis or treatment for alcohol or drug abuse at a federally assisted program and includes any individual who, after arrest on a criminal charge, is identified as an alcohol or drug abuser in order to determine that individuals' eligibility to participate in a program," 42 C.F.R. §2.12. Thus, someone referred to a program for an assessment who does not show up is not a client and may be reported to the referring entity because that person has not yet applied for or been given a diagnosis. This issue of identifying who is a client has become even more complicated because of the increasing clinical trends of providing outreach, early intervention and case management services. These engagement strategies coupled with the legal obligation of programs receiving federal block grant funds to provide "interim services" to certain priority populations, blurs the boundary of who constitutes a client and when "treatment" begins.

These persons may be considered clients for purposes of eligibility for services as well as defining professional behaviors and boundary lines for staff. On the other hand, these persons may not be considered patients under your state licensing laws, may not need a treatment record, may not be afforded the confidentiality protections and may not be covered under the terms of your agency's professional liability policy. Additionally, agencies that provide both mental health and addiction treatment services find that the definition of client may be more difficult to articulate because of the definition of "recovery". You should carefully consider all of these issues when defining a "client" or "patient".

♦♦ 66 ♦♦

You (supervisor) receive a formal complaint from the family member of a client alleging that a therapist at your agency is sexually involved with this client. Although your agency has a personnel code which explicitly defines sexual activity with a client as unethical, the therapist, in response to your questioning, makes the following points:

1) The therapist says that he was not sexually involved with the client when she was receiving services from the agency.
2) Treatment has been terminated and the woman is no longer a client at the agency.
3) Since the woman is no longer a client, what she and the therapist do is a private matter and none of the agency's business.

Discussion Questions

How would you respond to this situation?

What ethical issues are involved?

Does a client ever lose the status of client as it relates to references to "client" in standards of ethical conduct?

While the ethical prohibition against sexual activity with clients is consistent across the human service disciplines, there is an avoidance of and variance on the issue of sexual activity with former clients and a lack of consistent definition of when, if ever, a client ceases to be a client. The following are representative.

> *"Sexual activity with a patient is unethical. Sexual involvement with one's former patients generally exploits emotions deriving from treatment and therefore almost always is unethical." The Principles of Medical Ethics with Annotations Especially Applicable to Psychiatry, American Psychiatric Association, 1986.*

"Sexual intimacies with clients are unethical." Ethical Principles of Psychologists, American Psychological Association, 1981. A proposed 1986 expansion of this statement to include former clients raised such complex issues and triggered such intense debate that a decision was made to continue study and discussion before any modifications could be made.

"The social worker should under no circumstances engage in sexual activities with clients." Code of Ethics, National Association of Social Workers, 1979. A 1985 revision of this code added the following: "Clinical social workers do not initiate, and should avoid when possible, personal relationships or dual roles with current clients, or with any former clients whose feelings toward them may still be derived from or influenced by the former professional relationship."

While the National Association of Alcoholism and Drug Abuse Counselors Code of Ethics does not explicitly define post-termination sexual relationships between counselors and clients as unethical, a number of state alcohol and drug counselor associations have begun to address this issue. The Minnesota Chemical Dependency Association, for example, prohibits sexual relationships with former clients during the first year following termination of services.

Minnesota has taken the lead in defining criminal and civil penalties for sexual exploitation of a client by a psychotherapist. The Minnesota Criminal Sexual Conduct Code, §§609.341-609.351, was revised in 1985 to make psychotherapist sexual exploitation of a client a felony. This revision included as a violation, sexual activity with former clients under two circumstances:

1. The former client is emotionally dependent upon the psychotherapist.
2. The sexual contact occurred as a result of therapeutic deception.

Minnesota created avenues for civil redress of sexual exploitation by professional helpers through Chapter 148A Minnesota Statutes. This statute allows suits to be filed if the sexual contact between the client and professional helper occurred within five years of the action that gave rise to the suit.

Each helping agency must define the status and tenure of the designation of "client" based on the nature of vulnerability of their service recipients and the degree of power (potential for exploitation) implicit within the service delivery process. Gary Schoener (1989) has prepared an excellent review of the clinical/ethical/legal issues involved in the debate over post-termination sexual relationships.

To determine whether the therapist violated the law and the facility's corresponding obligations, you need to answer the following questions:

- *Is the client a minor? (If yes, it most likely will be considered child abuse under your state statutes and may also be statutory rape.)*
- *Does your state facility licensing laws or regulations expressly prohibit sexual relationships with clients?*
- *Does your state counselor/professional licensure requirements prohibit sexual relationships with clients?*
- *Does your state licensure requirements mandate a report to a licensing body, an investigating body or an office of inspector general?*
- *Do any state laws or regulations differentiate between current and former clients?*
- *Do any state laws or regulations provide time frames that permit relationships (i.e., adult client has not been engaged in treatment for two years)?*
- *Does your code of ethics or personnel policies clearly define the prohibitions and outline mandated reporting responsibilities for client sexual abuse?*
- *If your agency has a broad range of human services, does your code of ethics address whether staff providing one service may become involved with a client receiving another service?*
- *Does your code of ethics or personnel policies prohibit client relationships with clinical staff, administrative staff, support staff, maintenance staff, volunteers, or all or some of the above?*

In the event your code of ethics does not prohibit sexual intimacies with former clients who have ceased services for at least two years, you should consider the seven factors listed below to determine whether the client was exploited. Section 4.07 of the American Psychologist Association ethical principles recommends that the following factors be considered and that the therapist bears the burden of demonstrating no exploitation occurred:

- *The amount of time that has passed since therapy terminated.*
- *The nature and duration of the therapy.*
- *The circumstances of the termination.*
- *The client's personal history.*
- *The client's current mental status.*
- *The likelihood of adverse impact on the client or others.*

* *Any statements or actions made by the therapist during the course of therapy suggesting or inviting the possibility of a post-termination sexual or romantic relationship with the client.*

◆◆ 67 ◆◆

It has come to your attention that a therapist you supervise is involved in an intimate relationship with a family member of a client being served within the program in which the therapist works. The relationship was initiated by the therapist following the family member's participation in a "family night" educational meeting at the agency. While the agency personnel policies explicitly prohibit sexual relationships with clients, the issue of whether family members of "identified patients" are included within this prohibition has never come up.

Discussion Questions

What ethical issues are involved in this situation?

Should family members be included within the definition of "client?"

How would you respond to the therapist in this situation?

Are family members involved collaterally in agency services included within the definition of "client?" Would a sexual relationship with a sister of a client whom the involved staff member met while the sister was attending family week be prohibited? Would the degree of the family member's involvement in the service process make a difference in our judgment of the appropriateness or inappropriateness of the therapist's actions?

If family members are included in the dual relationship prohibition, does this include a non-traditional definition of family, e.g., paramours, and other persons of significance, involved in the identified client's treatment?

How should prohibitions related to dual relationships differ, if at all, for agency staff who were not directly involved in the provision of services?

Is a client's vulnerability lessened and the staff member's power decreased if the staff member is the executive director rather than the primary counselor of the client? What if the staff member involved is an accountant or a receptionist at the agency?

Here is one view; what is yours?

If we are to articulate ethical and professional standards governing the relationships between agency personnel and clients, then we must first explicitly define who is and is not included within the parameters of "client." A growing number of human service agencies are developing family centered models of treatment, education and support, yet our thinking about ethics continues to be tied to the relationship between a professional helper and an individual person with a presenting problem. The concern in this situation is that a therapist could use his or her position of power to exploit the vulnerability of a family member in the same manner that the vulnerability of the individual client could be manipulated. Two issues appear critical. First, we must expand our definition of "client" in our ethical discussion to include the family network in which the individual client is nested. Secondly, we must stretch our definition of "family" to include those individuals whose involvement in the service process and whose importance to the client warrant the designation, "family of choice." Family of choice would include those significant others in the client's life who with or without benefit of blood or law perform the functions of family. Family of choice would include everyone from domestic partners and paramours to intimate social networks that serve as a surrogate family structure for the client. It is imperative in our organizational communications that professional helpers understand that ethical mandates referring to "client" encompass family by both blood and function.

An agency's personnel polices should clearly define client. From a legal perspective, the clearer the standard, the greater likelihood of reduced unintentional breaches of policy, as well as consistent enforcement and discipline. Below we provide a sample definition for consideration:

> XYZ Center recognizes that addiction and mental illness are often long-term disorders and that many clients will go through varying periods of remission and relapse. Given that clients who have completed treatment at one point may at a later point in time seek further services, all references to "client" in this Code shall include both former (no service contact for two full years, or in the case of adolescents, until their 22nd birthday) and currently active clients. The terms "patient", "client" and "consumer" are to be used synonymously. In this context, the term "client" applies to individuals who are currently receiving or have formerly received therapeutic or counseling services from XYZ Center. The term "client" excludes clients who are organizations, employers, government agencies, or other customers that have agreements with XYZ Center. The standards apply when XYZ Center staff have first hand knowledge that an individual is or has been a client of a clinical intervention or treatment program at XYZ Center.

The policies should further prohibit intimate social relationships with known clients/families that could jeopardize the ability of the agency to provide effective services to that client/family. The code should also specify applicability to personnel such as clinical staff, administrative staff, janitorial or support staff, and externs and volunteers. Some agencies address this issue by making the standard applicable to ALL agency employees (including consultants, interns and volunteers).

♦♦ 68 ♦♦

Joan has been a therapist at your agency for the past three years. Three months ago she began dating Mark whom she had met through mutual friends. This past weekend Mark mentioned in passing that he was in counseling with his ex-wife at the agency before he and his ex-wife decided to divorce. This morning Joan enters your office to discuss this situation in light of the agency policy that prohibits social and intimate relationships between staff and clients (and former clients). Joan was not involved in a primary counseling relationship with Mark nor was she employed by the agency when Mark was a client. She was completely unaware of Mark's status of "former client" until this past weekend.

Discussion Questions

What ethical or professional practice issues do you see, if any, in this situation?

Should the ban on social/intimate relationships apply to this situation?

What is your response to Joan?

Many professional helpers would cite a case like Joan's to suggest that there are exceptions to the "once a client-always a client" policy, particularly when applied to:

- *staff who were not directly involved in the service delivery to the client*
- *staff whose relationship with the client originated from a context outside the agency*
- *clients who no longer receive services and who are unlikely to need services in the future.*

Joan clearly did not initiate a relationship with Mark with knowledge of his status as a former client nor did she possess special power based on Mark's pre-existing service history. While there is no exploitative intent and minimal exploitative potential in this situation, it would be appropriate to raise this situation as an issue in supervision. One ethics workshop participant, when given this critical incident, took the following stance:

> *"I would contact the former client to make sure he understood that a relationship with a staff person could preclude his future access to services at the agency due to our policy governing dual relationships. I would also tell him that the staff member with whom he was involved would not have access to his former service records. If the former client understood and agreed to these circumstances, I would wish him well and tell him that from this point forward the relationship was none of the agency's business."*

What would you do as a supervisor if such a situation was brought to you?

See Vignettes #66, 67 and 69 for legal guidance.

♦♦ 69 ♦♦

Jerry, who was once a client at your agency, has been hired as a detox technician.

Discussion Questions

Does Jerry lose his status of "client" now that he is a staff member of the agency?

Would socializing outside the agency or a sexual relationship between another staff member and Jerry be ethical or unethical?

What ethical issues might come up as part of Jerry's role transition?

Should there be any change in the disposition of Jerry's clinical service record?

If there is a recurring need for service, can Jerry be seen at the agency now that he is on staff?

There are a number of potential ethical and legal issues in the transition from client to staff member within an addiction treatment organization. The first ethical issue is whether Jerry's status as a client was prematurely terminated to meet the staffing needs of the program. The concern is that critical short-term staffing needs can contaminate the integrity of the clinical decision-making process resulting in a precipitous termination of a client's access to service and placement of a client in a situation that could undermine his or her health and long-term recovery. Some programs who employ former clients address this danger of exploitation by utilizing external consultants to review the client-to-staff decision-making process and/or by building in a required period of time that must pass following service termination before a former client becomes eligible for consideration in a staff position.

A second ethical issue involves whether the process of Jerry's transition from client to staff was managed honestly and with sensitivity to the potential strain involved in such transitions. Active management of this process would include such questions as:

- *Was there full disclosure related to the potential consequences inherent in the role transition? Was Jerry told that his taking on the role of staff member could jeopardize his access to future agency services? Was Jerry informed of the stress inherent within the role transition and the staff role he would be assuming?*
- *Was there a formal structure and process signaling Jerry's role transition to himself, his treatment peers and to all agency staff?*

A third ethical and legal issue involves the protection of Jerry's right to privacy as a staff member. The disposition of Jerry's permanent service record is an important dimension of what is now an issue of a staff member's right to confidentiality. Access to Jerry's prior service record by other staff members could violate Jerry's right to privacy by inappropriately revealing to his peers details of his personal and service history. Some agencies address this situation by removing the former client's record and placing it under the control of the Executive Director. Other agencies, where the law permits, make arrangements for the destruction of the client's record at the time the person moves into a staff position.

A fourth ethical and legal issue is the protection of records of clients who participated in treatment with Jerry. Even though staff within a treatment agency are permitted to share confidential information as a "communication within a program" under 42 C.F.R. §2.12(c)(3), Jerry should not be permitted to access any of those client records unless expressly authorized in writing by the client in accordance with 42 C.F.R. §2.31. See Vignette #71 for guidance on written consent.

What standards now govern relationships between Jerry and other staff members? Most agencies take the position that if Jerry is no longer a client, he and other staff are bound by whatever values and ethical standards govern social and sexual relationships between staff. This position is not without its ethical vulnerabilities. Though widespread, this stance leaves open the potential of a supervisor to prematurely terminate services to a client, move the client into a staff position, and then use the power derived from both the clinical and supervisory relationship for the purpose of sexual exploitation. See Chapter Seven for a discussion of sexual exploitation within the supervisor-supervisee relationship. See Chapter Nine for a discussion of the definition of "client" as it relates to prevention workers, trainers, and employee assistance counselors.

◆◆ 70 ◆◆

Rene has been court mandated into residential treatment at your facility under an agreement you have with the county court system. Rene's referral is part of a contractual arrangement whereby your agency is paid by the county to provide assessment and treatment services to addicted offenders. The court has mandated Rene's treatment, selected your program as the site for such treatment and will be paying your program for the costs associated with Rene's treatment.

Discussion Question

Who is the "client?"

The question of who is the client in this vignette is not a rhetorical question but an important avenue through which the problem of "double-agentry" may be examined. There exists in this case both an individual client and an institutional client, raising such important questions as: to which client is ultimate loyalty owed? Do the duties and obligations to the individual client conflict with those of the institutional client? How are conflicts of best interests of the respective parties decided? Where the financial interests of the individual therapist and the agency are dependent upon continued referrals from the institutional client, how can therapist objectivity be assured? It is important that professional helpers recognize situations that pose problems of "double-agentry," communicate the potential of such conflicts to their individual and institutional clients and have access to supervision to minimize the contamination of professional judgment via personal or organizational self-interest. The sensitivity of staff to problems with "double-agentry" is enhanced where organizations have identified via training and supervision the most common conflicts unique to their setting and have created procedures and processes to follow when potential conflicts of loyalty arise.

When providing information to the court in situations of mandated treatment, one of the ways to minimize legal conflicts down the road is to ensure the client executes a criminal justice consent form. Criminal justice consents must comply with all the requirements of written consent (See Vignette #71). However, criminal justice consents differ in three ways: (1) the consent is not revocable; (2) the duration of the consent is typically tied to the anticipated length of treatment and the need for information in connection with the final disposition of that criminal proceeding; and (3) the information may be redisclosed by persons in the criminal justice system as long as it is in connection with his/her official duties, 42 C.F.R. §2.35.

Informed Consent

◆◆ 71 ◆◆

Implicit within the concept of informed consent is the notion that an autonomous, competent client, having been informed of the potential risks and benefits of a prescribed treatment regimen, freely enters into an agreement to participate in the recommended treatment.

Discussion Questions

How do we apply the concept of informed consent to Rene whose status would preclude the definition of an autonomous agent and whose court-mandated treatment clearly surpasses the bounds of voluntary choice?

What ethical issues can arise when external coercion contaminates the normal meaning of informed consent?

Discuss potential ethical issues related to the following practices:

A. Admitting (via parental authority) an adolescent to a locked addiction treatment unit who has no desire for treatment and would run from an unlocked unit.
B. Seeking legal guardianship/payeeship of an alcoholic or addict.
C. Working with individuals entering treatment via court mandate.
D. Working with clients entering treatment to save their jobs.
E. Application of state mental health commitment laws to alcoholics and addicts via interpretation of "in danger to self or others."
F. Testifying on behalf of the prosecution in a probation revocation hearing initiated as a result of a client leaving court-mandated treatment against staff advice.

Is the informed consent process violated if the treatment center is in control of the external agent and is dictating to the family or court the threats and consequences which they should apply to the client if he or she fails to enter or complete treatment?

Consents for disclosure are governed by the federal confidentiality regulations, 42 C.F.R. §2.31, and must be in writing. To make a disclosure in accordance with these regulations, the following elements must be included in the written consent:

1. *Name of patient.*
2. *Name or general designation of program making the disclosure.*
3. *Kind of information and amount of information to be disclosed.*
4. *Name or title of person or organization to which disclosure is to be made.*
5. *Purpose for disclosure.*
6. *Date on which consent is signed.*
7. *Signature of patient.*
8. *Signature of parent or guardian, if applicable.*
9. *Statement that the consent is subject to revocation (except to the extent program has relied upon it).*
10. *Statement that the consent will terminate upon a specific date, event or condition.*

There is also the legal question of whether the treatment program should have used informed consent and whether clients were briefed on potential positive and negative effects of their public identification as addicts/clients. Legally, it is important to understand the distinction between consent, informed consent and the consent for disclosure required under the federal confidentiality laws. Although these concepts are related, they are not interchangeable and each has its own legal significance.

Consent means the voluntary agreement by a person in the possession and exercise of sufficient mental capacity to make an intelligent choice to do something proposed by another.

The federal confidentiality statutes and regulations, as discussed above, govern consent for disclosure. Prior to making a disclosure, a written consent form (containing the required elements of 42 C.F.R. §2.31) should be signed by the patient. For informed consent, see Vignette #4.

Informed consent is the linchpin in the contractual relationship between the professional helper and the helpee and yet situations like the above raise difficult issues in assessing the elements of competence and freedom from coercion so important to the concept of informed consent. Where the competence of the client is compromised through acute intoxication, drug-induced neurological deficits, or severe psychiatric impairment, a treatment site may have to rely on what Haas and Malouf (1989) call "substituted consent." Where competence to weigh risks and benefits of, and alternatives to, treatment is clearly lacking, the treatment site may have to rely on an independent party, e.g., parents, family member, advocate, or the court, to act on the client's behalf.

The question of autonomy versus coercion in the informed consent process can be a difficult one, particularly with the growing number of individuals mandated into treatment via the criminal justice system. To what extent do such clients have free choice in the informed consent process when refusal may mean violation of probation or parole and their potential incarceration? Is an informed consent valid under such circumstances? Most addiction treatment organizations who have wrestled with this question would answer that the consent is valid. They would posit that the informed consent does not imply that there may not be coercive forces pushing the client toward treatment nor will there not be painful externally imposed consequences resulting from the client's refusal to participate in treatment. The critical factor is that the treatment agency is not coercing the client into treatment nor does it have control over the external coercive agent, e.g., family, court, employer.

♦♦ 72 ♦♦

Jan, a fourteen-year-old adolescent, has contacted your agency requesting counseling services for problems that include her alcohol and drug use. She is adamant, however, in her refusal to allow you to contact her parents. Jan states that she will seek counseling only under the condition her parents know nothing about it. From the brief information you have collected so far, she is clearly in need of services.

Discussion Questions

How would you respond to this situation?

Does this client have a legal right at age fourteen to consent to treatment services?

Do you have any ethical or legal responsibilities to the parents in this situation?

Jan's story raises legal and ethical issues involving two separate issues:

1)   Can minors provide consent for their own treatment or must such consent come from parents or legal guardians?
2)   Can minors access services without the knowledge of their parents?

The age at which minors are legally competent to enter into financial contracts (i.e., loans), relationship contracts (i.e., marriage) or service contracts (i.e. medical treatment, counseling) varies from state to state. The legal mandates may also vary according to the type of services youth are seeking, e.g., recent trends toward increased ability to self-initiate substance abuse counseling without parental consent or decreased ability to initiate abortion counseling and abortion procedures without parental consent. Each agency must assure that it is working within the legal framework of state and federal statutes and regulations governing the consent process for minors.

In determining whose written consent is required for the disclosure of authorized client information when the client is a minor, the federal confidentiality regulations defer to state law, 42 C.F.R. §2.14. The federal confidentiality regulations provide that parental or guardian consent for disclosure (this includes consent by any other person legally responsible for the minor) is required only if the applicable state law requires parental or guardian consent before providing addiction treatment to a minor. Thus, if a minor client acting alone has the legal capacity under state law to apply for and receive addiction treatment, written consent for disclosure may be given by the minor only; parental or guardian consent will not be required under the federal confidentiality rules. This restriction includes the disclosure of privileged client information to the parent or guardian of the minor client for the purpose of obtaining financial reimbursement. However, the federal regulations do not prohibit a program from refusing to provide treatment until the minor consents to the disclosure necessary to obtain reimbursement. Programs must be careful about the refusal to provide treatment based upon their funding source agreements. The federal regulations also allow programs under certain circumstances to reveal facts relevant to reducing a threat to the life or physical well-being of the minor to the parent or guardian if the minor lacks capacity for rational choice.

Thus, if a minor of 12 years of age or older has the legal authority to sign into treatment, then under the federal law the minor has the right to execute the written consent to disclose confidential information. Neither the parent's nor guardian's consent is necessary. Despite the legal requirements, it is sometimes recommended from a liability perspective that both the minor and the parent sign the consent for treatment. Alternatively, if the state law requires the consent of the parent or guardian for a minor to obtain addiction treatment, written consent for disclosure must be given by both the minor and his or her parent or guardian.

Answering whether minors can legally consent to treatment does not in and of itself address the question of whether such consent is ethical. The ethical prerequisites of informed consent or refusal demand that: (1) the minor client be fully appraised of the risks, likely benefits, and alternatives to proposed service procedures; (2) coercion is not utilized to achieve consent; and (3) the client is mentally competent to make the consent or refuse decision (GAP, 1990). It is the third of these prerequisites that poses difficult ethical dilemmas with minors.

Grisso and Vierling (1978) suggest that the issue of competence must be addressed in three distinct situations:

- *Does the minor have the right to consent to treatment without knowledge of or with disregard of his or her parent's wishes?*
- *Does the minor have the independent right to refuse treatment which his or her parents wish to proceed?*
- *Does the minor have a right to active participation in discussions related to his or her treatment needs, but no right to consent or refuse treatment?*

The ethical dimension, as opposed to the clinical and legal dimensions, of these questions hinge on the question of competence of the minor to provide informed consent or refusal to treatment. Competence, at a minimum, must encompass sufficient autonomy of the minor client from parental influence and coercion to assure autonomous decision-making, the maturity of the minor client to project out of past life experience a realistic assessment of the risks and benefits of proposed services, and the cognitive ability of the minor client to analyze alternative forms of treatment in relationship to his or her future well-being. The clear presence of maturity, cognitive development and autonomous decision-making is so rare among minor clients that a substantial body of ethical literature from the human service professions has taken the position that parents or legal guardians should always be involved in the informed consent process except under circumstances where such consent would threaten the safety of the minor, e.g, child abuse. This stance may be even more justified for minors whose patterns of alcohol and other drug use and/or psychiatric impairment compromise the judgment required for informed consent. Most counseling organizations have taken the position that they will not see a minor child without first communicating with the parent and receiving the parent's informed consent for services to proceed. In many states, counselors may legally see a minor for a certain number of sessions without parental consent if the minor is seeking assistance for certain problem areas, e.g., drug abuse, sexually transmitted diseases. Even in these states, most agencies require a supervisory review mechanism to assure that counseling minors without parental consent is the exception rather than the rule. Agencies serving children and adolescents should formulate a clear philosophy and guidelines regarding the informed consent process for minors, the situations under which these normal guidelines may be excepted, and the situations that require a mandatory supervisory review.

♦♦ 73 ♦♦

"Informed" consent implies that a potential client is fully apprised of the potential risks and unexpected or undesirable effects that could result from a particular course of treatment as well as other available treatment alternatives prior to agreeing to initiate the recommended course of treatment.

Discussion Question

What potential risks or unexpected or undesirable consequences should clients be apprised of as part of the routine informed consent process within your program?

The exact nature of potential risks varies widely across addiction treatment settings based on the types of services rendered. Communication regarding potential risks to assure informed consent to treatment could include:

- *pain, discomfort or disability resulting directly or indirectly from a service procedure, e.g., potential medication side-effects*
- *inconvenience resulting from the service commitment*
- *inadvertent effects, e.g., stigma related to service affiliation.*

A client seeking outpatient counseling, for example, might be told the following as part of an informed consent process.

- *"Your decision to involve yourself in counseling will require the commitment of time and expense which we have just gone over."*
- *"You are likely during the counseling process to experience discomfort related to the exploration of painful events in your life."*
- *"You are likely to experience periods of stress related to the changes in how you see yourself and how you see the world that result from the counseling process."*

Communication of potential risks is balanced by communicating at the same time what the client can reasonably expect to gain from the counseling process. An additional critical step includes a brief and objective summary of alternative approaches to problem resolution that may be available to the client. With this step, for example, a client presenting herself at a methadone clinic would be informed of alternatives to methadone as part of the informed consent process. The counselor does not need to be competent to deliver all modalities of treatment but they must be knowledgeable enough to objectively represent these alternatives to the client. Once potential risks, benefits, and alternatives have been clearly summarized, the client is then able to decline participation in the proposed service procedures or provide informed consent to proceed.

Labeling: The Ethics of Diagnosis

◆◆ 74 ◆◆

An inpatient adolescent addiction treatment unit has aggressively marketed its services in your community and has achieved a very positive public image in its first two years of operation. The unit is becoming a "catch-all" for affluent kids with problems in your area. While the patterns, intensity and duration of alcohol and other drug use vary widely, all youth admitted to this unit are given a primary addiction-related diagnosis at admission and discharge. If the records were carefully scrutinized, they would reveal that adolescents are being regularly admitted and labeled as having an addictive disorder in spite of the lack of sufficient data in the record to justify such a diagnosis (or the rote listing of symptoms that match admission and/or diagnostic criteria). When asked about this practice, one is told that these kids need help regardless of the diagnosis and that such a diagnosis is required for the insurance company to cover the adolescent's treatment costs.

Discussion Questions

What ethical issues, if any, do you see in this practice?

To what extent does the dimension of informed consent include the exploration of the potential effect of the label "alcoholic" or "addict" on the developmental trajectory of such an adolescent?

How can the legitimate counseling needs of adolescents and their families be addressed without the misapplication and potential iatrogenic effects of a diagnostic label?

The vignette above raises a number of ethical issues. The vignette hints at the possibility that the program may be inappropriately admitting and diagnosing adolescents for the financial gain of the institution. The indiscriminate admission of troubled adolescents into an addiction treatment unit leaves the institution open to charges of financial exploitation. Even in the absence of malicious intent, where there is a true desire to assist the adolescent and the family, the placement of an addiction-related diagnosis on the adolescent for purposes of service reimbursement raises two concerns. The first is the potential iatrogenic effect of labeling. Placement of a diagnostic label, without the clinical data to justify such a diagnosis, ignores the potential impact of such labeling on the client. The admission to an addiction treatment unit and the accompanying diagnosis could have potentially harmful effects via social stigma, future occupational restrictions, or reduced insurability. A second concern involves the potential breach of contract with the reimbursing agent. To misrepresent a diagnosis breaches the expectation of professional integrity and honesty in the relationship between the service agency and the reimbursing agent. Where financial gain is involved, such misrepresentation leaves the program open to charges of fraud. Programs must guard against charges that they practice "checkbook diagnosis" or "administrative diagnosis", the misapplication of a diagnosis to achieve some programmatic or financial goal.

Addiction treatment programs, particularly those serving adolescents, have responded to this potential for client exploitation and financial fraud by establishing more rigorous criteria and standards for admission and by implementing both internal and external systems of utilization review to assure that the client's history and symptoms have been documented and warrant primary and secondary diagnoses and the intensity and duration of prescribed treatment.

Right to Treatment
Refusal to Treat

♦♦ 75 ♦♦

Your agency can accommodate 25 residential clients and 70 outpatient clients at a time. You are currently operating at capacity in both your residential and outpatient units, but have another 55 people who are seeking (and have been prescreened as appropriate for) admission. These 55 individuals present a diversity of demographic characteristics, a wide range of problem acuity and chronicity, financial resources ranging from the wealthy to the indigent, good and poor treatment prognoses, and varying referral sources. Their service requests are scattered over the past six weeks.

Discussion Questions

Who do you admit next?

What standards govern access to treatment at your agency?

What ethical issues can arise in the management of waiting lists?

When service demands outstrip resources, the management of the waiting list for services become the point of crisis through which conflicting needs and interests meet. Perhaps most critical in such situations is that there exists a clear set of standards that govern the decisions of who will be served, that such decisions are clearly communicated to all relevant constituencies, and that the standards are adhered to on a consistent basis. To create standards for waiting list management, the agency must identify how it will differentially apply the following principles:

- *Principle of fairness: first come, first served.*
- *Principle of greatest good: spreading resources to reach the greatest number of people.*
- *Principle of greatest need: allocating intense resources to those few clients with the greatest number and intensity of problems.*
- *Principle of client mix: selecting clients to enhance the best therapeutic chemistry within the treatment milieu.*
- *Principle of payee mix: allocating access across a formula of the best percentage mix between paying and non-paying and public pay and private pay clients.*
- *Principle of influence: allocating or bypassing normal access to accommodate favored persons or institutions.*
- *Principle of least needs: creating mix of client characteristics that minimize excessive time or emotional demands on staff.*

For those agencies that receive Federal Block Grant funds, federal regulations contained at 45 C.F.R. §96.131 require programs to provide preference in treatment to the following:

- *Pregnant injecting drug abusers*
- *Pregnant substance abusers*
- *Injecting drug abusers*
- *All others.*

In addition to these federal requirements, each state may define by statute or contract other priority populations such as persons involved in the child welfare system, criminal justice clients and those on TANF (temporary aid to needy families).

♦♦ 76 ♦♦

A social setting detoxification program has refused admission to a chronic public inebriate on the following grounds:

- The client has had dozens of admissions without exhibiting any sincere desire to stop drinking.
- The client uses detox for free food and to sober up until his next check comes.
- Based on the above, the staff believe that continuing to admit this client for services is a form of "professional enabling" and should be stopped.

Discussion Questions

What ethical issues do you feel are involved in this situation?

How do you view a client's right to treatment?

Under what circumstances, or through what procedures, could such rights be revoked?

Is this an appropriate or inappropriate application of the concept of enabling?

If this client dies shortly after refusal of assessment or admission services at the detox unit, do you feel the unit would be morally or legally responsible? Is this type of blanket denial of services a form of "clinical abandonment?"

What principles should govern clients' access to services?

See next vignette for analysis.

♦♦ 77 ♦♦

Marvin, a late stage alcoholic, was court mandated into residential addiction treatment following his third DUI. Within 48 hours of his admission, it is discovered that Marvin brought alcohol into the treatment facility and has been sneaking drinks since his admission. The program administratively discharges Marvin for failure to follow program rules. Marvin's family challenges this decision using the following logic: If Marvin has the disease of alcoholism, which is characterized by an inability to abstain from and/or loss of control over alcohol use, and if he was admitted to treatment because he lacked such control, then why should Marvin be excluded from treatment for exhibiting the primary symptom (drinking) of the disease for which he was being admitted?

Discussion Questions

If Marvin, in the hours or days following his administrative discharge, were to kill himself or others in some alcohol-related incident, would the program bear any moral responsibility?

What ethical issues can arise in the administrative discharge of clients from treatment?

When is the application of a clinical concept an ethical issue? Consider this view:

Refusal to admit previously served clients or the precipitous termination of clients, without objective clinical criteria, can leave a program or worker vulnerable to charges of failure to provide equitable access to treatment or charges of clinical abandonment. The concept of professional enabling (actions that inadvertently support continued pathology by protecting the client from the consequences of his or her behavior) has been proven to have great utility in the addictions field. Great care must be taken, however, that the concept not be misapplied to justify the exclusion or extrusion of undesirable clients from treatment. The concept of enabling presupposes that if those human and situational buffers that prevent the alcoholic from experiencing the consequences of his or her alcohol use are removed, a crisis of pain will result with the potential of igniting a change process. It assumes that there are still losses that can compete with the power of the drug relationship and that the alcoholic has the capacity to initiate action as a result of a crisis of pain. Great care must be taken in applying this concept to clients whose organicity or imbedded characteristics of dependency, passivity, helplessness and hopelessness leave them incapable of utilizing the experience of pain to spontaneously initiate a recovery process. To misapply the concept of enabling to such clients with the admonition that they must "hit bottom" is a form of abandonment that creates preconditions for treatment access of which these clients are constitutionally incapable of demonstrating, thus condemning them to continued addiction and high risk of death. While "enabling" has been an important concept to confront dysfunctional patterns of over-involvement with alcohol and drug dependent clients, it should not be used to justify the physical or emotional abandonment of these clients.

It is very important that poor-prognosis or chronically-relapsing clients not be denied access to services through elaborate philosophical justifications that may serve to mask problems of countertransference or counterresistance (negative feelings experienced by staff toward the client). Many programs address this problem by building in peer review, supervisory review and external consultation related to refusal to admit decisions, as well as decisions related to administrative discharge or premature termination decisions.

What is your view?

♦♦ 78 ♦♦

Sally, a client who has been seen for the past nine months at your agency will exhaust her lifetime benefit for chemical dependency treatment within the next month. Sally is facing severe financial problems related to her addiction history and does not have the financial resources to purchase continued services at their full cost.

Discussion Questions

How would you respond to this situation?

If agency policy dictates that clients cannot be seen if they are unable to pay for their services, what ethical issues and clinical standards should guide the process of termination?

The delivery of most human services involves a reciprocal contract of loyalty and continuity. The client commits himself or herself to the emotional effort and sustained time necessary to stabilize or resolve the dilemma for which they sought help. The agency, in turn, pledges itself to remain accessible to the client for the time required to address the identified problems. If the client's financial resources change in a way that jeopardizes this relationship, it is appropriate for the agency to assess whether an ethical duty exists to sustain client services. Many agencies/workers have built in administrative / supervisory mechanisms to review the clinical, ethical and financial issues at stake in such situations. Many agencies sustain what they believe to be their ethical duty of loyalty and continuity by:

- *exploring alternative sources of private and public funds to support the current or most critical level of client services*
- *providing continued services on a pro bono basis*
- *providing the services at reduced fees*
- *arranging extended payment plans for the client*
- *providing a structured period of termination through which services to the client may be transferred to an affordable treatment alternative.*

In addition to ethical principles, you may be legally required not to turn away patients for inability to pay. These requirements are often imposed on recipients of state grant dollars in their funding contracts. The requirement may also be contained in facility licensure regulations as part of a client's right statement or in the funding regulations.

Confidentiality

♦♦ 79 ♦♦

Jim, a good friend and a counselor who recently resigned from your agency to take another position, returns for a visit and, in casual conversation, asks you how Joe is getting along. Joe is a well-known and long-term client that Jim had transferred to you when he left the agency. Jim had worked with Joe for a long time and was quite concerned as he approached his exit date about how Joe would handle his transfer to a new counselor.

Discussion Question

How do you respond to Jim's question?

This vignette illustrates a common breach of confidentiality. While one tends to see Jim as having rights to information about Joe because of his long history of delivering services to Joe and his clear continued concern, Jim's right to access of this information ended the moment his employment with the agency ceased. Without a signed release of information specifying Joe's consent to release information to Jim, as well as specifications as to the scope of what may be communicated, no information about Joe can be ethically or legally communicated to include the acknowledgment that Joe is or has been a client of the agency.

♦♦ 80 ♦♦

You are at a mall shopping with your spouse and children when a former client appears, gives you a hug and tells you how glad he is to see you.

Discussion Question

How do you respond to the strange looks and inevitable "who was that?" from your family?

Persons who work in any community for a sustained period of time are likely to encounter situations like the above. The concern related to confidentiality is that agency staff members do not inadvertently identify to others that persons they encounter are clients of the agency. This restriction does not mean that you cannot talk to the person or acknowledge them. You are restricted from disclosing that the person was a client in addiction treatment. On a practical level, it is probably important that workers orient their family members to the mandates of confidentiality to which the worker is bound and request that family members respect this confidentiality through their silence in situations in which the family members could reasonable guess that someone was a client.

♦♦ 81 ♦♦

You work in a clerical position at an addiction treatment agency and part of your routine responsibilities involve typing dictations of client assessments. Today, in the midst of typing such dictation, you are shocked to begin hearing a dictation of an assessment of a young man your daughter just began dating. You had no idea this young man was an agency client and have not faced the dilemma of typing dictation or otherwise encountering information about someone you know in your personal life.

Discussion Questions

What do you do in this situation?

You have been worried about your daughter's choice of friends. Do you listen to the dictation?

If so, let's assume you hear information that alarms you to the extent that you want to confront your daughter and/or prohibit her from seeing this client.

What would you do?

The above vignette illustrates why it is so crucial to orient clerical staff to issues of client confidentiality and why it is important to protect both the client and the staff person in such situations. With no clear orientation or standard to guide his or her response to this situation, the clerical staff person would in all probability listen to the dictation and, in spite of declarations to the contrary, use the information gained to influence judgments related to the daughter's continued contact with the client. If the information gained led to a demand that the daughter terminate the relationship, the client would be quite justified in protesting that confidential information disclosed within the agency found its way outside the agency and resulted in harm to the client. To prevent intrusive or inadvertent breaches of confidentiality, staff access to information about persons with whom they are closely involved can be precluded or severely restricted. By creating a policy whereupon clerical staff are expected to communicate to their supervisor their involvement with a client, the above dictation could be transferred to another worker and the potential breach in confidentiality avoided. Some exposure to confidential information of

*neighbors, acquaintances, or associates may be inevitable within the small
...cy, where there are no backup roles through which such exposure could
...nited, or within the rural catchment area where "everybody knows
...body." Regular orientation on the ethical imperative to guard such
...lation is a crucial preventative measure.*

♦♦ 82 ♦♦

...rry, a client you have seen in counseling for the last month, reports that
...thing horrible has bothered him for a long time that he's never been able
...lk about with anyone. He wants to talk to you about it but says he will only
...so if you swear never to repeat it to anyone.

Discussion Questions

How do you respond?

What situations could arise in which you might feel compelled to break
this promise?

*Many of us would experience a desire to provide Jerry an open invitation
to talk with our assurances of confidentiality and silence. To fully protect
Jerry's rights as a service consumer, however, we must communicate to Jerry
the limits of such confidentiality and the specific circumstances under which the
vow of silence would be broken. Confidentiality regulations provide exceptions
to the general rule and permit limited disclosures of patient identifying
information under certain circumstances. Each exception has specific
requirements and limitations. It is important to note that the regulations
authorize disclosure in these limited circumstances, but do not mandate
disclosure. The exceptions are as follows:*

- *Communications within a program, 42 C.F.R. §2.12(c)(3)*
- *Information given to Qualified Service Organizations, 42 C.F.R.
  §2.12(c)(4)*
- *Information given to law enforcement personnel investigating a patient's
  commission of a crime on the program premises or against program
  personnel, 42 C.F.R. §2.12(c)(5)*
- *Child abuse or neglect reports, 42 C.F.R. §2.12(c)(6)*
- *Patient consent, 42 C.F.R §2.31*
- *Medical emergencies, 42 C.F.R. §2.51*
- *Research activities, 42 C.F.R. §2.52*
- *Audit/evaluation activities, 42 C.F.R. §2.53*
- *Court order, 42 C.F.R. §2.60-67.*

All written and verbal communications about confidentiality must encompass both the scope (inclusions) and limits (exclusions) of confidentiality. Failure to communicate the latter can lead to an unintended, and often much more serious, breach of client confidentiality. It is also important to note that the contract of confidentiality is between the agency and the client. The counselor working for the agency is not an independent agent and may not on their own power and authority grant exceptions to agency policies governing confidentiality.

♦♦ 83 ♦♦

In an informal conversation between two outpatient counselors at your agency, Rodney shares with another counselor a very "interesting case" he is currently seeing. The disclosure identifies the client by name along with the details of the client's personal history, as well as the client's special difficulties in treatment.

Discussion Questions

Is such disclosure within the agency, outside the boundary of clinical supervision or formal clinical consultations, a violation of client confidentiality?

Is the informal discussion of case material with co-workers a breach of client confidentiality?

What standards should govern internal disclosure of client information?

What information is provided, verbally or in writing, to clients of your agency informing them of the types of internal disclosures that could occur with information they share with their primary caregiver(s)?

The above vignette illustrates an ethical quagmire rarely addressed in codes of professional ethics. Legally, staff may share information with other staff about clients (including name) under the "communications within a program" exception, 42 C.F.R. §2.12(c)(3). However, this exception is permitted among personnel having a need for the information in connection with their duties that arise out of the provision of treatment. If Rodney was sharing information in order to obtain insight into the difficult clinical issues, the disclosure was legal. If Rodney was gossiping with a fellow worker, the disclosure violated the client's rights. The ethical, as opposed to the legal, issues of confidentiality raised by this incident involve both the client's right to privacy and the nature and scope of confidentiality that were communicated verbally and in writing as part of the agency-client contract. If the client's orientation to confidentiality identified the exclusions to secrecy to include only clinical supervision, appropriate court order, legally mandated reporting of child abuse or imminent threat of risk to others, and emergencies in which failure to disclose would jeopardize the safety or health of the client; THEN the casual discussion noted above would constitute an ethical breach of confidentiality because it extended the boundaries of disclosure beyond those agreed upon with the client. If the discussion above could be broadly encompassed within the rubric of "peer supervision," such potential disclosures should be communicated to the client at the beginning of the service relationship. Perhaps more importantly, there seems to be no justification for utilizing the client's name in such discussion unless it is part of an interdisciplinary staffing with other persons who will be involved in the care of the client. Identification of client name or identifying data constitutes gossip where such disclosure is not strategically designed to benefit the client. There seems to be increased recognition among human service professionals that confidentiality must be protected as rigorously within the agency as one would protect external disclosure. In a survey of counselors (Wagner, 1981), 80% of those surveyed felt that informal discussion of case material with coworkers not directly involved with the client constituted a violation of confidentiality.

♦♦ 84 ♦♦

A client that you saw briefly in counseling discontinued therapy and some months later committed suicide. The parents of this adult client approach you with a request for any information that would help them understand why their son killed himself. They are in great pain and are each experiencing guilt over real and imagined sins of commission and omission in their respective relationships with their son. You possess information gained from the therapy relationship with their son which could absolve them of this guilt.

Discussion Questions

How would you respond to this request?

Is sharing information about the deceased client to his parents a breach of confidentiality?

Could similar information be shared with legal authorities investigating the client's death?

Does the moral imperative to not share confidentially disclosed information continue even after the death of the client?

Stein (1990), in his treatise on counselor ethics, states unequivocally that "the moral imperative not to share confided information remains viable even after the death of the client." This position has evolved in the clear belief that any compromise to this moral imperative would fundamentally diminish the safety and effectiveness of the counseling relationship. Clients who feared subsequent counselor disclosure to the client's significant others after death might very well withhold, alter and fabricate material, compromising the role of the therapist by casting him or her in the role of biographer.

A query of addiction treatment supervisors regarding their response to the above vignette revealed markedly different responses. Most felt that a fundamentalist interpretation of confidentiality would prohibit any disclosure to the parents without a signed consent. Others felt that full disclosure should be made on the grounds that the positive effect (emotional healing of the parents) outweighed the potential harm that could be done by disclosure. A third group felt the therapist could assure the parents that the suicide was not a response to their actions or inactions without divulging the true nature of the issues contributing to the client's suicidal intent.

Legally, information protected under the federal confidentiality laws apply to deceased persons, 42 C.F.R. §2.15(b). However, information relating to the cause of death may be shared pursuant to laws requiring the collection of vital statistics or permitting inquiry into the cause of death (i.e. a coroner's inquiry). Any other disclosure relating to a deceased client must be consented to in writing by the executor, administrator or other personal representative. If there is no such appointment, the person's spouse or, if none, any responsible member of the patient's family may consent. The consent must satisfy the requirements of 42 C.F.R. §2.31. In this case, if there was no appointment of a personal representative, the parents could legally execute consent and receive the information about their deceased son.

◆◆ 85 ◆◆

A residential treatment facility routinely holds its business and board meetings at this facility. To get to the meeting rooms, individuals must walk through the day room and living areas of the facility. Tours are also routinely provided through the facility to persons visiting the program.

Discussion Questions

Do such practices violate the confidentiality of clients in treatment?

How might these situations be managed to avoid inadvertent violations of confidentiality?

Hosting community meetings within human service facilities and the routine touring of service facilities to include client activity areas and residential dorms constitute potential areas of non-malicious, inadvertent violation of client confidentiality. The unannounced introduction of outsiders into the treatment facility exposes clients to individuals, who based on prior contact with the client, may identify the client as a service recipient of the agency. Such inadvertent breaches of confidentiality can be avoided by:

- *holding meetings outside of, or away from, client living and traffic areas*
- *conducting facility tours during days or hours clients are not at the facility or are in group activities in areas not visible to visitors*
- *announcing the presence of outsiders within the facility and providing clients with the opportunity to remove themselves from common areas during visits or tours.*

Additionally, treatment facilities should have visitors sign-in and the visitor log should include a few sentences such as "Federal law protects the confidentiality of persons in treatment in this facility. Visitors agree to comply with the law and respect XYZ Center's clients right to confidentiality. Disclosure of such information is a federal criminal offense."

◆◆ 86 ◆◆

Jeff, a client that Dan has been seeing for a short time in counseling, has not confided with his spouse about his involvement in treatment, partially because he is trying to sort out whether as a sober person he wants to invest energy in salvaging his marital relationship. Jeff has resisted Dan's efforts to involve his spouse and has made it very clear that he does not wish her to know about his counseling activities. An emergency arises which requires Dan to contact Jeff to change their weekly appointment time. When Dan calls, Jeff is not at home, so Dan leaves his name and a phone number and requests that Jeff call upon his return. Jeff's wife, who takes the call, calls the phone number and discovers that it is a well-known, local counseling agency. Upon Jeff's return, she confronts him about his involvement with the agency.

Discussion Questions

Did Dan violate this client's confidentiality?

How should such situations be handled?

To leave a phone message for Jeff in a manner that would allow those who took the message to directly or indirectly identify Jeff as a client of the agency is an inadvertent breach of confidentiality unless the agency has a signed release to communicate with the person with whom the message was left. While reasonable effort should be expended to contact Jeff regarding Dan's emergency, any message which linked Jeff to the agency should be avoided. It is best to discuss the potential of such situations and develop an agreed upon procedure for handling them with each client at the beginning of the counseling relationship. Such care and discretion takes on even more added necessity given the advent of caller ID services.

◆◆ 87 ◆◆

A client walks out of a treatment center after telling you that he has no intention of quitting his cocaine use, that he's been using cocaine every day in treatment and that he only came into treatment because of the threat of jail. Saying he'd rather do the time, he leaves the facility without saying anything to the other residents. An hour later in group, residents want to know what happened to this client.

Discussion Question

What do you say in response to their questions?

The area of staff-to-client communication about other clients represents ambiguous and ethically vulnerable territory in milieu-oriented treatment environments. The fact that the client is no longer involved in treatment is a fact that must be communicated to those clients whose treatment brought them into significant interaction with the client who left. The reactions of other clients to the client's absence can and should be explored. The reasons and circumstances under which the client left which were communicated to you alone are confidential and not proper to share within the broader treatment community. At a practical level, it is very appropriate to ask the exiting client what he or she would like communicated to other clients about their disengagement from services. This can often open the door to appropriate and approved explanations to other clients as to the client-in-question's status.

◆◆ 88 ◆◆

Lee works as a nurse in an addiction treatment program. A client admitted this morning reports that he is HIV positive.

Discussion Questions

What factors should Lee consider in determining which, if any, other staff members need access to knowledge of this client's HIV status?

Should other residents within the program be informed of the client's HIV status?

Ethical duties to protect confidentiality and to prevent harm to other parties must be carefully weighed in the care of clients who are HIV positive or who have AIDS. Most programs have infection control policies that have been updated to accommodate the new service complexities posed by the spread of HIV that will guide persons like Lee in the discharge of their duties. Both legal and ethical discussions of confidentiality of a client's HIV status in the health care setting focus on the phrase, "need to know." Need to know policies basically contend that only those staff persons who need to know a client's HIV status for purposes of more effectively serving the client or for protecting themselves (e.g., during invasive procedures or medical emergencies) should be provided this information. The confidentiality of HIV information is governed by state laws and regulations, which vary greatly among states. An excellent 50 state survey of those HIV laws is conducted regularly by the George Washington University AIDS Policy Center.

Some treatment agencies interpret this policy "medically," with only physicians and nurses informed of a client's HIV status, with no communications made to other staff and no seropositive documentation in the client's chart. The exception to this rule would be disclosure in the event of a life-threatening medical crisis. Even in this situation, a client may be encouraged to share his HIV status with other staff or the treatment community for purposes of support. In other agencies, the definition of "need to know" is expanded "clinically" to include the clinical supervisor and the primary counselor who will be working with the client. If your agency expands the need to know beyond medical personnel, it may be advisable to have clients sign an informed consent identifying to whom their HIV status will be disclosed if the client chooses to share the information with a staff member. The use of rigorous infection control procedures for all clients obviates the need to identify a client that needs special precautions. Given the risk of HIV infection among all addicts, special precautions are warranted with all clients seeking treatment.

Agencies also have a duty to reasonably protect other clients from exposure to contagious illness. This duty can generally be met without disclosing a client's HIV status. Agencies can reduce the risk of client-to-client sexual contact or needle sharing through one-on-one and group educational formats that clearly communicate the sources of transmission and methods of risk reduction. Many programs utilize peer educators to conduct such orientations for all clients entering treatment. Most agencies have treatment policies that prohibit sexual interaction between clients. If such activity occurs, you need to check your state laws regarding criminal transmission of HIV, partner notification laws, and duty to warn obligations. See Chapter 8 for a discussion of the federal confidentiality conflicts with a duty to warn.

Where all clients are being educated about HIV/AIDS and where the HIV positive client is cooperative (i.e., avoiding unprotected sexual activity), no disclosure of the client's medical status is warranted or legally permitted. Such disclosure is only permissible with the client's written consent or when the client voluntarily shares the information. Some states may also have regulations requiring your agency to have policies addressing situations of client self-disclosure during group counseling, client's HIV medications and mandatory training of clients as well as staff. One approach to HIV/AIDS education in situations where clients may find it difficult to talk to one another about HIV/AIDS is to indoctrinate all clients to act as if they and all persons they interact with were HIV-infected.

♦♦ 89 ♦♦

A long-term adolescent treatment program utilizes their residents to make anti-drug presentations to local school and community groups. These presentations are built in as a component of every adolescent's treatment experiences and may not be refused.

Discussion Questions

Does this practice constitute a forced violation of confidentiality and anonymity?

What issues are involved in such situations?

What guidelines would you suggest related to such activities?

While the treatment program may posit that such presentations are an effective tool to break down adolescent denial and a means to construct a new recovery-based identity, the ethical question is whether the role of coercion robs the adolescent and his or her family of their right to anonymity and confidentiality. To the degree that coercion (real or threatened consequences of client refusal to participate) restricts or removes the client's freedom of choice to participate in such programs, the practice is unethical. To use clients within such programs on a voluntary, non-punitive basis would not violate the client's right to confidentiality if the client executes a consent form meeting the requirements of 42 CFR 2.31 because the client is disclosing his/her identity as a substance abuser (See Vignettes #71 and 72 for the written consent requirements and the minor's rights to consent). Many programs have moved to the use of former clients who serve in a volunteer capacity to conduct such programs. This practice minimizes the potential compromise of anonymity and confidentiality through positive or negative coercion.

◆◆ 90 ◆◆

A famous sports figure has checked into your facility under conditions of duress following his most recent failed drug test. Within hours the sports media is aggressively trying to penetrate the veneer of secrecy surrounding this client's treatment. Numerous reports are already appearing in print quoting "reliable sources" about the client's drug choices, drug history, treatment duration and treatment prognosis. As days progress, the program administrator is being pressured from above to set up a public statement by the client regarding his treatment and future plans in order "to take the media pressure off the hospital." At the unit level, the client experiences verbal coercion to make a public statement as a "positive step out of denial." There are rumors within the hospital that the Public Relations Director has been feeding tidbits to the press and orchestrating the pressure for a public statement by the client from the hospital, all for the PR benefits of the hospital and the chemical dependency unit.

Discussion Question

What are your reactions to this situation?

There are at least two critical questions raised by the above vignette. The first is whether confidential information about the client has been released without the client's permission. The exploitation of the client's fame for institutional gain via the breach in confidentiality is clearly an ethical as well as legal violation. Such disclosure by an employee is grounds for immediate termination in nearly all hospitals. A second issue is whether the integrity of this client's treatment has been compromised for the potential benefit of the institution. The pressure from counseling staff for a public statement from the client as a "positive step out of denial" may be more aimed at enhancing the unit's occupancy rate than the client's recovery process. The furor and general excitement that inevitably surrounds the treatment of a famous person can often lead to a suspension of normal professional and ethical conduct. Rigorous supervisory review and the use of external clinical consultants in such cases can help assure the ethical and clinical integrity of the service delivery process.

♦♦ 91 ♦♦

Bernie, a client you are seeing in outpatient counseling, reports today during his counseling session that he needs you to write a summary of your intake assessment and a progress in treatment summary for his upcoming court date. To comply with this request, you prepare a letter to the probation officer briefly summarizing the material upon which you based Bernie's need for addiction treatment services and a brief synopsis of the course of treatment. Prior to sending the letter, you review its contents with Bernie and ask him to sign a written consent for release of the information to his probation officer. After reviewing the content of the letter, Bernie says he will sign a release for all information except the reference to one episode of relapse which he experienced during the early stage of his treatment. He is concerned that the mention of the relapse episode may result in a revocation of his probation rather than his release from probation.

Discussion Questions

How do you respond? Can a client selectively delete portions of clinical information to be disclosed to an outside source?

How would you respond if the deletion of the material which the client refused to have released substantively altered the overall content and meaning of the communication?

Would it be an ethical breach for the counselor to forward the report to the probation department with the relapse episode deleted?

While Bernie is free to withhold his consent to release information to outside sources, the counselor is free to assess when the selective withdrawal of that consent alters the nature and integrity of professional communication. Bernie may choose to permit or not permit his counselor to provide a synopsis of his response to treatment to the local probation office. If Bernie says he will provide permission for such communication but will not permit the mention of his relapse, then the counselor should refuse to provide such a factually distorted communication. We recommend executing a criminal justice consent at the onset of treatment so the parties expectations regarding release of information are clearly identified. See Vignette #70 for information regarding criminal justice consents.

♦♦ 92 ♦♦

Jerry works as an addictions counselor within a newly created treatment unit of a state penitentiary. Discuss which of the following client disclosures that you believe Jerry would be ethically bound to respect as confidential communication and which, if any, he would be ethically bound to report to institutional authorities or authorities in the wider community.

1. Client disclosure that a particular (named) prison employee is smuggling contraband into the institution.
2. Client disclosure that the client themselves is part of a drug trafficking system inside the prison.
3. Client disclosure that there are weapons in a particular cell block.
4. Client disclosure of a murder that he or she committed five years ago.
5. Client disclosure of a murder he or she plans to commit.
6. Client disclosure of having abused a child who is now an adult.
7. Client disclosure of a special method used by many parolees to beat the drug screening process used to monitor inmates being discharged into the community.

These questions are posed to underscore the fact that addictions counselors are working in ever-expanding types of settings and that our understanding of rules of confidentiality may vary as we move out of medically-oriented, free-standing addiction treatment settings and begin to move addiction treatment into the criminal justice system, the child protection system, and the workplace. While boundaries of confidentiality may vary in these settings, what should not vary is a clear definition of these boundaries to each client as part of the initial informed consent process. Counselors working outside the traditional addiction treatment settings would do well to clarify these issues BEFORE they encounter them in their clinical practice within these new settings. Institutions where issues of security and safety take precedence over treatment functions often impose different limitations on confidentiality. Every counseling relationship should begin with a clear communication of both the **scope** *of confidentiality and the* **limits and exceptions** *to confidentiality regardless of the institutional setting in which this counseling occurs.*

The legal answers as to whether such reporting to the prison or law enforcement authorities violates client confidentiality is as follows:

- *Prison employee smuggling contraband: can disclose without indicating the source to avoid breach of client confidentiality.*
- *Client self-disclosure of participation in a drug trafficking system: no obligation to report crime; however, counselors can report to law enforcement if the crime occurs against program personnel or on program premises (here the treatment program is in prison). Further, the treatment agency may have agreed by contract or licensure to comply with prison rules, including reporting crimes.*

- *Weapons on a particular cell block: similar to #1 above, you could disclose without indicating the source thereby preserving client confidentiality. Additionally, similar to #2 you could also legally report. Due to the seriousness of having weapons available to inmates and the threat of danger to staff as well as other prisoners, legally your obligation would be to disclose.*
- *Client disclosure of a murder five years ago: no obligation to report past crimes.*
- *Client disclosure of murder he is planning to commit: you need to do a duty to warn analysis. See Chapter 8 for an in depth discussion of duty to warn.*
- *Client disclosure of abuse of a child who is an adult: no duty to report past crimes and since the abused person is no longer a child, there exists no duty under mandatory child abuse reporting laws. If the child was under 18 you would have a legal duty to report and no confidentiality violation would exist because of the child abuse reporting exemption.*
- *Ways parolees are beating the drug screening process: once again you can disclose without indicating the source to avoid breach of client confidentiality.*

Respect

♦♦ 93 ♦♦

Your agency director has received a call from the mother of an adolescent client. The mother is registering a formal complaint related to the following incident. The mother confronted her son about swearing and demanded to know where he had heard that kind of language. The son defended himself by telling his mother that there was nothing wrong with his language because his counselor, who the mother forced him to see, uses that kind of language all of the time. The mother informed the director that she was a born-again Christian and would not tolerate her son being in a situation where such language was used. She announced that her son would no longer be allowed to come to the agency and that she was writing a formal complaint to the agency board.

Discussion Questions

What ethical and professional practice issues are involved in this situation?

How would the issue vary in different geographical and cultural environments?

The use of profanity or argot from deviant subcultures involves both clinical (is it effective?) and ethical (is it right? Is it potentially harmful?) dimensions. While some clinicians proclaim the need to talk at the client's level in language the client can understand, others (White, 1996) attack the frequent use of profanity and argot by professional helpers on the grounds that it reinforces the client's involvement within pathology-enhancing subcultures. Others contend that the use of profanity in some settings reflects an insensitivity to prevailing community values and that such insensitivity threatens the reputation of the agency and, as in the above case, the access of clients to the agency's services. The most central question is: is there any language used by agency staff that weakens the client/family-agency relationship or client/family-staff member relationship. There must be concern with any language that is offensive, demeaning or depersonalizing. The shaping of standards related to language is an important element in building a healthy, and ethical, organizational culture. What explicit or implicit standards exist within your organizational culture that are related to profanity or argot? Are there standards or values governing the use of derogatory language that reflect racism, sexism, or homophobia?

Respect for Personal/Political/Religious Beliefs

♦♦ 94 ♦♦

Roger, shortly after entering treatment, refuses to go to Alcoholics Anonymous (AA) meetings, because he feels that it is a religious program. As an atheist, Roger believes that forced attendance at such meetings is both offensive and counterproductive. He is adamant in his desire to address his alcoholism but demands that such treatment not involve religion.

Discussion Questions

How would you respond to this situation?

Would forced AA attendance or denial of treatment under these circumstances constitute a form of religious discrimination?

Where does one draw the line between respect for religious and political beliefs of clients and the responsibility to confront a defense structure or gambit that allows the client to escape the experience of treatment? The ethical issue is the mandate to respect a client's beliefs about religion, to include the right to refrain from religious belief. Several options might be considered in this case. If the program's philosophy and approaches are broad enough to encompass highly individualized approaches to treatment, then it may be quite *possible to address the client's need for treatment while exploring alternatives to 12 step or religious frameworks for long-term support for abstinence. If the program philosophy and design of treatment activities are not broad enough to explore alternatives to AA meetings and its related step work, it may be appropriate to explore alternative treatment approaches and sites through which the client could explore a recovery pathway congruent with his atheism. There is legal support for this position. Courts are consistently ruling that Alcoholics Anonymous meets the descriptive criteria of a religion and that court mandated (state coerced) participation in AA violates the Establishment Clause of the First Amendment. Thus, if a probation department or a prison substance abuse rehabilitation program requires AA participation, the client's First Amendment rights may be ruled by a court to have been violated. See <u>Warner v. Orange County Dept. of Probation</u> (U.S. Ct. App. 1999) and <u>Griffin v. Coughlin</u> (N.Y. 1996). Clients who profess atheism must be provided non-religious treatment alternatives and recovery support groups. The more well known of the latter include Women for Sobriety and Secular Organization for Sobriety/Save Our Selves. The literature describing these alternatives include works by Kirkpatrick (1978, 1981, 1986) and Christopher (1988, 1989, 1992).*

♦♦ 95 ♦♦

Jeremy has requested a formal evaluation from your agency to assist in getting his drivers license reinstated. Jeremy openly acknowledges his past addiction and is equally candid about his two prior DUI offenses that occurred more than five years ago, resulting in the loss of his license. Jeremy reports that he was "born again" in 1985 and hasn't had a drink since he turned his life over to Jesus. Jeremy has received no treatment and has no involvement in Alcoholics Anonymous or other formal addiction recovery support group. His sustained sobriety and church activities are fully corroborated through collateral interviews.

Discussion Question

How do you view such persons with Jeremy's history?

Respect for a client's religious and political beliefs also includes a recognition of the legitimacy of religious and political pathways to change. Many treatment programs and many administrative systems set up to assess the stability and durability of a client's pattern of sobriety and to assess a client's potential risk to public safety via future drinking and driving have a great deal of difficulty responding to cases like Jeremy's because the addictions field has provided them little if any understanding of non-traditional pathways of recovery. As the field matures, respect for religious and political beliefs will increasingly come to encompass the recognition of the role of religious and political beliefs as a medium of personal transformation.

If we are to recognize the legitimacy of religious pathways of recovery and respect the client's choice to explore this alternative, then we must resist attacking or undermining the client's beliefs and explore how to work within rather than in opposition to this belief system.

There are exceptions to the general mandate of respect for religious beliefs of clients. What should a clinician do when a client's affiliation with a particular religious or political institution escalates pathology rather than promotes health? (See Howard Clinebell's (1956) discussion of the distinction between salugenic (health-enhancing) religion and pathogenic (pathology-enhancing) religion in alcoholics.) While addressing such influences may be clinically warranted, ethical mandates require that the clinician take great care in assuring that his or her own religious or political beliefs are not biasing clinical judgment in such cases. Serious introspection and self-analysis as well as clinical supervision or consultation should precede discussing this with the client.

◆◆ 96 ◆◆

Bud, a late-stage alcoholic and recent admission to your treatment program, is the most racist, sexist, homophobic man you have ever met in your life.

Discussion Questions

To what extent, if any, are each of these dimensions of character an issue of addiction treatment?

If Bud becomes a sober racist-sexist-homophobe, is this successful treatment?

Bud's black-white thinking, rigidity, intolerance, excessive and unreasonable resentments may be treatment issues. His use of a racist, sexist or homophobic mask for purposes of defensive posturing could be a treatment issue. His verbalization of racist, sexist or homophobic remarks in violation of treatment norms or his commitment of acts that demean or injure others in the treatment environment would be treatment issues. If you are Bud's assigned counselor and your views are so conflicted with his views as to preclude the possibility of effective clinical work, then YOUR problem with counter-transference is an issue in Bud's treatment. Bud's beliefs are not a treatment issue unless they surface as a concrete obstacle to his continued recovery or unless it is Bud's choice to explore these beliefs as part of a broader treatment issue that he has self-identified. It is crucial that staff maintain a clarity of purpose in their service interactions and not get manipulated out of their service effectiveness by either the client's or staff's religious and political beliefs. While we may find a client's political views repugnant, the nature of the client's political beliefs are not a criteria for access or denial of services nor should they become a focus of, or an obstacle to, addiction treatment services.

Honesty

♦♦ 97 ♦♦

A counselor and a physician are both concerned about a particular client with a pattern of chronic relapse. Both are convinced that if something does not get his attention, this client is going to quickly drink himself to death. In spite of a chronic drinking history and a broad array of high risk activities (e.g., repeated drinking and driving), this client does not exhibit any significant alcohol-related medical diseases. As a last resort the physician grossly exaggerates the severity of the client's medical condition, suggesting advanced liver pathology in somewhat vague but ominous terms and talking about the threat of death to the client.

Discussion Questions

Is such a fabrication or exaggeration ethical if designed to benefit the client?

Would it still be unethical if this communication proved to be the turning point in this client's recovery?

See analysis after following vignette.

♦♦ 98 ♦♦

A counselor and a physician are both concerned about a client who has just been readmitted for treatment. The client's liver profiles reveal late stage liver-disease. The client is responding better to treatment this time than during any previous contact and the physician and the counselor are both concerned that an honest presentation of the client's medical condition will disrupt his fragile sobriety and lead the client to drink himself to death.

Discussion Questions

Is it ethical or unethical for the physician and the counselor to withhold information from this client about his medical condition?

What would you do in this situation?

Both of the above vignettes test the general rule of honesty as a value upon which helping relationships are based. Candor and truthfulness make up the foundation of the helping relationship. The helping relationship would seem so impossible without this bond of honesty that most helping professions have made the value of honesty a cornerstone in their respective standards of professional ethics. The question raised by the above critical incidents is whether lying or deception can ever be ethically justified within a helping relationship. Most texts on ethical issues involved in health and human services do not contend that there are never any circumstances in which it might be appropriate for a counselor to lie. They do, however, consistently contend that a lie, even a "noble lie," should be a last choice and chosen only after considerable deliberation. Bok (1978) recommends two tests in such a situation: (1) is there a truthful alternative to lying? (If so, choose the truthful alternative.) and (2) What moral arguments can be made for and against lying in this particular situation? The concerns about the effect of lying are many. It could lead to a severing of the helping relationship and damage the credibility of the profession in the eyes of the client. This could damage, not only the current relationship, but the client's willingness to seek assistance in the future. Lying disempowers the client, and places that power in the hands of the therapist, by depriving the client of all the knowledge available to influence his or her life decisions. How can a client begin a program of recovery based on honesty when the foundation of that recovery is a lie? Lying reflects poor role modeling by the professional helper, who holds up deception as a viable method of problem-solving.

Right of Privacy

♦♦ 99 ♦♦

You are seeing a 13-year-old in counseling who constantly seeks reassurance about the confidentiality of what she discusses with you. Her parents, who initiated her contact with the agency, are quite intrusive in their efforts to know the nature of the problems their daughter is discussing and the direction in which the counseling is proceeding.

Discussion Question

In working with children and adolescents, what legal and ethical guidelines help you balance the child's right to privacy and confidentiality versus the parent's traditionally defined right to know about and approve of the nature of care being provided to their children?

See Vignette #72 regarding a minor's right to confidentiality. Many addiction counselors have found that their effectiveness with adolescents hinges on the adolescent's ethical, if not legal, rights to confidentiality. To avoid conflict and crises later in the counseling process, the scope and limits of confidentiality and an explicit agreement of what will and will not be shared with parents is best completed at the beginning of counseling as part of the informed consent process.

◆◆ 100 ◆◆

A client signed a release of information allowing her counselor to disclose information to her probation officer related to her attendance in treatment and the results of random urine testing which had been performed at the program site. In responding to this request for information, the counselor forwarded a report that in addition to the information requested included disclosures of the client related to her sexual abuse as a child and confusion related to her present sexual orientation.

Discussion Question

Was this client's rights to privacy violated even though she had signed a release of information for disclosure of treatment information?

Professional helpers may ethically disclose only that specific information prescribed within the client's signed release of information and should take great care to avoid violating the client's right to privacy via professional gossiping. Clinical reports, whether presented in writing or orally, should include only data relevant to the role of the requesting party and only data that has been specifically sanctioned for release by the client. Release of the client's history of sexual abuse and current struggle with sexual orientation issues goes beyond the report of attendance and urinalysis results and as such constitutes a breach of client confidentiality and a violation of privacy.

Empowerment Versus Paternalism
   Cultivating Dependency Versus Autonomy

♦♦ 101 ♦♦

Rolanda, a client admitted to intensive outpatient treatment this past week, has just approached you (her primary counselor) and reported that she wants to look through her record and see what has been written about her. In this same record are notes from interviews with Rolanda's parents who reported that Rolanda was adopted, a fact they have not disclosed to Rolanda, and a psychiatric evaluation that catalogues an unending list of pathologies and notes that she has an extremely poor prognosis for recovery.

Discussion Questions

Do you feel clients should have full access to their clinical records?

Under what conditions could client access to records do harm?

Whose interests, other than the client's, must be taken into consideration in the decision to give a client access to his or her complete record?

There are innumerable legal issues governing clients' access to their records in the addiction treatment setting. Although individual clinicians and agencies have been given wide discretion on their client access to records policies, the trend has clearly been toward increased legal access to a client's own record, particularly in agencies that receive federal funding. The federal confidentiality regulations do not prohibit patient's access to his/her record, 42 C.F.R. §2.23. In fact, no consent or court order is required. Although the federal confidentiality regulations do not mandate access, most states have laws governing such patient's rights of access. Additionally, a trend exists on the federal level under privacy regulations that will be implemented pursuant to the Health Insurance Portability and Accountability Act to not only establish individual rights to access, but also to correct information, to be informed of an entity's information policies and to obtain an accounting of all records disclosed, 42 U.S.C. §1301 et seq.
   The ethical issues involved in clients' access to their records hinge to a great extent on differing views of autonomy and paternalism. Autonomy dictates full client access to records; paternalism dictates no client access to records. The growing exploration of ethical issues within the addictions field has led to decreased paternalism in many areas including a significant increase in client access to records within treatment programs. More and more programs are opening records to clients as part of increased client autonomy

and client rights. Programs may still confront situations in which an overriding reason exists to deny or limit client access to information from their clinical record. The most frequent example would be when full disclosure of information in the record could harm the client or a third party. Particular care must be taken to avoid disclosing information to the client from other caregivers whose records were forwarded without the knowledge that they could be potentially shown to the client.

♦♦ 102 ♦♦

You have taken a position as clinical supervisor at a local addiction treatment agency. John, one of your most popular counselors, has a style of relationships with clients that alarms you the more you come to understand it. There seems to be a high level of dependency cultivated between John and his clients. John seems to be the primary focus of long term support for clients with whom he works. Former clients are constantly calling in emotional crisis. Couples (clients and their spouses) frequently request and receive marriage counseling from John in spite of his lack of formal training in this area. John's clients seem to be incapable of making decisions without first consulting him.

Discussion Questions

Although no clients are expressing harm resulting from John's approach (they, in fact, proclaim he has saved their lives), what ethical issues are raised by this vignette?

How would you respond to John as his supervisor?

The ethical value of autonomy posits that the helping professional should maximize the client's experience of personal freedom. Counselor interventions that inadvertently undermine a client's personal efficacy by cultivating dependency upon the therapist violate this value. As such relationships proceed, clients feel better and better about the therapist but worse about themselves. Cultivated dependence is a process of clinical disempowerment. As a supervisor, it would be very appropriate to monitor John's clinical work and begin a supervisory process aimed at supporting a restructuring of John's relationships with his clients. While many variations in counselor-client relationships can be attributed to nuances of personal style, dimensions of counselor style that undermine the freedom and autonomy of clients must be brought into the process of clinical supervision.

Restrictiveness of Treatment Environment

♦♦ 103 ♦♦

Psychiatric treatment programs have for some time attempted to operationalize the principle that clients have a right to treatment in the least restrictive environment that is capable of addressing their current needs. The addictions field has similarly, if not painfully, moved toward this position, particularly under the influence of the patient placement criteria of the American Society of Addiction Medicine (ASAM). Some have expressed concern that the addiction treatment field is being forced to move from a one-size-fits all inpatient/residential model of addiction treatment to a one-size-fits all brief outpatient model of addiction treatment.

Discussion Question

While the above-noted shift has obvious economic and clinical dimensions, what are the ethical issues involved in fixed level of care treatment?

What value on this issue should guide decision-making of staff as they make recommendations and decisions regarding the choice of treatment modality for each client?

There are several ethical values that offer us guidance here. The first is a command to address the problems of each client with the least possible infringement on the freedom and autonomy of the client. When the addiction treatment field relied almost exclusively on residential treatment models, the restriction of client freedom became automatic rather than a matter of clinical necessity based on the assessment of an individual client's needs. Such modality biases result in unduly restricting the freedom and autonomy of many clients whose problems could be addressed without removing them from their home and work place. In a parallel fashion, denying access to residential services by prescribing that all clients utilize brief outpatient violates the promise that clinical decision-making would be based on an assessment of the client's individual needs. Such undue limits on client freedom and breaches in our promise of individualized care can be minimized by:

- *developing a continuum of care that contains many levels of care reflecting varying degrees of restriction of client freedom*
- *developing and adhering to clear admission procedures that define clinical criteria by which clients are placed in more or less restrictive treatment environments*

- *developing rigorous programs clinical review to monitor admissions, continued stay and level of care decisions*
- *imparting information to clients about levels of care alternatives as part of the informed consent process.*

◆◆ 104 ◆◆

As an intake worker in an addiction treatment program, you encounter a situation today that is becoming all to frequent in an age of managed care and increasing restrictions on addiction treatment benefits. A client presents himself to treatment dependent upon cocaine and alcohol, a pattern of great chronicity and intensity that has severely affected nearly every sphere of this client's life. The client has prior histories of failure in outpatient treatment, has acute medical problems that need to be assessed and treated, and lives in a drug-saturated social milieu. The managed care firm controlling this client's access to treatment informs you that they will grant two days of inpatient treatment and will then pay 80% of up to five outpatient sessions.

Discussion Questions

What ethical issues are raised by this vignette?

How does one maintain clinical integrity at a personal and programmatic level in an age where the modality and intensity of services available to a client are dictated by external agents based on criteria of cost containment rather than client needs?

Counselor patience can be stretched to the breaking point in a system where days of service or number of counseling sessions are being doled out by benefits managers with minimal regard for the history and needs of the client. To maintain personal and professional sanity in situations like the above, the counselor is left with several options. The first is to become an advocate seeking to broker the largest amount of resources required to address the client's needs. This requires not only assertiveness, but a gift for the details of documentation involved in appeals and extended stay requests. Beyond the scope of these resources, the counselor can work with the client to select the best possible services that are commensurate with the client's resources. The counselor can also respond to this situation at a broader level by speaking out in his or her professional associations and adding support to counter the current trend toward erosion of substance abuse benefits.

On the legal front, patients have tried to sue managed care companies for malpractice for dictating inappropriate lengths of stays. Most courts have ruled that such malpractice claims are barred by ERISA (Employee Retirement

Income Security Act), a statute governing employee benefit plans, including medical insurance, 29 U.S.C. §1001 et seq.. The United States Supreme Court affirmed ERISA bars such malpractice suits. See Pegram v. Herdrich, 2000 WL 743301 (U.S.). As a result, Congress would need to enact legislation in order to protect patient rights in this context.

Stewardship of Client Resources

♦♦ 105 ♦♦

A client presents himself for admission to an addiction treatment program via a court ordered mandate for treatment. The client presents a fourteen year history of opiate addiction, extensive involvement in predatory crime, and deep and long-term enmeshment in the illicit drug culture. The program that is assessing this client is a traditional short-term, step program whose program design has been very successful in treating high functioning alcoholics and polydrug users who are at early to middle stages of addiction and who retain strong social supports that can be enlisted in the treatment process.

Discussion Questions

What should be the response to this client's request for admission?

Are there ethical issues involved in accepting clients into a treatment modality that has neither the intensity nor duration of contact that is likely to address their problems?

Looking at the above critical incidents, what do you feel are the ethical issues related to the "overtreatment" or "undertreatment" of clients?

The above vignette raises the question of whether it is unethical to admit a client into a treatment modality with a structure and intensity that is unsuited to address the chronicity and severity of the client's problems. Acceptance of the client into the above program communicates to the client and the court that the client has a reasonable chance of addressing his or her problems within the structure of the program's treatment activities. If the client fails to respond to the program via initiation of a sobriety-based lifestyle, the client may be penalized by both the program (denial of re-admission) and the court (probation revocation) for failing to respond to a treatment structure that had little likelihood of success. The misplacement of clients with severe and chronic addiction problems in low intensity modalities, whether out of naiveté or financial exploitation, constitutes a type of shame-based treatment system. Clients not only fail to respond to such systems, they exit such programs with their original problems intact, but have their potential for future recovery diminished by the experience of treatment failure. The experience of failure by misplaced clients breeds passivity, dependence, helplessness and hopelessness and enhances the likelihood that the client will enter the pool of chronically relapsing clients within the addiction treatment system. To the extent that clients are inappropriately accepted into modalities within which there is a high probability of failure, undertreatment is indeed an ethical issue. There may be circumstances under which the admission of chronic clients into low intensity treatment regimes may be appropriate, but the potential and probable benefits must be ethically weighed against the potential iatrogenic effects of likely treatment failure.

♦♦ 106 ♦♦

"The goal of business is to make money. The goal of the counselor is to meet the needs of the client." (Wright and McGovern, 1988)

Chris is assessed and determined to be in need of addiction treatment services. Benefits provided through his employer provide for addiction treatment but set a lifetime financial cap on such treatment. The assessment worker places Chris in the program's already downsized but still struggling inpatient unit where Chris remains until the financial cap of his benefits have been reached. Upon Chris's discharge, there are no benefits remaining to support outpatient or aftercare services or any future need for services. What ethical issues present themselves in this situation?

While there may be issues related to conflicts of interest in the decision to place Chris in the inpatient program, a more clearly evident issue is the question of stewardship of this young man's resources. In most cases, spreading resources over multiple levels of care and reserving some resources for services that might be needed during later stages of recovery are a wiser allocation of resources than exhausting those resources completely in one level of care. The value of autonomy would further suggest the need to inform the client of the pros and cons of the choices available to him and to place the client in the primary decision-making position regarding this allocation of resources.

Experimental Counseling Techniques
Special Treatment Procedures

♦♦ 107 ♦♦

Bill, an outpatient therapist at your agency, recently attended a two day seminar in which he was exposed to a new technique of rage reduction. In this technique the client is physically held by the therapist and goaded into rage reactions related to key areas of developmental trauma. Bill began using this technique immediately following the seminar. Other therapists are complaining to you that the approach is highly experimental and that there is no body of literature documenting the clinical effectiveness of the technique. Parents of two of Bill's clients have called the agency to express concern that their children have been emotionally upset and volatile following their most recent appointments.

Discussion Questions

How would you respond to this situation?

What standards should guide the use of new and experimental counseling techniques with agency clients?

Should there be some supervisory or peer review process before a therapist uses strategies or techniques that fall outside standard clinical practice in the field?

To protect the health and safety of clients and the reputation of the agency, many organizations have established mechanisms of clinical privileging which are designed to assure: (1) that clinical practices (procedures, interventions, techniques) performed by staff are within the boundaries of the agency's mission and scope of services; and (2) that the staff person performing such procedures is practicing within the boundaries of his or her education, training and expertise. Other agencies have instituted special procedures of supervisory review, or staff committee review, related to the implementation of new or experimental methods or techniques within the agency. To protect clients from potential harm, the establishment of mechanisms for prior approval and on-going monitoring of experimental techniques is essential. Implementation of behavioral management techniques or any form of physical restraint should be carefully reviewed by your legal counsel. Many states have regulations addressing physical interventions and restraints, especially those involving children. Such activities could also raise liability concerns if appropriate policies, procedures, informed consent and training is not provided to the staff. If the treatment provider elects to assume such risk, the workmen's compensation and professional liability insurance policies should be reviewed for coverage.

♦♦ 108 ♦♦

"Pops" is a late stage alcoholic with numerous alcohol-related health problems and a well-documented failure to sustain voluntary abstinence. The only history of any sustained sobriety was several Antabuse-aided experiments at sobriety several years ago. Pops' medical problems would normally contraindicate the use of Antabuse. Both his age and medical history could make drinking on Antabuse life-threatening. On the other hand, Pops' medical problems have reached a point where his death is imminent if nothing intervenes to disrupt his cycles of prolonged intoxication. Both the medical and counseling staff are split on the potential risks and benefits of Antabuse in this situation.

Discussion Questions

What is the best procedure through which this risk-benefit analysis could be conducted at your agency?

Are there special procedures or guidelines to be followed in reviewing special treatment procedures that pose potential risks to the client?

Our discussion here will focus, not on the pros and cons of Antabuse, but the process utilized within a treatment program to evaluate the potential use of treatment procedures that may pose substantial risks to the comfort and health of the client. The adage, "first, do no harm" is operationalized within many treatment centers by procedures that require a justification, review and approval process prior to implementation of any experimental or high risk procedure. Such processes include preparation of a detailed procedure justification noting the likely benefits and potential risks, review of the proposed procedure by the medical and clinical directors, review by a special committee of the clinical staff, assurance of voluntary informed consent of the client prior to procedure implementation, and a definition of monitoring procedures and indicators that would call for cancellation of further use of the procedure.

Freedom from Exploitation

◆◆ 109 ◆◆

Many residential and intensive outpatient addiction treatment programs have incorporated "work therapy" into their daily regimen of treatment activities. In many cases the work involved is work that, if not done by clients in treatment, would require the hiring of additional staff or the completion of such work through contracted labor.

Discussion Questions

When is work "therapy" and when is work exploitation of a client?

What guidelines do you think should exist to prevent the potential exploitation of client labor?

Work assigned to clients can be therapeutic and it can be exploitive. Programmatic review of the following questions can help separate appropriate and inappropriate use of work within a treatment milieu.

- *Is there any aspect of work therapy duties that would pose a risk to the health or safety of the client?*
- *Are there any aspects of work therapy assignments that are demeaning or disrespectful?*
- *Does the institution, or do individual staff members, reap any direct financial benefits or gain from client labor?*
- *Are work assignments determined by client need for knowledge and skill development or by programmatic need (what the client is already capable of doing)?*
- *Do work therapy duties make up a disproportionate allocation of time in the treatment day compared to other more traditional therapy activities?*
- *Are the objectives, benefits, skills, and perspectives the client is to achieve through work therapy clearly identified and communicated?*
- *Is the client's response to work therapy assignments reviewed and documented within the broader framework of treatment progress?*

Depending on the "work therapy" program parameters, the client may be considered an employee entitled to wages and other protections under state and federal employment laws. Similarly, if the clients receive any compensation it could trigger payroll tax, workers' compensation and unemployment insurance issues. Such issues should be reviewed with your local attorney.

Self-Disclosure

♦♦ 110 ♦♦

Jim, a recovering alcoholic counselor actively involved in Alcoholics Anonymous, is currently working in an addiction treatment program. One of his current assignments is to provide a series of lectures to clients on the steps and traditions of AA.

Discussion Questions

Is it appropriate for Jim to self-disclose his own recovering status and speak of the steps and traditions of AA from his experience as an AA member?

Would such disclosure violate the anonymity tradition of AA?

How can the agency avoid placing recovering staff in situations that might violate principles of their personal recovery programs?

The question of counselor self-disclosure encompasses practical issues (Is self-disclosure an effective counseling technique?), ethical issues (Are there circumstances under which self-disclosure could be harmful?), and personal issues (Does self-disclosure violate group traditions to which a counselor may be bound as part of his or her own personal recovery program?). In the above case, disclosure of the counselor's recovery status and AA affiliation would not be generally considered a breach of AA traditions as the demand for anonymity within these traditions extends only to disclosures involving print, TV, radio, films or other public media. It would be important, however, for the counselor to emphasize that he is speaking as an individual recovering person and as a professional alcoholism counselor and not speaking as a representative of or on behalf of AA. (See A.A. Guidelines for A.A. Members Employed in the Alcoholism Field available from the General Service Office of A.A.) Program managers and supervisors should be knowledgeable of various mutual aid traditions and guidelines and avoid assigning individuals work activities that might conflict with and undermine the staff member's personal recovery process. Some agencies have addressed this issue of self-disclosure in their codes of ethics and personnel policies. Some programs also have policies allowing "appropriate disclosures" while others prohibit any personal disclosures, especially in adolescent programs.

◆◆ 111 ◆◆

Jack is an "old-style" recovering alcoholic who has worked for many years in halfway houses and residential treatment programs. His style of counseling involves a high level of personal self-disclosure (telling his story). Many persons have been deeply touched and personally inspired by Jack's story as it unfolded through their counseling sessions and others were not.

Discussion Questions

Are there any ethical issues you see that could arise from such self-disclosure?

How would you distinguish appropriate from inappropriate self-disclosure?

Counselor self-disclosure has been used effectively by counselors as a relationship-building tool, as a technique for reducing client resistance, and as a means of teaching principles about addiction and recovery. Some would say there has also been an over-reliance on self-disclosure at the expense of more effective counselor interactions. Ethical dimensions of counselor self-disclosure involve circumstances under which the timing or content of self-disclosure could undermine the counselor-client relationship or do other potential harm to the client. Counselor self-disclosure, for example, that was poorly timed or through its intensity created an expectation of the client to respond in like manner could so discomfort the client as to precipitate a flight from treatment. A more common concern is the danger that self-disclosure defocuses the attention of the interview from the client to the helper. Self-disclosure can represent a disengagement from the focus on client problems and needs and an overinvolvement with the client to meet the support needs of the professional helper. Like the role reversal in a dysfunctional family where children take on caretaking responsibilities for their parents, here we could have the client thrust into the role of caretaker (listener, supporter) of the counselor. The overreliance on self-disclosure as a counseling technique further violates client autonomy by inadvertently trying to program the client's experience through that of the therapist, a process that inevitably communicates: "This is the way I did it; this is the way you must do it." Developing a programmatic philosophy related to the appropriateness or inappropriateness of counselor self-disclosure and providing training and supervision related to issues of counselor self-disclosure are recommended.

Countertransference

♦♦ 112 ♦♦

Julie, an addictions counselor, has become increasingly exasperated with Ted, a client with many prior treatment admissions. He is by anyone's definition hostile, resistant, and manipulative. He has, in fact, been "administratively discharged" from the last three treatment programs he entered. At this same point in time Julie also has another person in treatment, Robert, who might be called the ideal client—hard-working, insightful, articulate and appreciative. Julie has been doing everything she can to avoid Ted while spending excessively long sessions with Robert. (She and Robert have even talked about their mutual exasperation with Ted). While having nightmares about Ted, Julie must remind herself that Robert is a client because she is so at ease with him. When Ted disrupts group today (one more time), Julie, in a very unsettling confrontation, terminates Ted with the admonition that he seek treatment elsewhere. She is so distraught over this event, she and Robert spend a good portion of his individual session talking about the incident in group.

What is your perception of what is going on here?

What strategies should Julie have pursued in managing her relationship with both Ted and Robert?

What are the ethical issues in this situation?

John Imhof has defined countertransference as the "total emotional reaction of the treatment provider to the patient." (Imhof, 1991) The ethical concern with countertransference arises when our extreme feelings (positive or negative) toward a particular client cloud our clinical judgment and alter the service relationship in ways that are detrimental to the client. Julie's distancing maneuvers from Ted and her progressive overinvolvement with Robert are both examples of countertransference. While such emotional reactions to clients occur in all helping professions, these reactions seem to be particularly extreme in the addiction treatment arena. The addict's potential hostility, self-pity, dependency, narcissism, perfectionism, pessimism, intellectualization, and intrusiveness (to name just a few) can arouse strong counter-reactions in the therapist. This can lead to doing too much or too little for the client. It is far easier to define the clinical problem in the character of the client rather than in our own feelings toward the client, but it is this latter process that is required. As Imhof has so clearly stated, "It is only through examining our own thoughts, feelings, and attitudes toward our patients that we may be able to provide the most objective and effective care that each individual seeking treatment is entitled to receive." (Imhof, 1991) Julie's option here is to use clinical supervision as a framework for such self-examination. Where competent clinical supervision is not available, the counselor has a responsibility to seek peer supervision or seek such supervision on their own outside their primary agency.

Dual Relationships

The concept of "dual relationship" embraces the existence of any relationship between the institution/worker and a client outside of the service relationship. The ethical concern is the way in which dual relationships can compromise the quality and integrity of the service process. In the professional helping relationship, the institution/worker takes on a special duty for the well-being of the client that assumes objectivity, honesty, advocacy, availability and continuity. Any pre-existing or secondary role relationships with the client may jeopardize these conditions, leading to a deterioration of service effectiveness and potential breaches in ethical conduct. The vignettes below will explore a number of issues related to dual relationships.

Casual Encounters

♦♦ 113 ♦♦

Naomi, an addiction counselor who has worked in the same community for the past decade, runs errands for four hours on Saturday. Through the course of her tasks, she ran into five different current or former clients.

Discussion Questions

What ethical issues, if any, might arise in the following encounters?

- You have a client who lives in your neighborhood and you occasionally encounter each other while on walks and in neighborhood stores.
- You have a client who has a son in the same classroom as your daughter, creating periodic contact between you and the client at school events.
- You frequent a store where one of your clients is employed as a sales clerk.
- You live in a small, rural community in which you seem to always encounter clients outside the service setting.

While such encounters as the above may cause fleeting awkwardness and while great care must be taken not to inadvertently violate client confidentiality (by directly or indirectly acknowledging the person's status as a client in the presence of others), these brief interactions do not usually fall within the rubric of dual relationships because the interactions possess neither the intensity nor the duration of contact to undermine the service relationship. It is best in such circumstances if the client is always in control of whether to acknowledge, address or otherwise initiate the contact. If the worker initiates contact, he or she may place the client in the awkward position of having to respond to a companion's query: "Who was that?"

Therapeutic Bias

♦♦ 114 ♦♦

Pam, a lifelong friend, calls you saying she feels she has a problem with alcohol and would like for you to assess her. She emphasizes how difficult this situation is for her and that she feels you are the only person with whom she would feel comfortable talking about her drinking.

Discussion Questions

How do you respond to this request?

What are the issues to be considered in response to this request?

The primary ethical issue raised in the above vignette is whether the pre-existing personal relationship would eliminate your ability to perform your professional role. Does the intensity and duration of the pre-existing relationship destroy any pretense of objectivity? Will your prior relationship and hope for a continuing relationship with this person inevitably color your perceptions, judgments and recommendations? Are you being approached manipulatively by Pam because of what she hopes to be your lack of objectivity? Could information you have gained in the personal relationship be used in making clinical judgments and recommendations if you agreed to such an assessment? Would potential problems of role ambiguity and role conflict produced by mixing a personal and professional relationship not only undermine the personal friendship but decrease the integrity and quality of the service relationship? It is precisely the issues raised by these questions that has led to a general exclusion of service involvement with close friends, relatives and co-workers. While sharing general information about alcoholism, providing feedback on your perception of Pam's drinking, and encouraging Pam to seek assistance would all be helpful, referral of Pam to another assessment resource would be indicated. Many treatment agencies have provisions in their codes of ethics or personnel policies requiring clinicians to notify their immediate supervisor of any pre-existing relationship with a client that could bias the treatment relationship or jeopardize the client/family's feelings of comfort while receiving services.

♦♦ 115 ♦♦

You work as an intake worker at a residential addiction treatment program. A brother of a staff member who works as a counselor at the program is seeking admission for residential treatment.

Discussion Questions

What issues and concerns are raised by this request?

How would you respond to the request?

What guidelines should exist related to the treatment of family members, intimate partners, and close friends of staff by the agency?

See analysis for Vignettes 114 and 116.

♦♦ 116 ♦♦

The President of the Board of your agency calls regarding the assessment of his son's apparent alcohol and other drug problems.

Discussion Questions

Do you feel it would be appropriate or inappropriate for the agency to assess and/or treat a family member of a Board member?

What complexities could emerge from this type of dual relationship?

All of the above three vignettes represent situations in which the institutional-worker-to-client relationship could be compromised to the detriment of the potential service consumer. The ethical problems with dual relationships in these vignettes springs from pre-existing relationships with the clients that would compromise one's professional objectivity. A pre-existing relationship that elevates a client to the status of "special" almost always contaminates the integrity of clinical decision-making. In the case of the Board President seeking services for his son, there are at least two major sources of danger. The first is that the needs and interests of the child could be sacrificed to sustain a favorable relationship with the father. The father could, in such a case, exercise coercive power and control in his status as Board President to dictate clinical decisions in the service process to his son. Secondly, problems in the service delivery process could spill out to threaten the agency via arbitrary and capricious decisions of the Board President related to policies or personnel.

The potential for ethical breaches would always exist in the above described dual relationships. How programs respond to this differs widely. A growing number of programs explicitly prohibit the admission of persons who have pre-existing significant role relationships with staff persons of the agency. Other programs, particularly where alternative service agencies are not readily available, could utilize one or more of the following mechanisms to assure integrity of clinical decision-making:

- *the exclusion of the key staff person involved in the dual relationship from the service decision-making and service delivery process*

- *external clinical supervision or consultation to monitor the service delivery process so as to minimize the untoward effects of the dual relationship*
- *the use of an external consultant to actually conduct the assessment and provide the services required, thus providing services through the agency but outside the boundaries of the dual relationships.*

The Board member would also need to be aware of any conflict of interest provisions in the corporate bylaws or Board policies. This aspect of the conflict would focus on the financial arrangement of the family member accepted into treatment. (See Vignette #21 in Chapter 3.)

Social Relationships

♦♦ 117 ♦♦

Sherri hit it off with Renee from the second Sherri introduced herself as Renee's counselor in a residential addiction treatment program. Sherri greatly respected the effort Renee put into treatment and found herself genuinely liking her. There were so many parallels between their lives and so many shared interests that a special bond quickly grew between them. After treatment, Sherri had continued contact with Renee through a shared 12 step program. Over the months following treatment, a special friendship developed between Sherri and Renee. Within six months following treatment, Sherri and Renee became very close friends sharing a variety of social activities.

Discussion Questions

Comment on any ethical problems inherent within this relationship.

What special duties within the treatment relationship make social relationships with clients particularly problematic?

How would the issues be different if Sherri had met Renee while working as a secretary or outreach worker at the agency rather than as Renee's therapist?

When a social relationship is added to (some would say, replaces) a professional service relationship, the latter relationship is inextricably and irrevocably changed. Professional objectivity is lost. Professional honesty and candor is compromised because the worker does not want to jeopardize the friendship and the client's honest feedback on the service delivery process is compromised for the same reason. Both worker and client may find themselves experiencing role confusion, never being quite sure if they are interacting in the roles of helper-helpee or friend-friend. When the professional helper develops an investment and expectation in meeting his or her personal needs within the relationship with a client, the primary commitment and duty (the fiduciary contract) to care for the client has been at best weakened and at worst abandoned.

Sherri has, without conscious or malicious intent, left herself vulnerable to the charge that she has exploited the treatment relationship with Renee for her own personal needs. Both Renee and Sherri might deny such a charge, even perhaps making the points that no harm has been done to Renee and that their friendship has supported Renee's long-term recovery. By moving into a close personal relationship with Renee, Sherri has abdicated her potential to serve Renee in a professional role. If Renee should have the need to reinitiate services, Sherri's role as best friend would make it impossible to recreate their prior service relationship and would prevent Renee's access to the one professional person who could be in the best position to continue services. Future problems and conflict in this relationship could lead not only to a loss of a friendship, but to Renee's feelings of being used, feelings that could severely inhibit her willingness to enter into future helping relationships.

From a legal standpoint, such friendships may violate the agency's personnel policies prohibiting any relationships with former clients for a specified period of time. Further, counselor licensing and certification requirements should also be checked for applicability.

Editorial Note: Readers should be aware that there are some who would take exception to this portrayal of the importance of boundary management in professional helping relationships. One author, Carter Heyward, has even taken the position that such rigid boundary management is itself abusive. (Heyward, 1993)

♦♦ 118 ♦♦

Opinions regarding social contact with clients sometimes vary based on the level of functioning of the particular client or client group. See if the comments above apply to the following scenario.

You work in a dual diagnosis unit of a mental health and addiction treatment agency. Your primary clientele are people with chronic mental illnesses who also have alcohol or other drug-related problems. Larry, one of your lowest functioning and most socially isolated, but most successful (recovery stability, employment, treatment attendance) clients, is about to face an upcoming holiday without family or friends. When your efforts to find some positive environment in which your client can spend the holiday fail, you consider the option of asking this client to join you and your family for the day.

Your family has a long tradition of including those less fortunate in such family rituals, but you have never before invited someone with whom you were professionally involved. Discuss the pros and cons of this option from an ethical framework. What do you think your final decision would be?

Helping agencies in America have for nearly two centuries worked with families to support the family as a whole or to provide assistance to one particular member of that family. With the loss of traditional safety nets (nuclear family, extended family and kinship networks, value-homogenous neighborhoods, healthy surrogate family structures), growing numbers of clients present themselves to addiction treatment with almost no families or a family network so riddled with problems that it has little potential as a source of support for the recovery of the client. In fact, many such clients come to us deeply enmeshed in drug and criminal subcultures. As a result of this change, helping organizations are shifting from working with families to serving as the family for an increasing number of clients. This evolution from professional helping agency to surrogate family structure will raise new and complex ethical issues in the coming decades. Our understanding of appropriate boundaries will need to evolve in tandem with the changing characteristics and needs of our clients.

♦♦ 119 ♦♦

Lisa has a 16 year old son who has a different last name due to her remarriage. Lisa's son brings home his new girlfriend to meet his family. The girlfriend is a client that Lisa has been seeing in counseling for the past three months. They are both surprised to encounter each other under these circumstances.

Discussion Questions

Discuss special complications that could arise in this situation related to confidentiality, therapeutic bias, role ambiguity and role confusion.

Should Lisa discontinue her clinical work with this client?

What guidelines would help staff address such difficult situations?

There are at least two types of risks posed by the above situation. The first is that the fact of the client's relationship with Lisa's son or problems which arise in this relationship could affect Lisa's professional work with the client. Problems of role confusion and role conflict may be inevitable for both the mother/counselor and the girlfriend/client. The second risk is that Lisa's knowledge of this client in their professional relationship could spill out of the professional setting to effect her relationship with her son. Suppose, for example, this young client had disclosed her past sexual promiscuity and fear that she was HIV positive. How does this privileged information not influence Lisa's communications to her son regarding this new relationship? How could the risk of inadvertent or conscious breaches of confidentiality be avoided under such circumstances? The health of all three parties in this situation may be best protected by the transfer of this client to another counselor. The general principle is: the greater the degree of intimacy in the service relationship, the greater the need for supervisory review to assure role clarity and role integrity. If the staff member in the above vignette drove a bus providing transport of the client to and from the center, there may be no significant conflict. If the staff member is the client's primary counselor, however, there is likely to be the potential for substantial conflict.

Mutual Aid Relationships

♦♦ 120 ♦♦

You are a recovering alcoholic working as a counselor in a chemical dependency treatment program. While you are at an AA meeting, a client involved with your agency comments on his difficulties maintaining sobriety and makes references to several recent relapses and his lack of honesty with the treatment staff. The client has not disclosed this information to his counselor at your agency and the counselor is proceeding under the assumption the client has maintained continuous sobriety since counseling started.

Discussion Questions

How would you respond to this situation?

What information about this client, gained at an AA meeting, if any, would be appropriate to share back to your agency?

What ethical issues in your professional role and/or in your role as a recovering person would shape your decision?

What standard could be articulated to guide agency expectations of staff in such situations?

See analysis to Vignette #122.

♦♦ 121 ♦♦

A client you see has asked if you would be his/her AA sponsor.

Discussion Questions

How do you respond?

What special issues could arise in the dual roles of counselor-sponsor that could present problems for the client and yourself?

How do (or might) you feel about attending AA meetings at which clients are present or at which current or former clients are speaking?

See analysis to Vignette #122.

♦♦ 122 ♦♦

A "Minnesota Model" addiction treatment program has all of its clients attempt to address the first five steps of Alcoholics Anonymous while in primary treatment. Each client is thus expected to complete a Fourth Step inventory and complete their Fifth Step just prior to discharge from treatment. Fifth Steps are usually conducted by volunteer priests and clergy but, when scheduling problems occur, recovering counselors are sometimes expected to fill in for these volunteers.

Discussion Questions

What potential problems could arise from this practice?

Should this special type of dual relationship be avoided?

All three of the above vignettes address special problems that can arise in dual relationships in which there are overlapping roles of counselor-client and mutual aid group member to mutual aid group member. Given the number of persons working in the addiction field who are involved in 12-Step and alternative support programs, this is a particularly common problem area.

The guiding principle governing responses in all three vignettes is the desirability of clearly separating one's professional helping role and one's peer or helping role within a mutual support structure. The first vignette tests the confidentiality of client disclosures within the mutual support meetings. While confrontation or encouragement for the client to initiate a more honest stance with the treatment staff would be appropriate in one's peer role as a mutual support group member, the disclosure of the information of the client's relapse behavior to the staff member's fellow treatment professionals would violate the expectation for confidentiality related to communications within support group meetings. The counselor may choose to confront the client about the issue of honesty but this communication would be in the role of AA member to AA member, not counselor to client.

The second and third vignettes raise the question of whether it is ever appropriate to intensify role confusion in the helper-helpee roles by performing the role of both professional counselor and support group sponsor and/or by mixing a professional counseling role with the sharing of a client's Fifth Step ritual. The concern with such situations is that the contractual relationship with the client loses its clarity through the assumption of multiple role relationships with the client, and that conflict or problems in one relationship may lead to problems in the other relationship. Folk wisdom within treatment agencies and mutual support programs suggests that such dual relationships can pose risks to the long-term recovery of both the client and the staff member.

At a practical level, the recovering counselor may need to set up special guidelines to avoid such dual relationship problems. Perhaps equally important are the special efforts that may need to be expended to sustain supports for his or her own recovery process. Many recovering counselors find it crucial to their health to find sources of support that allow them to escape the role of helper and focus on their own needs. Regularly seeking out meetings and retreats away from one's local professional helper identity and seeking peer supports from others who wrestle with such "two-hat" issues are examples of such personal caretaking by the recovering counselor.

Statements of belief related to this special type of dual relationship may be captured in codes of professional practices as standards, aspirational values or simple statements of collective wisdom on this issue. Codes of Professional Practice can be a framework to capture collective lessons of experience, a mechanism to crystallize oral history into a form through which it can be transmitted to future generations of recovering workers who might find themselves in such situations.

(One resource that tackles some of the "two-hat" boundary issues as well as such sensitive issues as sexual exploitation within self-help groups and ethical issues involving treatment-coerced fifth steps is Charlotte Davis Kasl's (1992) Many Roads, One Journey.)

Financial Transactions and Gifts

♦♦ 123 ♦♦

Jed, a detox technician, has been patiently saving money to buy a new CD/tape player for several months. One of the clients in detox mentions to Jed in passing that he has a court fine due in one week and will go to jail if he is unable to pay it. The client further mentions that he will be all right if he can find someone to buy his CD player. The client is willing to sell this $750 CD system for $250 so that he can pay his fine. Jed buys the CD player from the client after stopping by the client's home. The client expresses gratitude to Jed for helping him out of a jam.

Discussion Questions

What issues do you see inherent within this transaction?

What problems might this transaction create for the client or the worker?

How might this transaction impact the relationship between the worker (agency) and the client?

How might the client's family view this transaction?

There are a number of potential ethical issues involved in financial transactions between professional helpers and their clients. There is the potential of a worker to exploit his or her position of power and the client's vulnerability for the worker's financial gain. There is the potential of the client's family (or members of the community) to perceive any transaction benefiting the worker in terms of manipulative exploitation, such that the reputation of the worker and/or the agency is damaged. There is the potential that the consequence of this transaction, whether good or bad, will alter the nature and integrity of the service relationship. Anyone who has witnessed the range of problems that have occurred through such transactions could speculate on the potential for such problems in the above vignette. A sample would include the following:

- *The client, though initially appreciative, quickly develops a resentment of the worker over the loss of the CD player.*
- *The worker's sense of owing the client opens vulnerability for manipulation by the client.*
- *The worker becomes quite angry and resentful toward the client when the CD player turns out to be a "lemon."*
- *The client's family perceives the transaction in terms of exploitation and discourages the client's continued service involvement.*
- *The CD player turns out to be stolen and the worker is later questioned by the police about receipt of stolen goods.*
- *The CD player turns out to be owned not by the client but by the client's parents who show up to demand the return of their property.*

- *The CD player is stolen from the Jed's house a month after its purchase. Jed's suspicion of the client's involvement in the theft severely disrupts their service relationship.*

Financial transactions between professional helpers and clients (outside those involving reimbursement for professional services) in which the helper financially benefits can represent a misuse of the inequity of power in this relationship even when such misuse is unconscious or unintended. It is the client's vulnerability and the helper's power in this relationship that has led to prohibitions and restrictions on financial transactions and gifts between clients and helpers. Many agencies include provisions in their codes of ethics and personnel policies prohibiting any financial transactions between staff and clients. However, some codes may allow gifts of nominal value.

♦♦ 124 ♦♦

You have decided to buy a new vehicle and when you get to the dealer you are met by a former client now working as a salesperson. The former client is very happy to see you and expresses appreciation for your past role by offering to sell you the car of your choice at cost.

Discussion Questions

What things might be considered in your decision to accept or decline this offer?

How does this situation differ from an encounter with a client working as a cashier in a grocery store who checks out your groceries?

What standard should govern financial transactions with clients?

In an earlier discussion (of sexual relationships with former clients) in this chapter, the question was raised whether the special power of the professional helper was lost even after the service relationship was terminated. The general belief that such power is not lost is the basis for why the question of ethical conduct must be examined in the above situation. This point is further underscored in service settings that address diseases or disorders characterized by episodes of remission and relapse. All interactions with former clients must be conducted based on an awareness of the client's potential need to reinitiate the service relationship. In the grocery store situation, the worker receives no special benefit based on his or her pre-existing service relationship with the client. At the auto dealership, however, such a benefit based on the helper-helpee relationship does exist and makes the acceptance of the client's offer ethically questionable. The primary concerns are that the benefit received from such an offer could alter the client's future comfort re-initiating services and that the helper's potential acceptance of the financial benefit would represent a transformation of the relationship from the professional to the social. See analysis in Vignette # 123.

♦♦ 125 ♦♦

The family of an adolescent currently in treatment at your agency hears of the agency's fund drive for a new facility and offers to donate $10,000 toward the construction of the new facility.

Discussion Questions

Would you accept this donation?

Describe the issues considered in your decision.

Are the principles you are advocating here consistent with the policies you would advocate governing acceptance of gifts from clients by direct service staff? If not, describe how the ethical dimensions of client-institution gifts differ from that of client-counselor gifts.

The first ethical question raised by the above incident is whether the family "hearing about" the agency's capital fund drive was, in fact, an attempt by a staff member or the institution to financially exploit the family's current vulnerability and dependence. If no such action or intent occurred, there is still the question of whether the institution's acceptance of the $10,000 will alter the service relationship to the detriment of the adolescent and/or family. Would the acceptance of the gift potentially contaminate clinical decision-making? Will the gift inevitably produce the status of "special client?" Will feedback that needs to go to the family be withheld or will clinical decisions be altered for fear of losing the family's favor? Would acceptance of the gift influence the designation of "successfully completed treatment" if the adolescent was placed as an alternative to incarceration with the stipulation that he or she successfully complete treatment. Perhaps a broader issue is whether the same standard established to guide (or prohibit) financial transactions between counselors and clients also applies to the relationship between the institution and clients. One practical option might be the following: Assuming that the family's greatest vulnerability for exploitation is during the period of active service delivery, it could be explained that the program desires to avoid even the most subtle forms of exploitation and to avoid any transactions that could be perceived by other potential service consumers as exploitive. Given this *desire, it would be best if the family's decision to donate to the building fund could be postponed until after their son or daughter has completed primary treatment and aftercare. If at that time they still desire to make the contribution, their gift would be graciously accepted. It is best for the protection of clients and the agency if the roles of active service recipient and patron or benefactor are not mixed. See also Vignette # 123.*

♦♦ 126 ♦♦

Jason, a withdrawn adolescent who has been slowly emerging from his shell, enters your office and offers you a gift he purchased in your hospital's gift shop. The gift is a silk rose flower in a small glass vase. Jason says this is his way to say thanks for "hanging in with him."

Discussion Questions

What would be your response to Jason?

Are there any circumstances in which the refusal of a gift would be clinically or ethically inappropriate?

What kind of protocol should guide the acceptance or refusal of gifts from clients?

Agencies have attempted to address potential ethical problems related to gifts from clients through such mechanisms as the following:

* *establishing a prohibition on the acceptance of personal gifts by any agency employee*
* *establishing a value (such as $10) of a gift over which an employee may not accept, or*
* *establishing a supervisory review mechanism through which all gifts must be reported and reviewed for any potential problems.*

Barry (1983) offers seven factors that should be considered in the ethics of giving and receiving gifts.

1. *What is the value of the gift?*
2. *What is the purpose of the gift?*
3. *What are the circumstances under which the gift was given?*
4. *What is the position and sensitivity to influence of the person receiving the gift?*
5. *What is the accepted business practice in the area?*

6. *What is the company policy?*
7. *What is the law?*

Our concern in the case of Jason is the potential harm to the therapy relationship that could result from refusal of the gift. If programs implement gift policies to protect clients from potential exploitations, it is important that such policies be communicated to clients BEFORE clients extend the offer of gifts. Communicating and repeating the nature of this policy prevents clients from feeling hurt or rejected when their efforts at reciprocity in the helping relationship are met with refusal. Allowing token gifts to be accepted on behalf of the agency is a compromise position that protects the client from exploitation and the feeling of rejection that could accompany gift refusal. Check facility licensure regulations governing clients' rights and your applicable counselor licensure or certification codes of conduct for any prohibitions on gifts.

◆◆ **127** ◆◆

Rick is requesting therapy services in your private addiction counseling service. He is unable to pay for these services with cash, but he has proposed a bartering of services to pay for his counseling.

Discussion Questions

Describe your response to a proposal to trade any of the following for counseling services: housecleaning services, works of art, clerical services, plumbing services, yard work, or auto repair.

What special clinical and ethical issues do you see potentially arising from such barter arrangements?

There are at least two troublesome issues that can arise through the use of barter to obtain counseling services. The first is an issue of the equity and fairness in assessing the value of labor and how misunderstandings over the barter negotiations can spill into, and lead to a deterioration in, the helping relationship. How does one practically compare the value of a piece of art to therapy services? Is there a differential assessment of the value of one hour of therapy and one hour of yard work? The therapist may be open to charges of exploitation of Rick's vulnerability in the comparative assignment of value in the bartering process. A second issue is the extent to which fulfilling the barter agreement leads to a breakdown of intimacy barriers in the professional relationship. Would a client performing housecleaning and laundry services in barter for therapy services inevitably lead to such a breakdown? Would the regular presence of the client in the therapist's house (the inevitable mundane social intercourse outside the normal structure of the therapy process, trivialize and degrade the helping relationship? Could potential disagreements over missed or poor quality cleaning insinuate itself as a source of diversion from the helping process? While there are potential problems in the practice of bartering, it is probably best viewed within a cultural context. In cultural settings in which bartering is common and the value for various products and services is clearly defined, this medium of exchange may pose few ethical complexities. It may be important for the counselor to explore the practice of bartering within the client's cultural context before making a decision as to the appropriateness or inappropriateness of such an arrangement.

Physical Touch

♦♦ 128 ♦♦

An addiction treatment agency, well known for its warm, family atmosphere, has evolved a ritual of frequent hugging between staff members and clients.

Discussion Questions

Are there situations in which such familiarity could be experienced by the client as disrespectful or a violation of appropriate boundaries in the therapy relationship?

How can we be supportive and nurturing without being disrespectful and invasive?

Is there a value or standard that helps staff define appropriate and inappropriate touch at your agency?

Does the value or standard explicitly define the parameters of touch as a component of counseling technique and the counseling relationship?

Values and standards related to physical touch in health and human service agencies will vary according to local community cultures, the nature of the client population, the nature of the services rendered, the education and training of staff and the unique organizational culture. Defining the boundary line between appropriate and inappropriate touch must be done with an understanding of these contexts. Jeanette H. Milgrom (1992) of the Walk-In Counseling Center in Minneapolis, Minnesota conducts workshops on "Boundaries in Professional Relationships" for a wide variety of health and human service workers. She utilizes a framework for exploring personal and agency standards that goes beyond abstract philosophical discussion to examine the appropriateness or inappropriateness of specific helper behaviors (see chart which follows). Using a three column discussion worksheet with the headings "Always OK," "Sometimes OK" and "Never OK," participants are asked to define for themselves or for their agencies under which categories certain behaviors should be placed. When the answer to any category is "sometimes," respondents must then clarify when the particular behavior would and would not be okay. This structure can be used to explore a broad number of client-staff boundary issues. On the following page is a worksheet through which prevention and treatment staff can specifically explore values and standards related to physical touch. This format is exceptionally helpful as a training aid in helping addictions workers explore ethical issues related to physical touch.

There may be any number of factors that make the issue of physical touch a particularly important clinical, ethical and legal issues within the field of addiction treatment. There is a growing body of evidence documenting the number of men and women entering addiction treatment with histories of physical and/or sexual abuse. Many of our clients not only have histories of sexual abuse, but have a much higher proportion of traumagenic factors associated with such abuse, factors such as early onset, extended duration, multiple perpetrators, more boundary invasive forms of sexual abuse, and failure to be believed when silence was broken to significant adults. Given the intensity and duration of such trauma, great care must be taken in protecting the physical and psychological safety of our clients within service relationships. That safety is assured through a rigorous sensitivity to actions that could be experienced by the client as a sign of imminent seduction, violation or abandonment. Physical contact of any kind, regardless of its intent, can be violating if it is made without the non-coerced consent of the person on the receiving end of such contact. Client participation in rituals of physical nurturing such as hugging should be an option rather than a mandate. Some, including the authors, would question whether non-coerced consent is even possible given the power imbalance in the helping relationship. The greater the power differential, the less freedom available to the client to assert his or her own boundaries of comfort related to physical touch. The physical and psychological safety of clients requires great sensitivity to the multiple meanings of physical touch.

From a legal perspective, certain types of touches may be deemed child abuse, patient abuse, sexual molestation, sexual harassment or inappropriate under licensure rules. Legally, no physical contact is the safest. Obviously, along the continuum, certain types of touch may be clinically and ethically appropriate but could cross that legal line. Asking for client verbal consent and documenting such consent could minimize potential legal liability.

*The Boundaries of Physical Touch

Behavior	Always OK	Sometimes OK	Never OK
Frontal hug (face to face position; arms around client with bodies touching)			
Holding a client on your lap			
Kissing a client on the cheek			
Touching a client's breasts or genitals			
Asking a client for a massage			
Touching a client's knee			
Side Hug (Side to side position: one arm around client's shoulder)			
Touching the client's face, as in wiping away a tear or a hand on the client's cheek.			
Brief holding of hand			
Massaging a client's face			
Massaging a client's neck and shoulders			
Kissing a former client on the lips			
Sexual intercourse with a client's relative			
Patting a clients arm or shoulder			
Sustained holding of client's hand			
Giving a client a full body massage			
Asking client to remove article(s) of clothing			
Asking client for touch			

* Adapted from *Boundaries in Professional Relationships: A Training Manual,* Jeanette H. Milgrom, Available from Walk-In Counseling Center, Minneapolis, Minnesota.

Verbal Intimacy

♦♦129 ♦♦

Marjorie works as an outpatient addiction counselor at your agency. She is young, energetic and effusive in her warmth to both clients and other staff. She can be heard with great animation exclaiming or joking, "You're beautiful," "You're the greatest," or sharing other terms of affection and appreciation to staff and clients. Joshua, the other outpatient therapist in her unit, seems to spend an inordinate amount of time on sexuality issues in his counseling work with clients.

Discussion Questions

Are there verbal intimacy barriers that can be violated in the counselor-client relationship?

What kinds of verbal communications with clients would be considered invasive or abusive?

As noted in the introduction to this chapter, the physical and sexual abuse of clients within helping relationships is often the last step in the progressive movement of helper disengagement or over-involvement. By seeing sexual abuse, for example, as the end of a progression of violations of intimacy barriers, earlier stages can be identified as targets of intervention and prevention. Through such scrutiny, we have the capacity to not only decrease the sexual abuse of clients, but to also decrease the other boundary violations that often precede such abuse. The above vignette opens the discussion of different levels of verbal intimacy that may or may not be appropriate depending on the agency, one's role, and the characteristics of particular clients. It can be very helpful for agencies to explore values that define the boundary lines between communications that are professionally appropriate and those that violate boundaries of appropriate intimacies or are otherwise abusive to clients. On the following page, there is another worksheet using the same format developed by Jeanette Milgrom which was displayed in the last vignette. This worksheet can be used in small group discussion or individually to help staff explore boundary issues within their communications with clients.

Sexual Relationships

♦♦ 130 ♦♦

Robert works on the maintenance staff at your agency. He met a young woman who frequently comes to the agency for services and subsequently

Nature of Verbal Communication	Always OK	Sometimes OK	Never OK
"You're very attractive."			
Using profanity with or directed at a client			
"We've become very close since we first started seeing each other."			
"You're very special to me."			
"There are times I forget you're a client."			
Talking with client about sexual issues			
Answering client questions about your personal life			
"I like you."			
"I'm going through a difficult divorce myself right now."			
Increasing the frequency and duration of client interviews			
Asking questions about the client's personal life not related to presenting problems			
Calling the client by his or her first name			
Using client's time to discuss the counselor's interests or hobbies			
"I'll always be here for you."			
Using terms of endearment with a client, e.g., Honey, Sweetheart, etc.			
Calling the client at home			
Meeting client outside of office			
"I love you."			

asked her for a date. Robert met her at the agency and asked her out while she was at the agency for an appointment with her therapist. They have become sexually involved and there is now a conflict with the woman's family because Robert has asked this client to move in with him. The family has written a formal complaint to the agency claiming that a staff member took unfair advantage of their daughter.

Discussion Questions

Did Robert's asking the client for a date constitute a breach of ethical conduct in the agency-client relationship?

Does the traditional prohibition against sexual involvements with clients extend to non-clinical staff of the agency? If so, how should such expectations be communicated?

What if Robert was himself a former client who had been hired to work at the agency? Would this make a difference in your view of this situation?

There are a number of potential ethical issues present in the above critical incident. These would include:

- *Does Robert's sexual involvement with the client constitute an exploitive abuse of power derived from his employment at the agency?*
- *Would the situation be viewed differently if Robert knew the client in the past and the initiation of the relationship did not occur through contact at the agency?*
- *Will the client's sexual relationship with Robert pose risks to her continued service relationship with the organization?*
- *Will the perception of Robert's behavior damage the professional reputation of the agency in the eyes of the client's family or in the eyes of other potential service consumers?*

If we accept the notion that there is an institutional-client relationship in addition to a worker-client relationship; if we accept that the worker-client relationship flows out of the more fundamental contractual relationship between the institution and the worker; and if we assume that it is the institution that holds forth the primary commitment to protect the client's vulnerability through ethical and professional conduct and that each worker acts as an organizational agent bound by this commitment, then all persons who represent the organization—paid employees, board members, volunteers, consultants—are bound by this contractual relationship. For any agency representative, regardless of the role, to approach the client with the primary agenda of meeting the representative's own needs would constitute a breach in the fiduciary contract governing the agency-client relationship.

This vignette offers an excellent illustration of the differences between professional codes of ethics and agency codes of professional practice. Whereas agencies rely on the former to guide ethical conduct of employees, we typically find, as in Robert's case, a number of agency employees who have no such code of ethics and who quite likely have not been fully oriented to boundaries of appropriateness in their relationships with agency clients. In contrast, agency codes of professional practice cover all employees and involve all employees in training and orientation related to boundary issues in client relationships. See the legal analysis in Vignette # 66.

Verbal/Physical Abuse

♦♦ 131 ♦♦

Therapy groups within the addictions field have historically been much more confrontational than in any other sector of human services. Some groups modeled on the early "Synanon game" could be viewed as brutal by today's standards.

Discussion Questions

How do we distinguish appropriate confrontation from verbal abuse and disrespect of a client?

What standard could define and distinguish appropriate interventions from client abuse?

Like the relationship between computer hardware and computer software, treatment technology (software) must be selectively matched to the characteristics (hardware) of a client. There are ethical issues in the inappropriate use of treatment techniques when such techniques are demeaning, have little likelihood of success or pose iatrogenic (harmful) risks. The application of confrontation techniques designed to penetrate the rigid defense structure of the street/prison-hardened addict-con to the client whose defense structures are fragile and underdeveloped could pose serious iatrogenic risks. Such misapplication of clinical technique violates a number of basic explicit and implicit elements of the contractual relationship between the client and the agency/worker. It violates the commitment of the agency to base its intervention with the client on an individualized assessment of the client's needs. It also violates the commitment to not harm the client.

Mechanisms to avoid ethical breaches that occur through inappropriately applied treatment technology include:

- *rigorous screening that excludes potential clients for whom a program's standard treatment protocol may be ineffective or harmful*
- *utilization of an interdisciplinary assessment and individualized service planning process that allows for the strategic deletion of potentially harmful service modalities or activities*
- *a clear mechanism (e.g., clinical supervision, team meetings) through which workers may voice their perception of client-treatment mismatch issues.*

Some states have begun passing statutes and regulations governing verbal abuse of patients. A local attorney should check your jurisdiction to provide up to date guidance to your agency on any legal restrictions.

Assisted Suicide

♦♦ 132 ♦♦

Robin went through inpatient treatment more than three years ago and has continued outpatient counseling episodically since his discharge. He has maintained uninterrupted sobriety since entering treatment and most of the continued counseling support has focused on issues surrounded the diagnosis of AIDS made during Robin's initial treatment contact. Robin's health has deteriorated significantly during the past six months in spite of many changes in his medications. This week he announces in the counseling session that he has decided to plan his own suicide. He has been with two close friends through the final terminal phase of AIDS and has consciously made a decision to take his life before he reaches this final stage of deterioration. He has heard about "assisted suicides" where the suicide (by drug ingestion) takes place within a ceremony in which the person with AIDS is brought together with loved ones for tribute and farewell.

Discussion Questions

Describe your response to the following:

- Robin expresses his wish to use the counseling time to plan and emotionally prepare himself for this event. How do you respond?
- Robin seeks your technical knowledge about drugs in the selection of an appropriate drug and dosage to assure that his death will be as quick and painless as possible. How do you respond?

- Robin asks you if you will attend the ceremony. What factors would influence your decision to attend or not attend the ceremony?
- You know the time and date of the ceremony at which Robin plans to end his life. Would you take any action to stop this event?
- What ethical issues do you see arising in the above situations? What standards or procedures could guide staff facing such a situation?

This vignette raises some very complicated ethical issues that would have to be carefully sorted out in the process of clinical and administrative supervision. The use of counseling time to help Robin emotionally prepare himself for this ritual of suicide first and foremost raises the issue of whether the counselor would be overstepping the bounds of his or her competence to assent to this request. Assent would imply competence on the part of the counselor to both clinically understand and counsel dying persons and the ability to ascertain whether the client's exploration of suicide is being made out of free choice or compromised mental status. If the counselor's clinical training and experience does not assure such competence, then referral to other resources for these specific services would be indicated. Referral options might include hospice programs, HIV/AIDS support groups, and psychiatric/ psychological consultation. Referral of Robin for mental health consultation would help assess the degree to which Robin's current suicidal thinking is being influenced by transient change in mental status, e.g., depression, that warrants active treatment. If the counselor was clinically competent to assent to this client's request, a more fundamental issue is whether the counselor could ethically support the decision of this client to take his own life. This would immediately force an examination of the values of the counselor and the values of the agency that would guide this decision. In some agencies, (e.g., Catholic social service agencies) organizational values derived from religious sponsorship would rigidly preclude any such involvement. In other agencies, the option of whether to respond to Robin's initial request would require a more involved analysis of agency policy and the values of agency staff and leadership. The obvious conflict between the value of autonomy (Robin's right to make decisions controlling his own destiny) and the value of nonmaleficence (the counselor's obligation not to harm Robin) would need to be seriously weighed.

Providing Robin technical knowledge to actually commit the suicide act would in nearly all cases fall outside the competence of the addiction counselor. Such active assistance would abdicate the counselor's role to objectively explore the client's emotional health and life options and place the counselor in the role of advocate of a particular course of action. Moving out of this position of neutrality, for example, could decrease the ability of the client to reconsider his decision at a later time. An important discussion point is whether referral of the client to a source for the information he is seeking would also abdicate counselor neutrality and loyalty to the welfare of the client. The concern is that such a referral is seen in the eyes of the client as approval and encouragement for him to proceed with his decision. There are important lines between understanding a suicide decision, providing continued emotional support to the client considering suicide, providing technical support to actually effect the suicide and advocating suicide as an option.

The decision to attend or not attend the suicide ceremony involves both counselor values and agency values and the analysis of a number of key questions. Would the counselor's presence at the suicide ceremony violate any core values of the counseling profession or the agency? If the counselor attends the ceremony, would he or she be in attendance as a private citizen or as a representative of the agency? How will the counselor's presence effect the willingness of other persons with HIV disease to seek services from the agency? How will attendance potentially effect the reputation of the counselor and the reputation of the agency?

Knowledge of the time and place of the ceremony and the decision of whether to intervene would have to be carefully weighed based both on the clinical data provided by the counselor on Robin's mental status and on the values of the counselor and the organization. If the counselor judged Robin's decision as not reflecting a rational decision (the value of autonomy) but a consequence of acute depression, then he or she would have an ethical duty to protect Robin from harm (the value of beneficence).

Situations like the above raise very complex clinical, ethical and legal issues. If part of the function of professional practice codes is to protect the health and integrity of clients, staff, the agency and the community; then what is most clear is that decision-making in such situations should not be made alone and that the best resources possible are brought together to guide our responses to such situations. Most states have criminal statutes prohibiting assisted suicide. In addition to the ethical implications, legal consultation should be sought to determine what level of participation in a suicide decision rises to the level of a criminal act.

Documentation

♦♦ 133 ♦♦

You have just finished the assessment of a client in which there was the admission of numerous acts of cocaine-related criminal activity, e.g., drug transactions, embezzlement, armed robbery and the prior physical abuse of the client's spouse. The client, in reporting these incidents noted, times, dates, places, and other persons involved.

Discussion Question

What would you consider in determining what, if any of this information, is recorded in the client's permanent medical record?

Numerous forces come together to shape the parameters and content of what gets documented in a client's service record. External regulatory and funding agencies dictate both elements and processes of data collection. The agency's clinical philosophy shapes the designation of what should and should not be documented. Ethical dimensions of the documentation process could involve such things as:

- *the accuracy of clinical documentation*
- *the degree to which client self-report, clinical observations and clinical judgment are clearly delineated*
- *the degree to which judgments, diagnoses, and recommendations are within the scope of the education, training and competence of each person recording such data*
- *the exclusion of material that lacks clinical relevance and could do potential harm to the client if inadvertently disclosed*
- *cognizance of problems related to secondary breaches of confidentiality or violation of confidentiality by persons or organizations to whom clinical information has been released via signed client consent.*

Ethical issues in the vignette above would be influenced by one's setting and role. If this was an evaluation conducted by a forensic psychiatrist or psychologist, documentation of a high level of detail might be warranted to elucidate the client's state of mind at the time of the criminal offenses and to detail the exact relationship between the client's addiction and the client's criminal activity. If, however, this assessment is an intake to a substance abuse treatment program, different documentation criteria would apply. In the latter setting, it is the fact of drug-related criminal activity and the frequency, intensity, duration, and variety of criminal activity that is clinically relevant in assessing the person-drug relationship, not the details of when, where and with whom such crimes were committed. The latter detail not only lacks clinical relevance but its documentation could potentially harm the client via inadvertent or secondary breaches of confidentiality.

It is important to note that any information contained in a record that would be used to criminally investigate or prosecute a patient must follow the court order procedures in 42 C.F.R. §2.65. If the employer receives information even pursuant to consent, the employer is prohibited from redisclosing any information in those records to prosecuting authorities, insurance companies or others attempting to establish a case against John for embezzlement and his other crimes. Specifically, Section 2.32 of the confidentiality regulations prohibits redisclosure without client consent and further warns recipients of information that the federal rules restrict any use of information to criminally investigate or prosecute any alcohol or drug abuse patient, 42 C.F.R. §2.32.

Staff members who have been trained to rigorously document nearly all clinical data may have difficulty understanding the need for such care related to documentation. After all, some would say, the clinical records are confidential and the dangers of secondary disclosure are remote. The following story is illustrative of the possibility and potential consequences of accidental disclosure of nonessential information.

John completed treatment related to his cocaine dependence in a reputable inpatient chemical dependency unit within the local hospital in his home community. During the early assessment interviews John disclosed that he had sold cocaine to fellow employees and had embezzled funds from his employer to sustain his cocaine addiction. John's primary counselor noted the details of these actions (how, when, where, to whom) as John had reported them within the "Psychosocial Summary" form used by the unit. As John's treatment progressed, he spent considerable time expiating feelings of guilt related to his drug-related criminal activity, particularly as it related to the embezzlement of funds from his employer who had been extremely supportive of John. Deciding that he could not have the guilt and risk of eventual discovery hanging over his head, John called and set an appointment with his boss for his first day back at work, at which time he planned to confess his indiscretion and either work out a plan for restitution or "let the chips fall where they may." John signed a release of information for a "Discharge Summary" to be sent to his employer which according to company policy had to accompany his release to go back to work. The release which was forwarded to the Medical Records Department of the hospital within which the unit operated found itself in the hands of a new employee. Confronted by a thick file and forms unlike those used on all the other units of the hospital, she mistakenly pulled and forwarded the "Psychosocial Summary" from John's file instead of the "Discharge Summary." John's employer, expecting to find a routine release for John to return to work, was quite shocked to find a document detailing John's embezzlement of funds. When John arrived at the meeting with his boss on his first day back, he was summarily fired and told the information had been turned over to the local police department. John was eventually indicted and the hospital was subsequently sued. The hospital chose to settle out of court for what was an obvious and blatant breach of client confidentiality.

♦♦ 134 ♦♦

Cheryl has seen Gerald for the past seven months in her private practice addiction counseling service. The clinical record, if it were examined today, would include intake forms completed by the client and progress notes which contain only the repeated notations "client seen" following each date that Gerald has been counseled over the past months.

Discussion Questions

What kind of ethical issues do you see in this situation?

What kind of problems could arise due to the failure to document the course of treatment and the client's response to this treatment?

What special ethical issues, if any, could arise in your setting due to failure to adequately document assessment data, the course of client treatment, and the client's response to treatment?

A client's service record has multiple functions. These functions include documentation of services related to service reimbursement, documentation to meet regulatory requirements for accreditation or licensure, and documentation related to potential legal defense, in addition to its utility in the clinical service process. A primary purpose of the service record is to capture a clear synopsis of the assessment data and conclusions, treatment procedures utilized, and the client's response to various treatments for the benefit of current and future caregivers. If Cheryl would be unable to continue seeing Gerald for any reason, the next caregiver would lack much of the significant clinical data that could speed the initiation and enhance the quality of the service delivery process. The failure to document significant clinical data about a client gathered through the counseling process could pose risks to the client or others just as a medical record that failed to document medication allergies could pose risks to the life of the client. The failure to document is an abdication of one's professional duty and responsibility to protect the current and future interests of the client. Some states have specific licensure regulations governing the documentation in clinical records, including necessary documentation of progress notes. Additionally, if a facility receives Medicare or Medicaid, certain clinical record documentation is required to demonstrate medical necessity and appropriate involvement of medical and clinical professionals.

♦♦ 135 ♦♦

When a Medicaid audit at an addiction treatment agency revealed inconsistencies between clinical records and client billings, the resulting investigation disclosed that one of the agency counselors had been fabricating a portion of their clinical contacts complete with clinical progress notes and the completion of billing sheets that were used to invoice Medicaid. This small agency that often struggled to make payroll was asked to reimburse Medicaid for 20% of its year-to-date billings (more than $90,000) as a result of the fraudulent clinical records and invoices.

Discussion Questions

What ethical issues are posed by this situation? Who could be hurt as a result of this staff member's actions?

While the actions of the staff member were a breach of law, they also reflect a breach in ethical conduct. While the staff member's actions violate the ethical principle of honesty, they also reflect a process of clinical abandonment in the service relationship. The actions of the staff member could do injury to his or her clients (injury resulting from failure to provide needed services), injury to the individual staff member via criminal prosecution and expulsion from the field, and injury to the agency and the agency's other workers. The authors are aware of agencies that were forced to close their doors as a result of such actions of a single staff member. See Chapter 2 for a discussion on corporate compliance programs and Chapter 3 for issues involving fraud and abuse.

Referral

♦♦ 136 ♦♦

Scott is an intake worker at an outpatient addiction treatment agency. Today a 22 year old client arrives seeking counseling services which Scott is able to easily arrange through the agency. The client presents another dilemma for Scott that is more personally troublesome. The client reports that she is three months pregnant, has used massive quantities of alcohol and cocaine over the past six months and is terrified of the prospects of a severely impaired baby. Because of this fear, she reports to Scott that she has decided to get an abortion. Given that there are no physicians or clinics providing abortions in the local community, the client seeks Scott's assistance in linking her to the closest such agency. Lacking any organizational policies or procedures to guide his response to such a request, Scott is thrust back on his own discomfort. Although Scott, a practicing Catholic, is very ambivalent about many of the church's teachings, including those on abortion, his active participation in the church is very important to him. He believes he could face ex-communication if he materially aids in helping someone get an abortion.

Discussion Questions

What are Scott's choices in this situation?

What organizational policies might aid someone like Scott who find themselves in a similar situation?

Staff working in addiction treatment programs may encounter a variety of situations in which their personal beliefs conflict with the performance of their job duties. While it is reasonable for the agency to assume an employee would not seek a job position whose performance conflicted directly with his or her personal beliefs (person opposed to methadone applying to work in a methadone program), such conflicts can arise in isolated instances or when an employee's job responsibilities have been fundamentally altered. What is critical is the availability of a mechanism through which the employee can escape or resolve the conflict without compromising the accessibility, timeliness and quality of client services. The mechanism in most cases is that of supervisory consultation. In the case above, Scott could seek the assistance of his supervisor, explain the nature of his conflict and ask if the supervisor or another staff person could respond to the client's request for referral information. If the agency, as a matter of policy, did not provide referral information for abortion, that policy could be explained to the client with the recommendation that she discuss her concerns with her physician.

Responsibility to Terminate
Responsibility to Refer

♦♦ 137 ♦♦

Cedric, a client you have been seeing in outpatient counseling for the past four months, has prematurely terminated outpatient treatment with other therapists on two previous occasions and has experienced several episodes of relapse during this tenure in treatment.

Discussion Questions

Should Cedric's course of outpatient treatment be terminated with a referral to inpatient treatment?

When does a client's lack of responsiveness to treatment ethically require termination and referral?

Where is the line between responsibility to terminate/refer and abandonment of the client?

The mandate to terminate and refer arises when a client is not responding to a particular regimen of treatment and there exists alternative approaches or settings to treatment that have a greater likelihood of success than the treatment the client is currently receiving. This ethical mandate is intensified in circumstances where the client may be pressured into staying involved in the current treatment due to the financial or emotional self-interests of the practitioner or institution. The mandate to terminate and refer is part of a broader concern of shame-based treatment: the placement of the client in a modality that has little likelihood of success and then blaming the client when they fail to achieve change in that modality. The NAADAC Code of Ethics is quite clear on this issue: "The NAADAC member shall terminate a counseling or consulting relationship when it is reasonably clear to the member that the client is not benefiting from the relationship." In contrast to appropriate decisions to terminate and refer, abandonment occurs when:

- *the decision to terminate is precipitous*
- *the client is not provided a reasonable period of time to process termination of the helping relationship*
- *the decision to terminate is based not on the clients needs, but the needs of the practitioner or the institution*
- *there is no reasonable effort to arrange for alternative services for the client.*

This chapter has explored a number of critical incidents through which individual workers and agencies must define boundaries of appropriate and inappropriate behavior in our service relationships with clients. Individually and collectively we must do three things:

1. We must define the boundaries of abuse and declare unequivocally that such behaviors are prohibited and, if exhibited, will result in the field's most severe consequences.
2. We must define those zones of marginality that involve increased vulnerability for clients and staff and elevate the frequency, intensity, and quality of clinical supervision to assure the protection of both clients and staff within this zone.
3. We must define the zone of effectiveness through the clear codification of clinical protocol and the articulation of our highest aspirational values.

Chapter Seven

Conduct in Professional Peer Relationships

What values and ethical standards should govern the relationships between helping professionals and helping agencies? While there is a long history of exploring ethical issues in helper-client relationships, the addictions field has only recently begun to fully explore the ethical dimensions in the helper-to-helper relationship. While there are parallels between these two ethical arenas (dual relationships, boundary violations, the values of respect, honesty, and fidelity), there are a growing number of unique ethical issues arising within this area of professional peer relationships. This chapter will explore ethical issues in professional peer relationships within two separate contexts: peer relationships inside the helping organization and relationships with professional peers and agencies external to one's primary work place. It is hoped that the case studies and discussions in this chapter will help move us toward what Leonard Haas and John Malouf (1989) have called the "etiquette of collegial relationships."

Critical Incidents

Internal Professional Relationships

Management of Human Resources
Staff Hiring

♦♦ 138 ♦♦

Sue has developed a reputation as an extremely competent and charismatic leader of a local addiction treatment agency. She has handpicked and recruited what many would call the "cream of the crop" of addiction treatment professionals within her community. Her ability to aggressively recruit highly capable and experienced staff has been described by some as "management genius" while others refer to her recruiting practices pejoratively as "raiding," and bitterly refer to their own agencies as training centers for Sue's agency.

Discussion Questions

Are there any standards (ethical or otherwise) governing how your agency recruits staff?

What would you consider to be unethical recruiting practices?

Most agencies that address this issue quickly achieve consensus on two issues. First, they articulate an ethical mandate to accurately represent job duties, salary, benefits, career ladders/paths and the realistic potential for advancement during the staff recruitment and interviewing process. Second, they articulate an ethical prohibition against misrepresenting or impugning the reputation, salary structure, career potential, etc., of the agency in which the person being recruited currently works. There is less consensus on where to draw the boundary line between aggressive recruiting and recruiting that is unprofessional or unethical. An even more complex issue is raised by the following question: Is it unethical to build the strength of one agency at the expense of the remaining local health and human service agencies? This question broadens the perspective and raises the possibility of practices which enhance one agency while weakening, and thus doing potential harm to, the broader community's health and human service system.

Other than recruitment regulations for incentives to physicians, the law is somewhat silent on ethical/legal recruitment practices. However, an agency can attempt to legally protect itself from competitors engaging in corporate raiding by having covenants not to hire in contracts with those agencies. Sometimes an agency can also restrict an employee by having a non-compete agreement. However, the non-compete strategy most likely would not apply to most staff because without an employment contract with independent consideration, such a provision would not be enforceable. The covenant not to hire provision is a way of protecting your business without using restrictive covenants or non-competes against the employee. These provisions are very important in joint venture relationships or where the agency provides staff to another entity or on premises of another organization.

◆◆ 139 ◆◆

You are a supervisor in an agency that has experienced, and is experiencing, extreme turmoil. The agency has undergone serious leadership problems, been subjected to numerous reorganizations, and experienced an extremely high rate of staff turnover. Staff morale is at an all time low. Your board is considering potential merger offers with other organizations.

Discussion Question

In filling the vacant staff positions, how much information do you provide to perspective applicants about the agency's current internal problems?

This vignette raises the question of whether there is an ethical mandate for "truth in hiring." There is a breach in the ethical principle of honesty if conditions within the agency were overtly misrepresented. It creates a situation in which the foundation of the agency-worker relationship is one of dishonesty and deception. Most workers know that morale ebbs and flows within any organization. A candid description of the organization's current stage of development, while potentially scaring a few candidates away, begins the relationship between the employee and the organization on a foundation of candor and honesty. While it may not be appropriate to indiscriminately disclose an agency's internal problems to every job applicant, it would seem reasonable that all candidates being offered a position would be apprised of such problems. A "no surprise" policy begins the person-agency contract on an ethical foundation of honesty and fidelity.

If you are in merger discussions it is common for the organizations to sign a confidentiality agreement, especially during the due diligence phase. This confidentiality agreement typically allows each organization to share information about its operations, business systems, financials, personnel and other proprietary information while placing an obligation on the receiving party that the information will remain confidential. Additionally, these agreements often include a "gag clause" which prohibits either party from making any public disclosures, including refraining from issuing press releases about the potential merger discussions. If such an agreement were signed, the information about the merger could not be shared with a prospective employee.

♦♦ 140 ♦♦

A local addiction treatment program has for more than two decades recruited the majority of its staff from the pool of clients who have gone through the program.

Discussion Questions

What kind of guidelines should govern the recruitment and hiring of recovering persons?

Are there special concerns related to hiring persons to work in a program in which they were also in treatment?

There may be a number of practical concerns involved with hiring recovering persons to work in the roles of professional helpers within addiction treatment programs, but the ethical issues generally involve the potential for exploitation by the hiring organization. The potential for harmful exploitation is illustrated through the following questions.

- *Are the interests and needs of the recovering person/client compromised to meet program needs? Has the client's treatment been shortened, for example, to speed his or her movement into a staff position during a period of high staff turnover?*
- *Is the recovering person being placed in a position that jeopardizes the stability and durability of his or her recovery? Does the recovering person have the length and stability of sobriety to manage the high stress work environment of substance abuse treatment?*
- *Is the person's status of recovery or his or her status of former client being unduly taken advantage of via lack of equity in salary, work schedules, working assignments, etc., in comparison to non-recovering staff?*

The most frequent attempt to address this potential for harmful exploitation is to establish time requirements for continuous sobriety when hiring recovering persons as staff. However, this could violate the Americans with Disabilities Act (ADA). The ADA prohibits employers from discriminating against a qualified individual with a disability in any terms and conditions of employment, including applications for employment, hiring, promotion, discharge, wages, and training. 42 U.S.C. § 12112(a). Drug addiction and alcoholism are recognized as disabilities. The illegal use of drugs is not. EEOC Interpretative Guidance on Title I of the Americans with Disabilities Act, Sections 1630.16(b) and 1630.3(a).

The ADA draws clear distinctions between drug addicts who currently illegally use drugs and alcoholics who currently abuse alcohol. The ADA permits employers to refuse to hire any job applicant who currently engages in illegal drug use and to terminate or otherwise discipline employees who are using drugs illegally. The rules for job applicants or employees currently abusing alcohol, however, differ and depend on the job involved. An alcohol or drug abuse counselor or supervisor must obviously be free of alcohol abuse in order to perform the essential duties of the job. Maintaining sobriety is generally an essential requirement of the job, because a person who has not overcome his or her own addiction is in no position to help others with their problems.

Minimum periods of sobriety are not uncommon in the addictions treatment field and may be justifiable and defensible in light of the duties of these jobs. However, we are seeing a trend of personal policies being silent on minimum sobriety requirements. These agencies are instituting impaired staff policies and other general drug-free workplace guidelines which treat performance problems related to the use of alcohol or other drugs like other performance problems related to health conditions. In these cases, the employee bears the responsibility for obtaining proper care and correcting performance problems. Other agencies have drug-free workplace policies that not only include the legal requirements under the Drug-Free Workplace Acts but also promote high work standards including the maintenance of a drug and alcohol free work place that maximizes safety, quality of care and productivity. Some agencies have gone a step further by imposing a responsibility on staff to provide a positive role model regarding their personal use of mood altering substances in the community (i.e. establishing a reputation in the community as fostering a drug and alcohol free environment, one which encourages the concept of a safe haven for clients).

This shift in thinking regarding silence on minimum sobriety requirements may be in response to legal concerns under the ADA as well as the recognition that treatment agencies are encountering other staff impairments (psychiatric illnesses, physical disabilities, violence in the workplace, etc.) which need to be addressed in their personnel policies.

On the other hand, a related and major concern for employers in support of some minimum sobriety requirements is one of negligent hiring and retention. It is conceivable that a client could bring a professional liability/malpractice suit against a treatment agency for retaining a staff member who was abusing alcohol or drugs. Additionally, sobriety requirements are supported because someone who has not yet succeeded in sustaining his or her recovery over a reasonable period of time will lack essential experience needed to assist others who are recovering. Others have also suggested that the mission of the treatment organization is to provide clients a safe environment which is conducive to their recovery. This environment begins with the sobriety of an agency's staff. Whatever the rationale, a program must make a reasonable judgment in setting its minimum sobriety guideline about what length of time in sobriety is necessary to qualify a person for the job. A six-month or one year period for a counselor is more likely to be upheld by a court than demanding a longer period of time in recovery. A period longer than a year might be found to be reasonable for an administrative or supervisory position. The key, however, is to use the period only as a guideline. Treating it as a hard and fast rule will violate the ADA's requirement that each person with a disability be evaluated individually. Less than one-year sobriety for one person may be deemed sufficient, whereas it may not for another.

The courts have generally held that employees/applicants with a physical or mental impairment which prevents them from performing the essential functions of a job, including with a reasonable accommodation, if requested, are not protected by the ADA. Several courts have ruled that "currently engaging in the illegal use of drugs" may extend days, weeks and months from usage. In Baptiste v. Khoury, 910 F.Supp. 277 (W.D. LA. 1996), a 1996 United States District Court case, an employee was terminated seven weeks after being caught with and arrested for possession of an illegal drug. He argued that he was enrolled in a drug treatment program and seven weeks drug-free at the time of his termination. The Court ruled that seven weeks was not a sufficiently long enough period of time to be classified as a recovering drug user. Similarly, in, Shafer v. Preston Memorial Hospital Corporation, No. 96-1412 (4th Cir. 1996) a United States District Court, indicated in a footnote that individuals who had been drug-free for one year were not current users or addicts under the FHA [Fair Housing Act]. However, the court did not decide whether individuals who had been drug-free for less than a year were current users. This reference, although not as legally persuasive as a court holding, does suggest the timeframes courts may consider reasonable when evaluating these issues.

Exposure under the ADA and other anti-discrimination laws would be reduced if agencies eliminated minimum sobriety requirements and adopted an individualized approach using minimum sobriety timeframes as a guideline in evaluating the person's qualifications for performing the essential functions of the job. We believe that court precedence would not support a timeframe beyond one year. Furthermore, the Equal Employment Opportunity Commission of the U.S. Dept. of Labor guidance and other court cases suggest that even lesser guidelines or no restrictions should be used for persons not involved in direct client contact.

Nepotism

♦♦ 141 ♦♦

You are an executive director who has been recruited from out of state to take over the management of a rural addiction treatment agency with a multi-county catchment area. Confronted with your inability to recruit qualified staff into your locality, you are considering hiring your spouse to run the agency's residential services. Your spouse is academically trained, is a certified addictions counselor, and has prior supervision experience.

Discussion Questions

What problems could be created by this choice?

What ethical issues are raised via the hiring of family members?

There is a substantial amount of folk wisdom within the addictions field, and almost all other fields, on the risks inherent in hiring one's own family members. This wisdom posits that the selection and placement of one's spouse could prove disruptive to the organization and pose potential risks to the health of the marital relationship. In short, the folk wisdom says: "Anyone who hires his or her own partner is just asking for trouble." A closer examination would reveal writings within the field (White, 1997) that have even generated principles like the following to predict the degree of organizational and personal impact from such situations:

- *The smaller the organization, the greater the repercussion.*
- *The closer the roles and the more functionally interdependent, the greater the conflict within the organization and the marriage.*

The major problem of such situations is similar to those described under the section entitled Dual Relationships with Clients. The dual roles of husband-wife and supervisor-supervisee contaminate the normal chemistry of team relationships. At its worst, it turns the organizational environment into a soap opera.

While the decision to hire one's own spouse in a particular situation may pose risks or be an unwise decision, that does not in, and of itself, make the decision unethical. In what way does the hiring of one's own spouse violate some ethical principle or do potential harm? The most frequent principle violated by nepotism is a generally held principle of equal access and equal consideration of all candidates. This principle of justice says that access for consideration is open and that the criteria upon which the hiring decision is made are objective and that everyone is competing under the same ground rules. Equity of access is violated when objectivity and fairness are compromised by the personal and/or financial self-interest of the person involved in the hiring decision. Even where objectivity and fairness may lead to the selection of the director's spouse, the PERCEPTION of the inequity in the hiring process may damage internal morale and the agency's external professional image. The potential for such damage must be factored into the hiring decision. The potential disruption of team relationships and the effect on the quality of service delivery must also be calculated into the decision-

making process. To justify such hiring, equity of access to the position should be rigorously assured and the skills and potential contributions of the related job candidate should outweigh the potential for problems inherent in the dual relationship. The objectivity and credibility of the selection process can be enhanced by precisely defining the selection criteria and by bringing others into the selection design, interviewing and decision process. In fact, because the Executive Director would be considered a "disqualified person" under the intermediate sanctions laws impacting tax exempt organizations, we would recommend having the Board of Directors approve the hiring, salary and establish parameters for ongoing review by a staff person other than the Executive Director. For a more in depth discussion on the intermediate sanctions law and conflict of interest issues see Vignette #21 in Chapter 3.

Patronage

♦♦ 142 ♦♦

As the director of the local human service center in an economically depressed county, you have become one of the largest employers in the county, a fact that has not gone unnoticed by politicians in the area. In the past five years, key members of the local political party have worked their way onto your agency board of directors and in the last year have made the following changes:

- Job applications must be picked up at the County Clerk's office rather than at the agency (the county clerk is on your board).
- Personnel committee members participate with supervisors in the selection of which candidates will be interviewed.
- Personnel committee members participate in the face-to-face interviews.
- Supervisors must recommend three acceptable candidates to the board for each open position.
- It is the board rather than the supervisor who makes the final selection.

Discussion Questions

What ethical issues are raised by these changes?

As the Executive Director, what recourse would you have in this situation?

There are serious management issues raised by the above vignette (e.g., boundary issues between the authority of the board, the executive director and the management team) some of which may have ethical dimensions. Patronage is an ethical issue if, and to the extent to which, it:

- *compromises or degrades standards of education, training, experience, or competence of workers*
- *injects politically-influenced coercion into the decision-making processes of supervision*
- *violates the integrity of the clinical decision-making process*
- *degrades legal and ethical practices related to the management of personnel (hiring, evaluation, promotion, firing) and the conduct of the agency's business practices*
- *decreases client access to services due to the deterioration of the public and professional reputation of the agency.*

Under the law, the role of the Board of Directors is defined by statute and further refined in the articles of incorporation, the corporate bylaws and corporate policies and procedures. Common law also imposes certain fiduciary obligations upon board members to oversee the operations of the agency but does not necessarily encourage the level of micromanagement occurring in this vignette. In general, boards of directors should establish policy, approve budgets, monitor the fiscal health of the agency by reviewing and approving financials on a regularly basis (no less than quarterly) and establish committees to provide guidance to the management team (i.e., personnel committee to review policies, a finance committee to review investments, etc). It is also required under the law that the Board be involved in Corporate Compliance Programs establishing Codes of Ethics. (See Chapter 2 for further discussion on Corporate Compliance). On the personnel issues, the Board should approve salary grades, overall budgets which include salary increases, new positions, bonuses and evaluate the CEO/Executive Director but not be involved in day to day hiring decisions. For additional resources on guidance for not-for-profit boards, consult the popovitslaw.com website. To avoid confusion of responsibility, we recommend detailing Board responsibility and delineating management responsibility in Board orientation materials and procedures.

Issues in Authority Relationships
Confidentiality

♦♦ 143 ♦♦

Mary reported to James, her supervisor, that she was divorcing her husband and that she would be needing some short periods away from work for meetings with her lawyer and for court appearances. Marjorie, a co-worker of Mary's, complained to James a week later that she was having increasing problems working with Mary on their team assignments. James took Marjorie into his confidence and explained to her that Mary was going through a rough time right now with a divorce and that Marjorie should be patient with Mary during this highly stressful period.

Discussion Questions

Was James' disclosure of Mary's impending divorce a breach of confidentiality?

Is there a standard of confidentiality that applies to the supervisory relationship?

Under what conditions, if any, should a supervisor disclose personal details revealed to him or her in the context of the supervisory relationship?

The structure, process and style of supervision varies greatly from agency to agency and may also vary greatly from supervisor to supervisor within the same agency. If there is an ethical mandate regarding confidentiality in supervision, it is the implicit demand that the scope and limits of confidentiality should be discussed and defined as a contractual foundation of the supervision relationship. While the scope of what is determined to be confidential communication in supervision varies considerably, exclusions nearly always include information disclosed in supervision that reveals a threat to a client or the agency and information that, if withheld in an emergency, could jeopardize the staff member's health or safety. Discussing and adhering to agreed upon boundaries of confidentiality in the supervisory relationship reflect values of honesty, trust, and respect for privacy and reinforce the general discouragement of, or prohibition against, gossip.

♦♦ 144 ♦♦

You recently terminated an employee that you supervised on the grounds of a breach in ethical conduct (a sexual relationship with a client). This former employee is communicating to other staff members and other community agencies that he was fired for the following reasons:

• You are racially prejudiced.

- The employee had discovered you were doing something funny with agency funds (described vaguely, but implying embezzlement).
- The employee had confronted you about having an affair with another staff person that you supervise.

Discussion Questions

How would you respond to this situation?

What information, if any, can be shared with other staff or other agency representatives about personnel actions, e.g., the conditions under which an employee left the agency?

There are multiple interests in the above situation: potential threats to future clients of the fired staff member, the reputation of the discharged staff member, the reputation of the supervisor and the agency, and the relationship between the supervisor and other workers at the agency. While there are potential legal nuances in this vignette, the ethical challenge for the agency is to simultaneously respond to all of these interests. The manner in which the agency responds to these interests in the face of such allegations will influence future supervisor-staff relationships and agency-community relationships. Indiscriminate release of personnel actions to persons not in a need to know position constitutes gossip and violates the generally held principle of confidentiality governing supervisor-supervisee relationships. The most frequently used response is to talk about principles without talking about details of a particular personnel decision. Upon questioning by other staff, for example, the supervisor could refuse to talk about the status under which the former employee left but could acknowledge his or her awareness of the former employee's allegations and rumors surrounding the agency and respond to those allegations and rumors.

From a legal perspective, we recommend not discussing any facts relating to the termination of an employee with other employees. The more statements made, the greater the difficulty in addressing employment actions, potential defamation claims, regulatory agency investigations, civil lawsuits by the client or the client's family or law enforcement prosecutions if the terminated employee engaged in criminal conduct. These discussions should be limited to the supervisor, program director, director of human resources, legal counsel and, if appropriate and depending on the severity of the issue, the compliance officer, executive management and possibly the Board of Directors. However, it is advisable to take steps with remaining staff to positively reinforce through policy review and training acceptable conduct/boundary issues with clients.

As for other agency representatives, we also recommend that agencies tread very carefully when providing references for any employees, including those terminated for cause. With the increase in workplace violence, negligent hiring and regulatory mandates for background checks, subsequent employers must conduct reference checks. Prior employers, however fear being sued for defamation. See Vignette 59 for ways to reduce liability for providing reference information.

Mandatory Training
Right to Privacy

♦♦ 145 ♦♦

A residential addiction treatment agency under new charismatic leadership launches a new staff training program. This mandatory training requires that all direct service staff participate in 60 hours of intensive training. The training is scheduled for one weekend a month (the training session runs from Friday evening to Sunday afternoon) and involves a training format that is highly experiential. In short, staff learn the techniques by actually experiencing the techniques in a process group with other staff. Within this group training context, there is immense pressure for staff self-disclosure. Staff who fail to get emotionally involved in the process have both their personal integrity and professional competence and commitment challenged. The training is conducted by the new director.

Discussion Questions

What are your thoughts about this situation?

What is the boundary between therapy and training?

What kind of mandatory staff training might be considered a breach of ethics in the relationship between the institution and its staff members?

Chapter Six described a continuum of intimacy that exists in the relationship between professional helpers and their clients. There is a parallel continuum of intimacy upon which relationships between professional staff of an organization can be conceptualized. The zones of appropriateness, marginality and abuse also exist in a parallel manner between staff-client relationships and staff-staff relationships. The boundary lines delineating these zones may vary considerably by treatment setting, treatment role, and the dominant treatment philosophy and techniques. Mandatory staff training of the experiential variety described above raises such ethical concerns as the following:

- *Can experiential training be mandated, when such a mandate was not communicated to the employee as part of the contractual relationship with the organization?*
- *Does the concept of "informed consent" apply to staff members? If there are potential risks or unpleasant side effects from such mandated training, should staff be informed ahead of time of such risks and have the freedom to agree or refuse to participate?*
- *Does mandated experiential training that includes coerced self-disclosure violate the right to privacy of participating staff members?*
- *Does mandated training infringe on personal decision-making when the content of training pressures staff toward certain beliefs or decisions unrelated to their work performance?*
- *Does mandated experiential training unduly violate the boundary between the staff member's professional and personal life?*

For a personalized account of the abuse that can be masked in the name of experiential training, see Jeffrey Moussaieff Masson's (1990) *Final Analysis: The Making and Unmaking of a Psychoanalyst* Reading, MA: Addison-Wesley Publishing Company, Inc.; and Carol Lynn Mithers book, *Therapy Gone Mad* (1994). Temerlin and Temerlin's (1982) paper on psychotherapy cults also provides important insights into such boundary violations in professional peer relationships.

Socializing Outside of Work

♦♦ 146 ♦♦

Many organizations have encountered problems related to staff relationships outside of the work environment. Such problems include:

- conflict in social relationships outside of work affecting team functioning
- internal decision-making (e.g., promotions, assignments) contaminated by external relationships
- issues of staff inclusion and exclusion (scapegoating) exhibited through social relationships outside of work
- staff developing a work-dominated social network (a factor seen as contributing to burnout)
- a process of inversion characterized by an intense focus on the personal and interpersonal problems of staff

- a process of diversion through which most staff-staff communications at work revolve around external social events.

Discussion Questions

Do we possess any collective wisdom or values related to what staff relationships should look like outside the work environment?

How would you articulate such values?

Most organizations completely ignore this issue until it detonates into some kind of crisis. Organizations that try to address the issue proactively usually do so in two ways. The first is to articulate an aspirational value or to otherwise capture and transmit folk wisdom about the advisability of such relationships. Examples would include the following:

- *Given the stressful and emotionally draining nature of our work, staff are encouraged to develop a rich network of replenishing activities and non-work oriented relationships.*
- *It has been our historical experience that a work-dominated social network can contribute to personal and professional depletion of those working for the agency.*
- *We recommend that when social relationships with co-workers exist outside of the work environment that such relationships supplement rather than replace outside social supports.*

A second response is to articulate a performance expectation. An example would include the following:

- *Issues and problems in outside personal relationships between staff will be addressed as an issue in supervision when, and only when, such issues and problems affect either individual or team performance in the workplace.*

Role Stressors

♦♦ 147 ♦♦

T.R.I. is a community mental health and addiction treatment agency with a long history of aggressive community service. T.R.I. has experienced funding cuts due to both state fiscal crises and a deteriorating local economy. In spite of more than a 30% cut in budget over two years, all service delivery statistics have stayed at the same level or have gone up during the past two years. Although the agency has been forced to cut staff, there has been no appreciable cutback in the range of services offered by T.R.I. Staff morale has deteriorated and staff turnover has begun to escalate because of unrelenting and excessively high workloads. A number of staff have begun to experience stress-related deterioration in productivity and in their personal health.

Discussion Questions

Does sustained role overload constitute an ethical breach in the relationship between the organization and its employees?

Describe potential responses to this situation.

The ethical principles noted in Chapter One, beneficence, justice, loyalty, honesty, fidelity, loyalty, nonmaleficence, apply to the agency-worker relationship as well as the worker-client relationship. Sustained conditions that undermine the health of the worker violate these principles. An agency that has not defined what it can and cannot do with available resources will inevitably have staff suffering from sustained role overload. Failure to appropriately match limitations on service provision with available resources not only threatens the health of workers, but eventually threatens the health and safety of clients due to stress-related employee impairment. Broad responses to sustained role overload include: (1) reducing role stressors (decreasing the load by redefining what the agency can realistically do with its constricted resources), (2) increasing staff supports (increased supervision, use of volunteers, improved technology and efficiency), and (3) strategic intervention to support workers who become symptomatic as a result of the overload (employee assistance programs).

Obedience and Conscientious Refusal

◆◆ 148 ◆◆

Zachary has been assigned to facilitate a new aftercare group at the agency by his supervisor. Although the assignment is clearly within his job description, Zachary refuses to accept the new assignment on the grounds that he is tired of doing groups and feels some other staff member should be assigned the group.

Discussion Question

While Zachary's refusal raises a performance and potential discipline issue, is there any ethical violation involved in this refusal?

There is a value of obedience implicit within the relationship between Zachary and his employing agency. This value was part of the promise Zachary made when he accepted employment with the agency. This value of obedience demands that Zachary follow the directives of his supervisor except when such directives demand action that is unethical, illegal or outside the scope of his professional duties. Zachary could seek to negotiate alternative duties with his supervisor or could resign to seek a position that better meets his needs, but his refusal in the above case is a breach of his promise to professional obedience and the value of fidelity.

◆◆ 149 ◆◆

A large prevention agency was experiencing severe staff morale and staff turnover problems. The CEO and the Program Supervisor met and agreed that this problem needed to be addressed. A plan was formulated whereby the Program Supervisor would confidentially interview each current staff member and a sample of staff members who had left in the last year. The Supervisor would then compile the findings of these interviews to list the major issues contributing to low morale and any recommendations that emerged from the interviews. The Program Supervisor and the Executive Director explicitly agreed that comments contained in the report would not be attributed to particular staff people in compliance with the agreement of confidentiality. The supervisor conducted the individual interviews as planned (recording the interviews to help capture the desired information) and then prepared and submitted the report as planned to the Executive Director. The Executive Director, after reviewing excerpted quotes from the interviews that were quite critical of his management style and recent management decisions, decided that it was essential for him to listen to the full interviews. The Executive Director demanded the tapes from the Program Supervisor and responded to the Supervisor's discomfort with this request by saying that the tapes were agency property and that the Supervisor would be disciplined for theft if the tapes were not immediately turned over.

Discussion Questions

If you were the Supervisor, what would you do?

What ethical issues are raised by this vignette?

The agreement that the Supervisor would be the only one who would know the identity of persons offering feedback or recommendations from the interviewer would be broken if the tapes were turned over to the Executive Director. The pledge of confidentiality by the Supervisor, as a designated representative of the agency, constituted a promise of safety under which the interviews were conducted. Any alteration in this arrangement would violate both the value of honesty and the obligation stemming from the pledge of confidentiality. The normal ethical duty of obedience does not apply to conditions under which an employee is directed to commit unethical or illegal actions. In a situation like the above, the ethical mandate is for conscientious refusal of the directive, even if this refusal opens up the Supervisor to punitive action by the Executive Director. Making an ethical choice does not free one from the potential for arbitrary and unjust punishment.

Typically, conversations cannot be taped legally without the consent of the individuals. In some states, it only requires the consent of one party. Pay attention to these wiretapping and other electronic communication laws and regulations. If the employees gave written consent and that consent limited the use or disclosure of the tape, the Program Supervisor legally, should not disclose the tapes. Violation of the federal wiretapping statute is a criminal offense. See 18 U.S.C. §2511.

Sexual Harassment
Abuse of Power
♦♦ 150 ♦♦

(The following story is taken from the author's book, *The Incestuous Workplace*.)

Faye took a position as a secretary in a community addition treatment agency against the advice of her husband who couldn't figure out why she would want to work around "crazy" people. Within three years, her intelligence and organizational skills had earned her the position of administrative assistant to the Agency Director. During these three years, she had found a whole new world of experience compared to her sheltered upbringing and married life. Her work also changed her social life, as staff socialized frequently away from work. This created some problems as her husband could not handle the "weirdness" of most of the staff. They reciprocated by applying a diverse range of diagnostic labels on her husband. During Faye's fourth year of employment, she was given the opportunity to participate in staff growth groups that demanded a high level of self-disclosure. The Director and others commented on her natural counseling aptitude, and it wasn't long before Faye was enrolled in college to prepare herself for a future career change. This was a very exhilarating time for Faye, but also a time of conflict as her husband was coldly unsupportive of her enrollment in school and her future plans. She increasingly sought support from the Director as conflict in the marriage increased. The Director became her trusted mentor, constantly providing encouragement and acknowledgment of her personal and professional value. Over the next year, Faye's school schedule and evening staff growth groups caused increasing conflict at home that was further complicated by her physical and emotional exhaustion. Partially through the counsel of the Director, Faye separated from her husband and got a place of her own. Faye had heard but didn't believe that the Director had been sexually involved with one of the counselors at the agency. The Director had never made sexual advances toward her, although there had been times that she wished he would. A month after her separation, Faye and the Director began their sexual relationship, an act in which she was totally willing to participate. She was in love, a fact unchanged by the Director's wife and family. Their relationship continued and became common knowledge at the agency. Other staff cooled their relationship with Faye, who found herself becoming increasingly dependent upon the Director. After four months, the Director informed Faye in rather painful terms that he could no longer handle her demands for time, that she put too much stock in the relationship and that the relationship was over. Emotionally crushed, Faye never returned to the agency. She did not even go in to resign as she felt she couldn't face the other staff.

Discussion Questions

Is the above a regrettable personal story, but one which has no professional/organizational implications, or does the story reflect the abuse of power by an agency manager?

Is this a story of sexual harassment? Are there ethical issues involved in any sexual relationship between a supervisor and a supervisee?

The task of any helping organization is to protect clients and staff from any situation whereby vulnerabilities could be exploited, but to provide such protection without undermining their freedom and autonomy. It is the implicit power in the supervisor's role and the potential for coercion and manipulation that brings ethical dimensions into such professional relationships when they extend to social, financial or sexual activity. In an earlier book (White, 1986, 1997) and a follow-up article (White, 1992), one of the authors offered two concepts on the sexual harassment and exploitation of workers within human service agencies. The first concept, presumptive vulnerability, places the primary responsibility for defining and maintaining appropriate boundaries in the co-worker relationship on that worker who has the greatest ascribed power. Presumptive vulnerability suggests that the power inequity in some relationships is so great that all sexual suggestions are by definition coercive. David Powell supports this view in his discussion of the ethics of supervision when he declares: "Sexual contact or a romantic relationship between supervisor and supervisee is clearly unethical and an unequivocal exploitation of the supervisory role." (Powell, 1992) The second concept is that of manipulation of vulnerability. It is the author's contention that a definition of sexual harassment in closed systems must include the phrase "manipulation of vulnerability." A supervisor, or other person with significant organizational power, can isolate staff professionally and socially, overextend staff in ways that deplete their physical and emotional energy, use his/her influence to undermine the outside intimate relationships of staff, and foster dependency in nurturing staff who experience conflict in their outside relationships. If the supervisor then manipulates the vulnerability and dependency of a staff member to meet his/her own sexual needs, then the supervisor has committed a type of sexual harassment every bit as demeaning as the more blatant behaviors associated with this term. These principles also apply to the relationships between supervisors and volunteers, interns and student visitors.

For an excellent analysis of the potential for abuse in the supervisory relationship, see: Conroe, R. and Schank, J. "Sexual Intimacy in Clinical Supervision: Unmasking the Silence," in Schoener, et. al., (1989) Psychotherapists' Sexual Involvement with Clients and David Powell's (1992) Ethical and Legal Concerns in Supervision. The Counselor, 10(6):24-27.

Many state laws and funding contracts require employers to provide a process for investigating and responding to allegations of sexual harassment. In 1998 the United States Supreme Court issued three unprecedented opinions further defining the law in this area (Burlington Industries v. Ellerth, 524 U.S. 742; Faragher v. City of Boca Raton, 524 U.S. 775; and Oncale v. Sundowner Offshore Servs. Inc, 523 U.S. 75). As a result, employers can be held vicariously liable for sexual harassment by their supervisory employees. Lessons to be learned from these three cases are:

- *Every employer should have a sexual harassment policy that is disseminated to all employees (this will enable an employer to raise an affirmative defense of exercising reasonable care to prevent and correct sexual harassment).*
- *This policy must be implemented in practice!*

- *The sexual harassment policy must include a complaint procedure that allows the complaining employee to bypass an alleged harassing supervisor.*
- *Employers should foster an environment which encourages reporting (i.e. eliminate the fear of retaliation or reduce the belief of futility).*
- *The policy should include no-retaliation provisions and promises to fully investigate.*
- *Employers and employees should recognize that sexual harassment is not limited to interaction between the opposite sexes.*
- *Sexual harassment will be measured from the viewpoint of a reasonable person in the plaintiff's position.*
- *The courts will also consider the social context in which particular behavior occurs and is experienced by its target.*

This is a hot area of the law that will continue to be further refined by common law interpretations. Consult an employment attorney for state-of-the-art guidance when revising your policy or when addressing allegations of sexual harassment.

Impaired Co-worker

♦♦ 151 ♦♦

You and several friends have decided to get out of town for a few days so you drive to another city three hours away. While at a comedy club, you are horrified to look across the room and see a counselor at your program, a highly visible and self-proclaimed recovering alcoholic, drinking a beer.

Discussion Questions

What would you do?

More specifically, would you communicate directly with this staff person and, if so, what would be the nature of this communication?

Would you communicate what you had observed to anyone else, e.g., your supervisor?

To the extent that the worker's recovering status was used to obtain his or her position and has been represented to fellow workers, professional peers, clients and the community, there is an ethical breach of honesty and a misrepresentation of credentials (the status of recovery). The vignette also raises issues related to potential threats to the reputation of the agency and potential threats posed to agency clients from an impaired counselor. While the ethical responsibility to confront this situation in some manner is evident, agencies have not provided clear expectations to staff on how to handle such an incident. Whereas the decision to approach and confront the counselor at the comedy club would be a personal one, most agencies set an expectation that such incidents are to be reported in a timely fashion to the supervisor of the staff member observing the incident. It is then the supervisor's responsibility to initiate an administrative review of the incident. If both staff members in the above vignette are certified addictions counselors, there may be additional mandates to the observing counselor to report this incident to the ethics committee of the certification board. Such mandates vary considerably from state to state. (See the analysis in Vignettes #32 and 37 relating to conduct on personal time.) You also should consult your personnel policies and codes of ethics to determine whether a violation existed. Depending on how those policies are drafted, you may have an obligation to come forward and inform the person's supervisor, the director of human resources or the corporate compliance officer (depending on if you have a compliance program and the mechanism for employee reporting.) If you fail to disclose the violation, you may face disciplinary action under your agency's code of ethics. See Chapter 2 for a further discussion on compliance programs.

Team Relationships

◆◆ 152 ◆◆

Phil is an extremely capable staff member in an intensive outpatient addiction treatment program. While technically skilled, he isolates himself from other staff and rarely participates in staff meetings or other group-oriented staff activities. While he performs the elements of his own duties with great precision, Phil never asks for support, nor offers support to other staff. His relationships with other staff are physically aloof and emotionally cool. It is almost as if Phil is conducting his own private practice inside the boundaries of this public agency.

Discussion Questions

While each of us have our own assigned responsibilities, what duties and obligations exist in regard to our relationships with one another as part of a treatment team?

What values should govern team relationships within our agency?

Examples of the values most frequently articulated by agencies who have attempted to define this process include elaborations of the following:

- *fairness in distribution of responsibilities and rewards*
- *expectation for mutual support*
- *expectation for participation in problem identification and problem solving*
- *expectation for honesty and candor; definition of and prohibition against gossip*
- *respect for role boundaries*
- *respect for team decisions.*

While Phil may be faithfully fulfilling what he perceives as his professional duty to his clients, he is failing to see that the term "professional" may also include duties and obligations in relationship to one's co-workers.

Managing Conflict

♦♦ 153 ♦♦

Terry and Paul are two counselors who co-facilitate counseling groups within a residential halfway house program. Today, Terry and Paul got into a disagreement following group that escalated into a shouting match and a mutual vow that each would refuse to facilitate group with the other.

Discussion Questions

In this small program, where there are minimal opportunities to transfer or reallocate staff, how would you respond to this situation if you were their supervisor?

What values or preferred methods of problem solving should guide staff experiencing conflict in their relationships with one another?

The style of managing, or refusing to manage, conflict jeopardizes the accessibility of client services and quite likely compromises the quality of services available to clients. Programs that help clients overcome chronic, self-defeating styles of living may have a greater mandate than other organizations to model healthy styles of problem and conflict resolution. There is a responsibility for staff to adhere to particularly high ideals related to conflict resolution when the manner in which staff respond to conflict is an integral part of the treatment milieu and treatment process. Conflict between staff is always uncomfortable and without an expectation and structure for problem-solving, small conflicts tend to escalate. Many agencies have attempted, in their development of a Code of Professional Practice, to articulate values related to the resolution of conflict within the agency. Such values often include:

- *the acknowledgment that conflict is inevitable within the high stress environment of addiction treatment*
- *the expectation that disagreement or conflict will be addressed face-to-face with the involved parties*
- *the expectation that this exploration of disagreement or conflict will occur in a timely manner*
- *the expectation that involved parties have an overriding responsibility to keep any conflict from compromising the service delivery process to clients*
- *the demand that conflict affecting service delivery or other aspects of team performance, if not resolvable by the parties involved, be brought to the attention of the supervisor(s) for assistance with problem-solving.*

Professional or Ethical Misconduct / Whistle Blowing

♦♦ 154 ♦♦

You have information which all but confirms that another staff member of your agency is sexually involved with a client. What complicates this particular situation is that the staff person involved is your supervisor.

Discussion Questions

What would you do?

What procedures are built into the organization through which staff can raise issues of ethical misconduct involving supervisory and administrative personnel?

What recourse would there be if the staff member attempted to raise this issue only to have the response be a perceived cover-up and lack of apparent action by the administrator/board?

Without significant structural supports for ethical conduct built into the organization, the staff member in such a situation is extremely vulnerable to be scapegoated and forced out of the organization if he or she attempts to raise the issue of the supervisor's conduct. Any organization that wishes to make the highest level of ethical conduct a crucial and visible component of its organizational culture must establish clear channels of communication and redress involving perceived ethical breaches by supervisory/administrative staff. Codes of Professional Practice or personnel policies can, for example, direct staff to move to the next highest level to report allegations of supervisory misconduct (e.g., the conduct of one's immediate supervisor would be reported to the person administratively above the supervisor, the conduct of an Executive Director would be reported to the personnel or executive committee of the board). While the precise procedures may vary, it is the establishment and communication of such reporting channels that is paramount.

A staff member's response to a perceived cover-up of unethical conduct by administrative/supervisory personnel could vary depending on the nature of the ethical breach and the degree of imminent threat posed to clients or the public. At a practical level, the challenge is to address any issues that compromise the quality of services by using those methods that can correct the situation with the least potential damage to the reputation of the agency. The ultimate value is not the existence of the agency, but the accessibility, continuity, and quality of client services. The consideration of external redress via reporting the allegation of misconduct to outside licensing, funding, accreditation, advisory bodies or the press can be best judged by this value. The staff member's choices in such a situation may also be tempered by an articulated organizational value that requires internal sources of redress to be exhausted before such external redress is sought.

Bowie (1982) in his excellent analysis of whistle-blowing (employee disclosure to the public of institutional acts that breach boundaries of ethics and law) has defined six conditions in which whistle blowing is ethically justified. He feels the potential damage to the organization and its employees can be practically and morally justified if: (1) the motivation for whistle-blowing is moral rather than personal; (2) the whistle blower has exhausted internal channels of redress; (3) there is overwhelming evidence of harmful actions; (4) action is taken only after a careful analysis of consequences of the moral or legal breach; (5) his or her action is within one's responsibility for avoiding and/or exposing moral violations; and (6) the whistle blower has some chance of success.

In addition to licensing, accreditation and funding agencies, depending on whether the client is an adolescent and the way your state defines caregivers under abuse and neglect laws, you may have a legal obligation to report this incident to your state child abuse hotline. Your agency should have specific procedures for child abuse reporting in accordance with state law. Additionally, if your agency has a compliance program, you could report the violation to the Compliance Officer. One of the key components of a compliance program is an employee reporting policy. Government agencies that scrutinize the implementation of compliance programs look to see if the employee reporting mechanism: (1) identifies the procedure for reporting; (2) allows access directly to the Compliance Officer; (3) encourages reporting by having a no retaliation provision and by enforcing discipline for failure to report; (4) accepts anonymous reports; and (5) provides discipline for deliberate false reporting.

Staff Termination

♦♦ 155 ♦♦

Over the past four years, Integrity, Inc., an addiction treatment agency, has evolved the following patterns related to staff termination. A number of staff have been fired capriciously and asked to leave immediately. Staff who resign, while paid for the required two week notice period, are given a few hours to clean out their desk and are asked to then leave and not work the remaining days. A number of staff have become extremely negative and embittered in the weeks preceding their resignation; it's as if people have to get mad and fight their way out of the organization to leave. Other staff have left precipitously with no notice in a kind of explosive, adult runaway behavior.

Discussion Question

While these conditions are clearly far from ideal, does the vignette raise any ethical issues about the relationship between the organization and its employees?

There are ethical issues raised by the above vignette to the extent that the methods of termination violate the promises inherent within the contractual relationship between the worker and the organization and to the extent that quality of services to clients is compromised by the deteriorating morale surrounding these terminations. Ideally, the termination process should be structured in a manner that facilitates emotional closure of the employee, facilitates a smooth transfer of service responsibilities to minimize disruption and discomfort to clients, and provides rituals through which the team can positively redefine itself in the absence of the exiting member. How terminations are managed involves ethical dimensions because these processes affect the health of clients, the health of workers and the health of the organizational system. Because termination of employment can have such an effect on an employee and his or her family's economic and emotional health, particular care should be taken in managing the termination process.

Continued respect for the employee, even at the point of termination, is reflected in psychological preparation for the prospects of termination (progressive discipline), courtesy and professionalism in the termination interview, adequate termination notice and structuring of the termination process. Some organizations supplement these efforts with outplacement counseling and job search assistance. The goal is to make the process as painless as possible for all persons involved. Principles of fairness (justice), kindness (beneficence), and honesty apply to employees as well as clients. Precipitous termination should be the rare exception reflecting extraordinary circumstances, not the norm.

Unfortunately, lawyers are not always as humane as ethicists and social service providers. The lawyer's focus will be on the best interests of the agency and the remaining staff. Sometimes a terminated employee can negatively impact staff morale, so it is prudent to remove the terminated individual as soon as possible. Similarly and more importantly, terminated employees can pose significant security risks. Their anger could result in workplace violence as well as lead to destruction and sabotage of company property. Prior to a termination occurring, your agency should have procedures in place for informing appropriate computer personnel so passwords can be changed or the employee about to be terminated could be denied access. Key codes for entrances intro buildings should be changed or locks altered.

If you have a personnel policy that requires employees to provide two weeks notice, courts generally impose that same obligation on the employer. Thus, if you terminate someone immediately, you may have to pay the two weeks wages in lieu of notice. If you have no notice provision, the law does not require that an employer pay any severance to an employee that has been terminated, laid off or resigned. The employee may be eligible for unemployment compensation. If, however, you have a employment contract, a union contract or implied contract in your policy handbook then some payment may be required by the agency. Make sure your personnel policies/policy handbooks clearly state in the beginning that "this handbook does not constitute a contract and your employment is employment at will."

External Professional Relationships

Value of External Relationships

♦♦ 156 ♦♦

Agencies, like family systems, vary in their degree of connectedness to the outside social and professional world. Some are characterized by a high frequency and intensity of boundary transactions with the outside world, while others are highly isolated from external professional relationships.

Discussion Question

To what extent does this connectedness to the outside world influence the health of the organization and the ethical conduct of its members?

Sustained organizational isolation leads to a deterioration of technical skills and professional support of staff as well as a reduction in resources available to address clients' needs. The xenophobic position that there is something wrong with all other agencies and workers, that we must meet all of the needs of our clients, inevitably leads an agency staff into practicing significantly beyond the boundaries of their individual and collective competence. Some agencies attempt to articulate the value of external relationships in their Code of Professional Practice. For example: "Center staff shall maximize the resources available to client/families through the fullest possible utilization of other community health and social services. Valuing external resources implies a value of respect and appreciation for the knowledge, skills, perspectives and commitments of other helping persons, seeing such persons as kindred spirits rather than competition."

Multiple Service Involvement

♦♦ 157 ♦♦

Laurie arrives for an assessment seeking your advice regarding her need for treatment. She has long suffered from severe and persistent addictions problems. She is now being actively seen by a psychiatrist who is promoting controlled drinking and maintaining her on high doses of minor tranquilizers and sedatives.

Discussion Question

Describe your response to: A) Laurie and B) the psychiatrist.

While there are any number of clinical issues raised by the above situation, most agencies identify four primary ethical concerns to which they most often respond to in the following manner:

- *Clients should be presented differences of opinion on treatment philosophy and technique between agencies or professionals with the greatest possible objectivity and least possible personal acrimony.*
- *Clients receiving treatment from another professional that is both outside the mainstream of current treatment approaches and which poses risks to the health of the client should be informed of such divergence and risks by the person/agency being consulted.*
- *Where the client faces imminent harm from the proposed treatment, the agency/professional being consulted should take whatever action is necessary to protect the client. This could range from bringing the risk to the attention of the psychiatrist, informing the family members of the client (with the client's permission), or notifying a higher authority regarding the psychiatrist's threat to his/her patients. Such higher authority could range from any administrative or clinical authority under which the psychiatrist works, the medical director of the hospital (if the services are provided through a hospital) or an external professional practice review panel.*
- *There should be a refusal to do concurrent treatment where goals or methods conflict or where concurrent treatment would result in decreased likelihood of problem resolution. The potential risks and benefits of the alternative treatment approaches should be explained to the client and outside sources of consultation should be offered. The client should also be told that he or she must make the judgement as to which approach will be best for him or her.*

Commenting on the Competence of Other Professionals

♦♦ 158 ♦♦

You are having lunch with representatives from four other agencies who you have known for quite some time. In the course of the luncheon conversation, one of them asks you for your candid opinion on a new psychiatrist that has recently begun practicing in your community. It so happens that your experience with this psychiatrist has been extremely negative and that you have stopped all client referrals to the psychiatrist until a meeting can be held to iron out what appears to be major philosophical differences related to the appropriate treatment of addictive disorders.

Discussion Questions

How do you respond to the question regarding the psychiatrist's competence?

What ethical or professional practice issues are involved in commenting on the competence or incompetence of other professionals?

At a practical level, it is probably crucial to reserve communicating one's judgment of a professional peer while there is some process continuing whose goal is to clarify and resolve professional differences. Most agencies that explore this question wish to strike a balance between two extremes. On the one hand, they want to define professionalism as it relates to commenting on the competence or approaches of others. This professionalism is usually defined in terms of objectivity or in terms of prohibitions against personalized or derogatory indictments or gossip. On the other hand, they want to avoid the criticism that professional disciplines represent closed guilds that protect through silence their least competent and their most impaired professional peers. A general guideline in commenting on the competence of another professional is to state first the nature and extent of the experience upon which your judgment is based and then state as objectively as possible your judgment of their performance.

If you choose to comment, you should be very careful because of the potential for allegations of defamation or tortious interference with a contractual or business relationship. It may also constitute a violation under your licensing or certification ethics codes. For example, Principle 10 of NAADAC's code of ethics provides "the NAADAC member shall treat colleagues with respect, courtesy, fairness and good faith and shall afford the same to other professionals". This principle needs to be balanced against Principle 9 stating "it is the responsibility of the NAADAC member to safeguard the integrity of the counseling relationship and to ensure that the client has reasonable access to effective treatment."

♦♦ 159 ♦♦

Representatives from two local addiction treatment organizations were asked to participate in a panel discussion about treatment on a local television show. The two programs had a long history of competition and mutual hostility that broke through initially during the television show in the form of attempted one-up-manship, challenges to the truth and accuracy of statements, and narcissistic posturing. In spite of the interviewer's attempts to focus the dialogue on issues that would be relevant to viewers, the discussion frequently involved a competitive bantering on arcane professional issues that the public neither cared about nor would understand. By the end of the show, the television host was barely able to keep the discussion from degenerating into personal attacks.

Discussion Question

What ethical issues are raised by the conduct portrayed in this story?

The participants in the above story, influenced by their historical relationship, defined the media opportunity as a debate rather than an informational panel. They had prepared and would evaluate their respective performances in terms of win or lose. The ethically questionable conduct involves the misuse of the media opportunity. Like a counselor letting his or her own needs and agendas interfere with effective counseling of a client, the workers above allowed institutional agendas to violate the integrity of their professional involvement in an educational forum. Time spent in competitive bantering constituted missed opportunities for public education. By failing to set aside institutional history or personal acrimony, the participants conveyed an image of the treatment field that diminished personal and institutional reputations and potentially decreased the willingness of potential clients/family members to seek services not only from the two programs but from ANY addiction treatment agency. To avoid demeaning the professional field, disagreements on philosophical or programmatic issues should be presented only in forums appropriate for such communication and should be presented with the highest level of professionalism and objectivity.

Allegations of Unethical Conduct

♦♦ 160 ♦♦

A client you are currently counseling reports that she was sexually exploited by her previous therapist. The therapist named by this client is a colleague who you have met at numerous professional meetings and who is still working as a therapist in another agency within your community.

Discussion Questions

Are there any actions you would take above and beyond your clinical response to this report?

What standard would capture the essence of what staff should do in response to hearing such an allegation?

The response to allegations of professional misconduct involves clinical as well as ethical issues. One quite poignant concern here involves the betrayal of the client through failure to take action. This parallels the frequent experience of sexually abused children feeling betrayed because family members and others did not believe them nor protect them from the sexual perpetrator within the family once the abuse was revealed. If the client in the above vignette had a history of such abuse, this potential recapitulation of her family of origin betrayal could be particularly devastating. Options available to the therapist in the above vignette would include the following:

- *Informing the client of her options of filing formal complaints or charges with the alleged abusing therapist's employer, funding sources of the agency in which alleged abuse occurred, regulatory agencies overseeing service agency or professional licensure or certification board, and filing a civil lawsuit or criminal complaint.*
- *Notifying in writing, with the client's permission, one or more of the above administrators or institutions about the nature of the allegation reported by the client.*
- *Providing on-going emotional support to the client through the formal allegation and hearing processes.*

Responding to a client allegation of sexual exploitation by a professional helper raises complex clinical, ethical and legal issues. Most agencies require that such allegations be immediately brought into the process of supervision to assure that such complexities can be identified and responded to appropriately. The supervisory process can be particularly helpful in providing the worker a means of preparing for any communication with the person about whom the allegation has been made. Supervision can help the worker:

- *Maintain the presumed innocence of the therapist by referring to the sexual activity as "alleged" or "reported".*
- *Determine the desirability or necessity of communication with the therapist.*
- *Select the best timing for such communication.*
- *Explore the best structure for such communication, e.g., in writing, by telephone, or face-to-face meeting.*
- *Determine what precisely should be said to the therapist and how it could be best communicated.*

Schoener (1989) has written an excellent review of the intricacies involved in filing complaints of unethical conduct against counselors and psychotherapists and has included an insightful section on the mechanics and risks involved in filing third party complaints on behalf of clients. Haas and Malouf (1989) provide the best discussion available on the ethics of confronting and being confronted.

Chapter
Eight

Conduct Related to Public Safety

Addiction treatment professionals have always had to address issues related to public safety. However, recent changes in the psychoactive drug menu, changes in the characteristics of drug consumers, and changes in the social context of illicit drug use in the U.S. have greatly intensified the public safety issues encountered by treatment professionals. The dramatic increase in predatory crime and violence and the spread of HIV infection within the culture of addiction have been supplemented by growing concerns about the risks posed by drug-impaired workers in American businesses and industries. Addiction treatment professionals now regularly face difficult ethical and legal issues surrounding the potential threats posed by clients to the health and safety of others. Treatment professionals are being called upon to assess and make judgements about a client's potential and imminent threat to public safety without either the technical training to conduct such an assessment or training in a clinical/ethical/legal decision-making model through which such judgements can be made.

Rather than responding to each vignette, the legal issues raised by this chapter can be summarized by evaluating the federal confidentiality obligations against: (a) state mandates to report child abuse and neglect; (b) statutory and common law duties to warn; and (c) public health reporting of HIV status and of notifying needle sharing and sexual partners. As discussed at length in Chapter 6, the federal confidentiality law governing the identity, treatment, prognosis, diagnosis and records of patients in substance abuse treatment programs is one of the most stringent confidentiality laws on the books. Unlike HIV laws which are state driven, federal law extends consistent confidentiality protections to persons in addiction treatment across all states. However, states may elect to adopt more stringent drug and alcohol confidentiality laws. To the extent of a conflict between the federal confidentiality laws, other state drug and alcohol confidentiality laws, state HIV-confidentiality laws, state duty to warn statutes or state child abuse reporting, the federal law supercedes (unless the state law is stricter). When confronted with one of the three public safety reporting mandates, these are the legal questions you should ask yourself:

___ Is there a way for me to report without identifying the client (maintain complete client anonymity)?

____ Is there a way for me to report without identifying the client as a participant in a drug or alcohol treatment program (give client's name but do not give your name or the addiction agency's name). Be wary of agency letterhead and caller ID!

____ If I cannot keep the client anonymous, is there an exception under the federal confidentiality laws?

____ If there is an exception, is there a limit to the information that can be shared under the exception?

____ If the situation does not fall within an exception, would the client consider granting written consent to disclosure or self-disclose him/herself?

____ If there is not an exception and the client will not grant consent, do I feel ethically the agency should pursue a court order to disclose?

____ If there is not time to obtain a court order should I disclose/warn despite the potential liability for breach of confidentiality because I believe a specific person is in imminent risk of harm and the client has a history of committing such violence, is capable of the violence, and has a specific plan?

For an in depth analysis of these issues, two excellent sources exist on confidentiality: the Legal Action Center's book on *Confidentiality and Communication: A Guide to the Federal Drug and Alcohol Confidentiality Law* and CSAT's TIP #13 on confidentiality. In general, the legal analysis for the three categories of cases described above are as follows:

1. **Child Abuse Reporting**

   The federal confidentiality laws require treatment programs to report child abuse or neglect as mandated by state law. However, follow-up information remains protected. What this means is that, without consent or appropriate court order, the child welfare agency may not access the record, counselors may not give testimony in court, and the child welfare agency may be limited in discussing issues of concern "outside the mandated report" with the addiction agency. In light of changes in public policy regarding permanency initiatives for children, this is an area that may change in the near future. Consult the popovitslaw.com website for additional information on the options for sharing necessary information with child welfare.

2. **Duty to Warn**

   Although a growing number of state statutes and common law have found therapists liable when they failed to warn someone threatened by a patient, the federal confidentiality laws supercede those state obligations. See 42 C.F.R. §2.20 and Hasenei v U.S., 541F. Supp. 999 (D. Md 1982). The federal regulations prohibit this disclosure unless you obtain a court order or you can make the report without identifying the individual who threatens to commit the crime as a patient. Most lawyers advise that if clear and imminent danger to a particular person exists, it is wise to err on the side of warning about the danger.

3. **HIV/AIDS Duty to Report**

    In most states, the public health reporting requirements and partner notification laws do not involve mandatory reporting of addiction agencies (it is typically for physicians, laboratories, public health authorities and hospitals). You should check your applicable laws and regulations on this issue. To balance the federally confidentiality protections against the public health report or warning of needle sharing or sexual partners, the following exceptions could be used: QSO agreements (see Vignette #16 in Ch. 3); written client consent (see Vignette # 71 in Ch. 6); or disclosure of non-patient identifying information. Of course, court orders are an option and in some rare cases, the medical emergency exception or the research option could be used.

The vignettes in this chapter have been selected to help the reader explore the ethical and legal issues raised by such threats to safety.

Critical Incidents

Physical/Sexual Abuse

♦♦ 161 ♦♦

You work in an addiction treatment agency. Ruth, a 16 year-old client that you have counseled for presenting problems of drug dependence, runaway behavior, and sexual promiscuity, today discloses that she was sexually abused by her father. Ruth reports that the abuse began at age eight and continued up until a year ago. Ruth has not been molested or otherwise abused during the past year. She has two younger siblings. She wants to talk about the abuse, but doesn't want her father reported since the abuse has stopped. She feels reporting him will "tear the family up" and make things worse for her.

Discussion Questions

How do you respond to Ruth's disclosure?

Would these circumstances ethically and/or legally require mandatory reporting to the child protection agency within your state?

begin again ↓

All fifty states have provisions for mandatory reporting of physical and/or sexual abuse of children. These statutes are based on the premise that the potential harm to children from abusive acts outweighs the potential harm that could occur through the violation of client confidentiality. The ethical command in the case above is to assure that the abuse of Ruth does not recommence and to assure the safety of Ruth's younger siblings (and perhaps the safety of other potential victims). How addiction counselors and addiction treatment reconcile their ethical and legal responsibilities differs widely. Three broad approaches are regularly encountered by the authors.

The first approach takes the position that the clinician should report only those cases of abuse that clearly fall under the definition of legally mandated reporting. This option makes compliance with the law the framework for ethical conduct. The risk here is twofold: first, that cases may arise in which there is an ethical mandate to protect which falls outside the legal requirement to report, and, second, that actions taken to protect—mandatory reporting—may, in some unique circumstances, do harm to those targeted for protection.

The second approach takes the position that the clinician should report only in those circumstances where there is a legal obligation to report AND when the action of reporting is judged by the clinician to be the best available vehicle capable of protecting the innocent parties and supporting the long-term health and safety of all parties involved. A judgment to not report with this option is an implicit assumption of responsibility and legal liability by the clinician for the welfare of those involved, but one deemed justifiable under certain circumstances. In fact, in some states, failure to report child abuse or neglect by a mandated reporter is typically a misdemeanor, and also grounds for disciplinary action by applicable licensing boards. To further encourage reporting, some states also have immunity provisions for those who report abuse and neglect.

The third approach posits that the clinician should report not only those cases that fall under the definition of legally mandated reporting, but also cases where the clinician feels an ethical duty to protect but circumstances are not of such severity as to legally require reporting. The risk in this option is in unduly violating client confidentiality and in adding non-critical work to an already overburdened child protection system. Once again, if the clinician reports in "good faith", some state statutes provide immunity for such reporting.

To reconcile the client's right to confidentiality with the duty to report, it is crucial that each agency clearly defines how it operationalizes both of these mandates within the span of the three positions noted above. Once that position has been determined, clients can be told of the exceptions to confidentiality in language precise enough to allow them to make informed choices regarding likely responses to their disclosures.

There are numerous variations on abuse situations that make it more difficult to sort out one's legal and ethical duties. The following worksheet, Exploring the Ethical Duty to Report, has been devised to help explore some of these variations. It is designed as a tool for discussion during inservice training or in staff meetings. The agency/clinician response to each situation can be discussed using the following questions:

- *Does the situation, as presented, warrant suspension of confidentiality and reporting to an outside authority? If yes, which outside authority?*
- *What actions in addition to, or as an alternative to, external reporting would enhance the protection of safety in the situation?*
- *Who will benefit and who will be potentially harmed by the proposed action?*
- *Which ethical values (see worksheet in Chapter Two) should guide our response to the situation?*

Duty to Warn (Threat of Physical Violence)

♦♦ 162 ♦♦

You work as the evening counselor in a residential addiction treatment program. Following a loud argumentative phone call, a client charges out of the facility threatening to kill his ex-wife and her new boyfriend.

Discussion Questions

Would contacting the ex-wife or the police constitute a breach of this client's confidentiality?

Would failure to warn the ex-wife constitute a breach of professional ethics?

What would you do in this situation?

In 1976, the California Supreme Court, in the now famous Tarasoff v. Regents of the University of California case, 17 Cal. 3d 425 (1976), ruled that therapists have a duty to warn potential victims of a specific threat of violence made by the therapist's client, even if such disclosure is not approved by the client. The Tarasoff decision intensified the ethical discussion within the

Exploring the Ethical Duty to Report	
Situation	Action Recommended (if any) (Confidentiality Versus Duty to Protect)
Minor client reports "sexual fondling" by foster parent with whom she is currently living.	
You repeatedly observe bruises on an adolescent client's face and arms, the client denies being beaten by parents or boyfriend.	
Adult client reports sexual abuse by father when he/she was a child. There are still minor children in the home.	
A 13 year-old client discloses initiating sexual fondling of younger siblings, ages 11 and 9.	
A 22 year-old client reports being sexually abused from ages 9 to 15 by her older brother.	
A 15 year old client reports current sexual abuse by the father of her best friend.	
An adult client reports sexual abuse by his/her father when he/she was a child. There are no minor children left in the home.	
A minor client reports sexual abuse by a pastor continuing up to time of present treatment admission.	
An adult client reports childhood sexual abuse by a pastor still working in your community.	

professional helping disciplines regarding the rights of clients to confidentiality and the rights of potential victims to be warned of threats to their physical safety. This tension between client privacy and community safety continues today. Since the Tarasoff decision, the "duty to warn" has become both an ethical obligation and a keystone within the ethical standards of most helping professions. The "duty to warn" is generally operationalized as follows:

- *All clients, as part of the informed consent process, are fully informed of both the scope and limits of confidentiality.*
- *A reasonable assessment of the client's potential for violence is conducted as a component of the intake assessment process.*
- *"Duty to warn" is activated when a client makes a threat of physical harm to an identified individual or individuals.*
- *A more intensified evaluation of the client's potential for violence is conducted in response to the verbal threat of aggression. Duty to warn applies where a threat of harm is deemed to be imminent.* ~happening approaching
- *The warning constitutes direct contact of the threatened individual by the helper with a concise explanation of the nature of the threat that was made.*
- *The helper should initiate all other possible actions to reduce the likelihood of harm to others. These actions may include dealing with the client's anger in counseling, increasing the frequency of client counseling, referring the client for psychiatric assessment, hospitalizing the client, asking the client to relinquish weapons, and initiating a no-contact contract between the client and the potential victim. (VandeCreek and Knapp, 1989).*
- *The details of the client's threats, the assessment findings of the client's potential for violence, the management options considered by the counselor/agency, and the actions taken are documented in detail within the client's clinical record.*

You should check your state laws and counselor licensing statutes for specific state guidance on duty to warn which may differ from the general common law principles articulated by Tarasoff.

♦♦ 163 ♦♦

You work as a receptionist in an addiction treatment program. Today a client arrives in a state of extreme intoxication for an interview. The client becomes irritated in the waiting room because the intake worker is running a little late for the client's appointment. The client says he's leaving and resists your suggestion that he wait for the counselor or talk to someone at the detox unit. Becoming increasingly belligerent, the client walks out of the reception room with his car keys in hand saying he's going to drive to a neighboring city to see his sister.

Discussion Questions

How would you respond to this situation?

Do the receptionist and the agency have an ethical responsibility to protect the public from this client?

The challenge in this situation is how to protect the public from the impaired driving of the intoxicated client without violating the client's confidentiality. Responses could include the following:

- *seek the assistance of any other available staff person to help you assess and respond to the situation*
- *communicate to the client that he is too intoxicated to drive and that if he gets in his car you will have no recourse but to call the police*
- *call the police informing them of your observation of an intoxicated person getting into an automobile, with the car's description, license number and location, without identifying the person as a client of your agency.*

If there was an extreme situation where the only way to protect the public was to acknowledge the person's status as an agency client, then such disclosure could be made ethically on the grounds that the imminent threat to public safety outweighed the client's right to confidentiality. However, you will be committing a criminal offense under the federal confidentiality regulations.

Allegations of Misconduct

♦♦ 164 ♦♦

You are at a social function with 50 other people. While in a small group of five to six persons, you mention in casual conversation that you work at a local addiction treatment agency. The person standing next to you says, with sarcastic amusement, that it must be a real interesting place to work there because her neighbor (mentioned by name) who is receiving counseling at your agency has been describing to this person the ongoing affair this client is having with her therapist (mentioned by name) at the agency.

Discussion Questions

How do you respond to this immediate situation as the five to six persons turn to you with great anticipation of your response to these comments? What do you say?

Do you share this information with the therapist about whom the allegation was made?

Do you share it with other staff of the agency?

The staff member in a vignette like the above is instantaneously thrust into potentially conflicting interests. The allegation raises concerns regarding the potential exploitation of clients as well as threats to the reputations of the individual staff member named in the allegation and to the agency as a whole. Discussions of this vignette most often raise the following points:

__Immediate Response__: The goals in responding to this allegation at the party are: (1) to protect the client named in the incident; (2) to obtain the necessary information that will allow a subsequent investigation of the charge (protection of client); and (3) to express that such a behavior, if true, would constitute a breach in both professional ethics and agency policy (protection of agency). The first goal requires that the staff member at the party not say anything that would inadvertently acknowledge the named client's status as a client. The second goal requires that the staff member obtains sufficient information (e.g., name of the person making the allegation) so that a subsequent investigation can begin. The third goal, which is designed to protect the agency, requires expressing the organizational value about sexual involvement between therapists and clients. This last intervention provides an opportunity to briefly educate community members about professional standards in this area–standards that may not be widely known given the proliferation of popular literature and movies depicting therapists' sexual involvement with their clients. The universal value of discretion calls for the staff member to bring the discussion to closure as rapidly as possible to reduce potential damage to the client, the reputation of the agency, and the reputation of the worker.

__Communication to Person Accused__: Staff vary in their responses to whether the person hearing the allegation should report it to the person about whom the allegation was made. Most are struck by how uncomfortable it would *be to communicate this information to another staff member. But most respond affirmatively to the question: "Would you want to be informed if such an accusation was being made about you?" What is helpful to the person in the quandary of how to respond to their awareness of an allegation of misconduct is that some consensus or standard has been defined within the agency as to the desired professional response in this situation. Most agencies take the position that staff members have a right to information in a timely manner on allegation that have been made about them. "The "timely," rather than immediate, notification is based on the fact that the safety needs of the client take precedence over the staff member's right to such information. Notification occurs only after safety concerns for the client have been assessed and addressed.*

*   **Communication to Supervisor**: Most agencies define in their Code of Professional Practice or their Corporate Compliance Programs the expectation that all staff shall convey to their direct supervisor any allegations of illegal/unethical conduct of board member, staff member, or agency volunteer. Many staff when they first brainstorm their response to this vignette respond that they would not want to communicate the allegation to their supervisor unless they were sure the allegation was true. After continued discussion, they usually realize the enormous burden this position places on them to determine the guilt or innocence of a co-worker and the enormity of the consequences if they misjudge the situation. The mandatory reporting to a supervisor is as much for the protection of the worker who hears such allegations as it is for the protection of the client. It also assures that the accused staff member is given full procedural rights in responding to the allegation.*

*   **Communication to Others**: What happens when you walk into the staff lounge for a cup of coffee Monday morning following this incident and everyone wants to know, "How was your weekend? Did you do anything exciting?" How do you respond? Most agencies try to incorporate into their Code of Professional Practice not only a mandate to report allegations of misconduct, but go further in restricting the range of subsequent disclosure of the allegation. Sometimes referred to as a "gossip clause," staff are prohibited from casual reporting or discussion of such allegations with others on the grounds that such communication is a form of professional gossiping that could damage both the reputation of the agency and the worker about whom the allegations have been made.*

♦♦ 165 ♦♦

You are in a state that has recently implemented a mandatory alcoholism assessment for all persons arrested for driving under the influence (DUI). This change has led to the rapid proliferation of DUI assessment programs and intense financial competition between the various agencies for DUI assessment referrals. One new agency in your community, whose whole business is DUI-related, has slowly evolved into a "hired gun" working closely with local defense attorneys to provide assessment conclusions and recommendations desired by the DUI offender and his/her attorney. It is your belief that this practice both hurts the reputation and integrity of the alcoholism field and poses a significant risk to public safety by its failure to identify and divert alcoholics into treatment or, at a minimum, play a supportive role in depriving actively drinking alcoholics of their right to legally drive.

Discussion Question

What would you do in response to this situation?

Most of us would agree that addiction treatment agencies and professionals have a responsibility to identify and, when possible, respond to threats to public safety. The potential threat to public safety and the alleged professional misconduct implicit in the above vignette should be brought into the process of supervision for review and strategy development. One's response in this situation must be measured to avoid the appearance that the agency is acting out of "sour grapes" in response to the other agency's financial success. Having the whole issue discounted as one of competitive back-biting will help no one. Responses could range from:

- *communicating to the director of the other agency feedback about their "hired gun" reputation*
- *communicating your concerns to the presiding judge in the circuit in which the agency's DUI evaluations are being submitted*
- *expressing concern to the state licensing authority regarding the agency's conduct*
- *expressing concern to the state counselor certification body that counselors may be compromising professional judgment in DUI evaluations for the financial benefit of the particular agency.*

AIDS and Risks to Third Parties

♦♦ 166 ♦♦

Toma, a client in outpatient treatment who knows he is HIV positive, has not yet informed his partner of this fact, in spite of their continued involvement in unprotected sexual activity.

Discussion Questions

> As Toma's primary therapist, do you have any ethical or legal responsibility to convey this information to his partner?

> What would you do in this situation?

Laws governing this situation vary from state to state and consensus is not easy on the conditions under which professionals may inform, or have an ethical duty to inform, third parties of their exposure to HIV. The professional, in balancing the client's right to confidentiality and the public's—or particular injured parties'—right to protect itself, may consider several possible courses of action:

- *convincing Toma to directly inform his partner regarding his HIV status and his or her potential risk—validating that such communication did occur and linking Toma's partner to testing and counseling services*
- *conducting a joint session with Toma and his partner to help to provide support and assistance as he informs his partner*
- *informing Toma's partner of Toma's status and his or her risk of HIV infection in spite of Toma's refusal to grant permission—such decision reflecting a judgment of an ethical duty to inform but most likely violates state HIV confidentiality laws and the federal confidentiality laws/drug and alcohol treatment records*
- *informing the third party (if it was someone other than the partner) of their exposure to HIV without informing them of the identity of the client*
- *inviting and involving John's family, intimate partners, and needle-sharing partners to HIV/AIDS education programs offered by the agency, and*
- *discussing consequences of possible pregnancy (if partner is female).*

◆◆ 167 ◆◆

Jessie is a client with AIDS who is participating in the intensive outpatient component of your treatment program. In spite of—or in reaction to—his AIDS diagnosis, Jessie is continuing a very sexually aggressive lifestyle, is consistently refraining from disclosing his infection status to his sexual partners, and refuses to use condoms. Of great concern to you is the fact that Jessie is also being sexually aggressive (seeking sexual activity) with a number of other intensive outpatient clients.

Discussion Questions

How would you intervene in this situation?

Do other clients have a right to know of Jessie's medical condition or would the communication of that knowledge be a gross breach of Jessie's right to confidentiality?

Under ordinary circumstances, Jessie's medical history, including his HIV status could not be disclosed without Jessie's written consent. The ethical concern here is the extent to which other clients' reasonable expectations of safety and protection from communicable disease in the treatment environment is being jeopardized by Jessie's actions and whether this threat supersedes his right to confidentiality. Balancing these conflicting rights and duties, staff might consider the following options:

- *confront the inappropriateness of Jessie's behavior in the treatment environment*
- *define and contract for restraint of sexual behavior in the treatment environment with clearly defined consequences for failure to comply, e.g., discharge from treatment, even though such contracting may have only minimal deterrent effect on Jessie's behavior*
- *intensifying HIV/AIDS education to clients, to include warnings of the high risk of sexual activity with other clients*
- *disclose Jessie's status to a public health agency with expressed concerns about his knowingly infecting other persons (pursuant to a QSO agreement or client consent to comply with federal confidentiality laws).*

Threats to Public Safety

♦♦ 168 ♦♦

You work as an addiction counselor in a local treatment agency. In the past two months, you have seen innumerable clients who report the same source for the enormous quantities of amphetamines they have been consuming. In each case, a local physician was named who is indiscriminately prescribing large quantities and varieties of psychostimulants and amphetamines. You suspect from recent personal contact with this aging physician is becoming increasingly impaired and is losing most of his traditional medical practice.

Discussion Questions

Does this physician constitute a threat to public safety?

Do you have an ethical responsibility to convey the information about this physician's prescribing practices to an appropriate public authority?

Would the disclosure of this information without identifying the names of the clients who reported the information constitute a violation of confidentiality since it was derived from treatment interviews?

What would you do in this situation?

What standards would serve as a guide to staff facing such dilemmas?

Data from multiple client interviews suggesting the escalating impairment of a physician raises concerns about threats to public safety both in terms of the doctor's contribution to the local drug abuse problem and the potential errors in professional judgment that may pose equally dire consequences to his or her other medical patients. Responses to this threat might include one or more of the following:

- *informing your immediate supervisor of the information obtained from the clients, expressing your sense of ethical concern about the physician's actions, and seeking consultation from the supervisor on potential courses of action*
- *involving the medical director of the agency as a consultant on potential courses of response*
- *approaching the physician directly with expression of concern about the ease with which he or she is prescribing and dispensing abusable drugs*
- *expressing concern about the situation to the physician's professional peers, if he or she is in group practice*
- *contacting the ethics committee of the local medical society*
- *notifying local law enforcement authorities, if all other courses of resolution fail.*

All communications in the above circumstances must involve a summary of findings reported by many clients and must be done in a way not to directly or inadvertently identify any persons as clients of the agency.

◆◆ 169 ◆◆

Lucinda works as a registered nurse in a hospital-based chemical dependency unit that utilizes multiple admitting physicians. A physician calls in an order for a medication that is both contraindicated for the particular patient and has been ordered at an excessively high dosage. After reviewing the client's medical history and reconfirming her understanding of the drug through reference texts in the nursing station, Lucinda is convinced that the administration of the medication could jeopardize the life of the client. When she calls the physician to express her concern, the doctor asks where she went to medical school and hangs up on her. The medication is scheduled to be given in one hour.

Discussion Questions

If you were Lucinda, what would you do?

How can Lucinda reconcile the duty to comply with directives from her superiors with the imminent threat to the safety of a client?

There are two ethical values that apply directly to this situation: nonmaleficence and conscientious refusal. The former demands that we not hurt anyone; the latter demands that we disobey illegal or unethical directives. While the doctor is demanding obedience to the order, the ethical obligation of obedience only extends to legal and ethically permissible directives. Lucinda's ethical recourse is to report the order of a medication that she believes will harm the patient and seek administrative review of the situation by soliciting consultation through the chain of command, e.g., nursing supervisor, director of nursing, chief of the medical staff.

◆◆ 170 ◆◆

Describe how, as an employee assistance program (EAP) counselor, you would balance or reconcile the protection of client confidentiality with the protection of public safety in the following situations:

• An inspector at a nuclear power plant admits falsifying safety inspections due to his inability to keep up with the escalating requirements of his job.
• A pilot for a major commercial airline self-reports flying repeatedly while being hung over and using cocaine and other stimulants to compensate for her alcohol-impairment.

- A nurse, who has been referred to the EAP because of performance problems, breaks down in the second interview and spills out the scope and intensity of his current drug involvement. The nurse discloses in tears his guilt over theft of drugs from the hospital, including the use of drugs ordered for patients.
- A young police officer has been recalled to uniform following four years of undercover vice work. Referred because of suspicion of psychiatric impairment, you discover a cocaine addict whose paranoia is increasing daily. He is hypervigilant and delusional—capable of misinterpreting very harmless cues as very threatening—and carries a gun around-the-clock.

There are numerous issues in these situations: the confidentiality of EAP service consumers, the vulnerability and reputation of the EAP counselor, the reputation of the EAP agency and the contracting company, and threats to the safety of parties outside the EAP helping relationship. Because of the ethical, legal and clinical complexities of cases like the above, the first goal is to keep the individual EAP practitioner from having to make and bear the brunt of such judgments by themselves. The first rule of action in such ethical complexities is to seek consultation. The goal is to bring the best collective judgment of agency personnel to bear on the situation. There are threats to public safety implicit within each of the above vignettes. The degree of imminence of harm and the degree of imperative for action varies. There is a mandate in each of the situations to collect sufficient information to determine the degree of threat to public safety. The first pathway of problem resolution is to seek an answer that allows the EAP counselor to uphold client confidentiality and protect the public safety. Such avenues could include enlisting the client's cooperation to disclose their status or actions to their supervisors, via a request for personal leave or medical leave to enter treatment, or to give the EAP counselor permission to speak with his or her supervisor. Offering to arrange, host, and support the client through such a meeting may increase the likelihood of this option being chosen by the client. Some EAP counselors use an either/or option to pressure the client to take action in order to remove the threat to public safety: "Either you talk to your supervisor and take a medical leave to enter treatment now or I will be ethically bound to report the theft and use of patient medication." Unless written client consent is given in this case, a disclosure no matter how ethical it feels would be a clear violation of confidentiality and may deter others from seeking assistance through the EAP program. The ethical value of self-interest not only demands that the EAP counselor seek consultation through this ethical quagmire, but also that the whole process be rigorously documented for the protection of the counselor and the agency. Such documentation should include:

- *details of the nature and intensity of the threat to public safety*
- *identification of the ethical issues involved, e.g., client confidentiality and duty to protect public safety*
- *the solicitation of consultation, the identification of the consultation resources used, and the nature of the advice given*
- *the clinical data that was most critical to the decision made*
- *the nature of the decision and how it was implemented*
- *the client's response to the action taken.*

See also Vignette #39 for advise when EAP client for advice when EAP clients seek counseling related to pending criminal or civil actions/investigations.

♦♦ 171 ♦♦

An employee of your agency who you supervise—a certified addictions counselor—was just dismissed following the finding (in an internal administrative hearing) that he had sexually exploited a client in treatment.

Discussion Questions

Does the agency have any ethical responsibility to communicate its findings to anyone outside the agency?

Should the agency notify the state certification board for addictions counselors?

Do you feel that there is an ethical mandate to communicate such information or would an agency be overstepping its boundaries and responsibilities in making such a communication?

Does the employee have a right to privacy regarding personnel actions of the agency under these circumstances?

While employees do have some claim to rights regarding the confidentiality of personnel actions in the employee-employer relationship, there are other interests involved in this situation: protection of service consumers, protection of the reputation of treatment agencies, and protection of the integrity and reputation of the profession. The ethical duty to protect clients and the profession is not fully met by discharging the employee. The employee may simply seek re-employment and continue the pattern of sexual exploitation. As a supervisor, there may be a number of actions to consider including the following:

- *Inform the abused clients of their rights to seek civil and criminal redress against the counselor (which could expose the agency to liability for negligent hiring, training, supervision or retention of the counselor). (See Vignette #51)*
- *Encourage the counselor to seek treatment and/or leave the field.*
- *Notify the state counselor certification board of the ethical breach by the counselor and the actions taken by the agency. (If you are certified, you may be ethically bound by your own certification to report this breach to the certification board.).*
- *Provide a strong recommendation for "no hire" to any future employer in the field contacting the agency for verification of employment. (See discussion in Vignette #59).*

There may be some conflict between what a person feels is his or her ethical duty and what one is informed are his or her legal vulnerabilities. One supervisor, confronting the systematic sexual exploitation of many clients by an agency counselor, discharged the counselor and took numerous steps to decrease the likelihood that the counselor would be able to stay within the field. When the supervisor was informed that he might be opening himself up to a suit by the now former employee, the supervisor responded: "Let him sue. I couldn't stay a supervisor in this business another day if I thought I hadn't done everything possible to protect other clients from that man's sickness. I will wear as a badge of honor having been found guilty of destroying his chances to ever make a living in this field!" Keep in mind, the best defense to a defamation action is the truth.

Alcohol and other drug-related threats to public safety are likely to increase in their severity and visibility within the coming decades. These threats will require an improved clinical technology in assessing the potential for violence and other behaviors that pose risks to the safety of individuals and communities. Addiction treatment and direct service practitioners will also need to come together to improve our ethical decision-making abilities in the midst of conflicting interests. When addiction agencies or counselors have sought legal advice on the difficult choice to make between one's ethical obligation (duty to warn because of a threat to public safety) and legal obligation (the obligation to protect client confidentiality), a lawyer would prefer to defend you in a breach of confidentiality lawsuit rather than a wrongful death lawsuit.

Chapter
Nine

Professional Standards Related
to Special Roles

The bulk of standards in the helping professions have focused on ethical issues in the relationship between a therapist and a client. There are many specialty roles within the addictions field to which these standards are inappropriate or not easily applied. This chapter will explore some of the ethical issues encountered by workers who are not in a traditional counselor-client relationship within an addictions treatment program. We will explore ethical dimensions of role performance in the areas of prevention, employee assistance, student assistance, outreach, training and research. The understanding of the ethical complexities that can arise in the performance of these roles is still in its infancy.

Critical Incidents

Prevention
  Personal Conduct

♦♦ 172 ♦♦

John is a youth prevention worker involved in drug education and alternatives programming in his local community. John smokes!

Discussion Questions

What ethical issues are raised by this behavior?

Given that so much of the focus of prevention programming is the teaching and promotion of principles of physical and emotional health, are there personal standards of conduct (related to physical and emotional health) to which prevention staff can and should be held accountable?

How would you articulate such a standard? What standard, if any, would apply to personal use of psychoactive drugs (nicotine, alcohol, etc.), obesity, workaholism, or other issues of personal lifestyle that may be highly incongruent with the prevention message?

See following vignette for analysis.

♦♦ 173 ♦♦

Tasha is the coordinator of a local prevention project. Somewhat to her embarrassment, she discovers that she has inherited from her just-deceased grandmother stock in a distillery and stock in a major tobacco company.

Discussion Question

Do Tasha's personal financial holdings represent an area of her personal life unrelated to her professional role or does her assumption of ownership of this stock potentially conflict with or compromise the performance of her professional role?

Both of the vignettes above implicitly ask whether there must be reasonable congruence between the life lived and the message preached and yet each also raises the question of the appropriate boundary line between the professional and private life of the prevention worker.   Prevention professionals, because of their visible advocacy of practices which promote individual and community health, may inevitably be held to a high standard of personal conduct.   There are ethical dimensions to any personal conduct that compromises one's ability to perform assigned role responsibilities within a prevention program.   The private behavior of a prevention worker involves breaches in ethical conduct to the extent that:

- *private behavior is so incongruent with the prevention message that the person's ability to carry this message is fundamentally negated*
- *private conduct in violation of prevailing moral and legal standards impugns his or her reputation to the degree it is no longer possible to effectively perform professional responsibilities*
- *financial relationships in one's private life pose conflicts of interest and loyalty that influence one's professional judgement and decision-making.*

The potential development of an ethical code of professional conduct for prevention workers must inevitably confront the visibility and power of these roles and the need for reasonable congruence between personal lifestyle and the prevention message.   To choose to be a change agent within the context of prevention work may demand a higher and more rigorous standard of personal conduct than is inherent in other roles within health and human service systems.   Some even believe that those who are promoting health have a higher obligation as a role model than those who are treating illness. The standards of prevention agencies may inevitably be more rigorous than agencies without the prevention-focused mission. Prevention workers will quite likely be expected to uphold a rigorous standard of personal conduct like other models of community propriety, e.g., the clergy and teachers.

Conflict between privacy rights and organizational accountability are likely to escalate in the coming decade. Both rights spring from legitimate foundations. The individual has a right to a private existence outside the reach of employer infringement. The organization has a right to protect itself and advance its interests by reasonably assuring that its employees exemplify character and actions congruent with the organization's mission. Reasonable people support both of these rights and have different opinions on how to reconcile them when they come into conflict. Each prevention organization must reach into the collective will of its members to forge a position that supports and protects both the individual and the organization. The articulation of rights and accountabilities in the form of values and professional standards will do much to insure the vitality and protection of the field.

It is the field's zeal for excess that poses dangers. We all have imperfections and fall short of complete adherence to our aspirational values. If a campaign were launched to "purify" the field with perfection as its criteria of inclusion, there would be no one left to work in the field. Someone once noted that programs whose goals are to stamp out sin usually end up stamping out sinners. Defining the line between privacy rights and organizational accountability as it relates to lifestyle must be done with great care and support to help people be included rather than self-righteously excluded. While the value of honesty demands reasonable congruence between organizational values and personal actions, the value of loyalty demands that we help persons achieve newly defined standards of professional propriety.

Role as Change Agent

♦♦ 174 ♦♦

Some persons, with a great deal of encouragement from the alcohol and tobacco industries, have launched an attack against prevention programs and workers. Today in your local newspaper there appears such an attack claiming that prevention professionals have become health police—seeking to suppress freedom of speech and action—in the name of some arbitrary standard of health purity.

Discussion Questions

How would you respond to this charge?

What is the boundary between educating a community and imposing one's beliefs on a community?

If the primary thrust of prevention activities is community change, what standards of ethics and values should govern our roles as change agents?

The ethical value of autonomy demands that prevention and treatment professionals honor the rights and freedoms of their consumers except under extraordinary circumstances, e.g., threats to the health of others. Each prevention program evolves implicitly or explicitly a philosophical position on the question of autonomy that defines the boundary between appropriate and inappropriate strategies for social change. What would be, for example, the line between advocating and dictating a health standard related to smoking? How far can one go in promoting attitudes and behaviors conducive to personal and community health? What would be "too far?" How does the question of autonomy differ in our approaches to legal versus illegal drugs?

Relationship Boundaries

♦♦ 175 ♦♦

Barry, in his role as a local prevention specialist, has been involved for the past three years in organizing alternative activities for youth. Those have included weekend retreats, educational and recreational trips, and prom and graduation sleep-ins. A local teen advisory group has served as the primary planning vehicle for these activities. Today you (as Barry's supervisor) receive a call from a father of an 18 year old graduating senior who has been president of the teen advisory committee for the past two years. He is enraged over his discovery of a sexual relationship between Barry and his daughter. The father says that he will file statutory rape charges against Barry if he can find any evidence of sexual activity before his daughter's recent birthday. He is extremely concerned that his daughter was taken advantage of by Barry. He wants to know what you, as Barry's supervisor, are going to do about this unethical behavior.

Discussion Question

How would you respond to this father and to Barry?

Much of the ethical standards development governing addiction treatment is based on the imbalance of power in the counseling relationship—power which the helping professional could exploit to the detriment of the client. Some prevention workers would attack the applicability of this model to prevention work, suggesting that the "professional-client" model smacks of classism and elitism and that no such power differential exists in the relationship between prevention workers and the people with whom they work. This position would raise some of the following questions that may be at the crux of any discussion of ethical issues in prevention. Are there any roles assumed or activities performed by prevention workers in which such power exists? Are there conditions under which prevention service recipients are vulnerable due to their special characteristics or the nature of the prevention service context? If professional status is eschewed and the status of client abolished, are there any standards of appropriate or inappropriate conduct governing relationships between prevention workers and their various constituencies? Does the prevention context lack the exploitive possibilities to which ethical standards are directed in the treatment context?

Assuming for a moment that the accusations of the father in the above vignette are true, let us explore what, if any, ethical issues are raised by the sexual relationship between Barry and the president of the teen advisory council. Is the sexual relationship a matter of free choice between two consenting adults that is none of the agency's business or does it constitute an ethical breach of job performance subject to disciplinary review and/or action? Factors that may have to be considered in weighing these questions include the following:

- *Context: Did the alleged exploitation occur during a prevention activity, e.g., retreat?*
- *Age of the Service Recipient: While the age of 18 may have arbitrary status under the law, the status of vulnerability—so critical to the discussion of ethical issues—may not be so arbitrarily determined. Would the potential ethical issues be viewed differently if the young woman was 16 or 14? Would it be viewed differently (based on the issue of age) if the sexual involvement was with the young woman's mother?*
- *Maturity and Mental Status: Does the cognitive and emotional functioning of the service recipient allow for informed (ability to anticipate pleasant and unpleasant consequences) choice and consent?*

Are there special vulnerabilities that must be recognized in prevention work with the mentally ill or developmentally disabled?

- **Coercion:** *Was there coercion or duress involved in the initiation of the sexual relationship? Was there deceit or manipulation involved in the initiation of the relationship?*
- **Service Intensity:** *What was the nature and duration of the service relationship between the prevention worker and the consumer of prevention services?*

Questions like the above help us explore two dimensions that open up the potential for exploitation: the power of the service provider and the vulnerability of the service recipient. If we look at the whole continuum of prevention services, these elements of power and vulnerability differ greatly. The prevention specialist has less power presenting information for 60 minutes to a group of 100 adults than in a two-year relationship with the president of a teen advisory council. The vulnerability of service recipients in these two situations would also differ greatly. Issues of dual relationships and issues of social, sexual and financial exploitation could be raised in the prevention context anytime that:

- *constituent characteristics potentially compromise free choice, e.g, the developmentally disabled.*
- *constituent characteristics create special vulnerabilities, e.g., children.*
- *there is an imbalance of power between the prevention service provider and the service recipient.*
- *the service delivery is of sufficient intensity or duration as to enhance emotional dependency even when no formal "treatment" or "helping relationship" has been defined.*

Due to the vulnerability for exploitation that exists when these conditions are present, there may need to be a particularly strict definition of boundaries governing social, sexual and financial relationships between prevention service providers and prevention service recipients.

Confidentiality and Limits of Competence

♦♦ 176 ♦♦

Alan functions as a prevention specialist assigned by a community treatment and prevention agency to work full time within county schools. Through Alan's classroom activities, leadership roles in a broad spectrum of alternative activities, and general availability, he frequently finds himself with young people who share personal confidences or seek his advice on personal problems. Since most kids will not accept a referral for counseling, Alan often finds himself involved in informal counseling relationships. In the course of the last month, Alan has interacted with a number of individuals who have shared information of varying levels of intimacy. Among these disclosures were the following:

1. A young neighbor approached Alan following a school presentation and disclosed her parent's intention to get divorced.
2. A school principal confided to Alan his concerns about allegations of sexual misconduct a student recently made against one of the most popular teachers.
3. A junior high student disclosed to Alan that crack was being sold for the first time at the school.
4. A professional peer disclosed to Alan her decision to enter an eating disorder program.
5. A young student disclosed her sexual abuse by an older brother and his threat of violence if she told anyone.

Discussion Questions

Alan is not a therapist or counselor, the students are not clients in any formal sense of this word, and there is no defined treatment relationship. To what extent do the normal rules of confidentiality within counseling relationships apply to Alan's relationships with students?

How does Alan appropriately determine the line between informal counseling and his need to refer a particular student/family for structured and on-going counseling services.

Are there any ethical restrictions on Alan's communications with parents, teachers, administrators, or community human service representatives regarding the status of a particular student that Alan knows through his prevention role?

Without the benefit of a formal counselor-client relationship, clearly codified confidentiality, informed consent, and clinical supervision, how does the prevention professional operationalize the value of confidentiality?

In which of the above situations would subsequent disclosure be a breach of confidentiality?

In which of the above situations, would there be an ethical mandate for subsequent disclosure to a third party?

The danger of informal counseling or advice-giving in the prevention field is that it lacks some of the specific safeguards of the formal counseling relationship: worker credentialing to conduct the counseling activity, informed consent, confidentiality, clinical supervision and continuity of contact. To the extent that Alan is involving himself in activities for which he has not been trained and for which he is not supervised, he is breaching the ethical principle of competence. This principle demands that we limit our activities to for which we have been trained and are competent to perform—a demand that is particularly compelling in situations where lack of knowledge and skills could result in harm.

The scope and limits of confidentiality should always be defined, even in the most informal of counseling events. The concern is that the same kind of harm can be done through the sharing of a confidence—or the failure to report that confidence under certain circumstances—in the prevention setting as can occur in the treatment setting. Each prevention agency should define and communicate to its staff and its service recipients the scope and limits of confidentiality within the various prevention service relationships. It is also essential that prevention workers have access to supervision to process responsibilities to refrain from any subsequent disclosure of information versus their duties to disclose in certain situations.

From a legal perspective, prevention programs most likely would not be bound by the federal confidentiality regulations (42 C.F.R. Part 2) because these regulations apply only to programs that specialize, in whole or in part, in providing drug or alcohol abuse assessment, diagnosis, counseling, treatment or referral for treatment. Typically, prevention programs would not be covered because these programs are of an educational nature and are not designed to provide individual assessment, diagnosis, counseling, treatment or referral. However, as a counselor in a prevention program, you may be required under state licensure or certification rules to maintain confidentiality under a state standard. Be sure to check your state laws for confidentiality restrictions even for informal counseling or advice.

Alliances

♦♦ 177 ♦♦

You are president of a local grassroots prevention task force that has been organizing and supporting a wide spectrum of local drug abuse prevention activities during its five years of existence. You are currently staging a fund-raising campaign to raise money for scholarships to send 50 inner-city youths to a prevention leadership camp. As the deadline for registration arrives, you have raised only enough money for 21 scholarships, due primarily to severe economic cutbacks that have hit local businesses and industries in the past year. A local business, reading of this dilemma in the paper, approaches the task force and offers to donate the $3,900 to reach the goal of financing 50 youths' attendance to the camp. The local business offering this financial support is the regional distributor for a national company whose primary product is beer.

Discussion Questions

What potential ethical issues, if any, would be raised by acceptance of this donation?

What course of action would you recommend to the task force as its president?

Ethical questions raised by acceptance of the above contribution would include the following:

- *What would it mean to the children to know that a brewery was sponsoring their participation in the camp?*
- *Would financial ties to the alcohol industry damage the reputation of the task force and decrease the potency of its prevention message?*
- *Would acceptance of the gift influence the task force's stand on labeling of alcoholic products or other issues related to promotion and distribution of alcoholic products, e.g., targeting of youth?*
- *Would potential publicity noting the brewery's contribution to support prevention activities divert public attention away from the fact that this company spends more than $1 million a day promoting their alcoholic products? Would acceptance of the gift by the task force create complicity in this diversion?*

A growing number of prevention organizations are taking the position that it is an ethical conflict of interest for a prevention program to accept funds from the alcohol industry at the same time it lobbies for or against issues that effect the economic interests of that industry. Groups like the National Association of Children of Alcoholics and Remove Intoxicated Drivers have adopted policies that prohibit acceptance of contributions from the alcohol industry. Groups like the National Council on Alcoholism and Drug Dependence, Mothers Against Drunk Driving and Students Against Destructive Decisions that once accepted such contributions have now discontinued this practice. Tobacco and alcohol companies are investing larger sums today in prevention programs because of criticism that they target youth in their advertising, and as a condition of various legal settlements. Such funds would better be channeled through some public health authority than to have local prevention agencies dependent upon or accountable to alcohol and tobacco companies.

For a review of ethical issues involved in the relationship between prevention agencies and the alcohol, tobacco and pharmaceutical industries, see White and Tolnai, 1998.

◆◆ 178 ◆◆

A local citizen, publicly notorious for his role in opening the first adult book store in your community, calls your local prevention program with the following requests. First, he has seen a number of your agency's prevention posters around town and would like to get some to put up in his store. Second, he is very concerned about the drug abuse problem and would like to know how he could become a volunteer to support various prevention activities.

Discussion Questions

How do you respond to these requests?

How would the situation differ, if any, if the person wishing to volunteer was the single person most associated with an anti-abortion (or pro-choice) campaign in your local community?

In sorting through its choice of alliances, each prevention agency through the deliberation of its board, managers and staff must address such questions as the following:

- *Is the person/agency seeking to use the affiliation with the prevention campaign in order to divert the community's attention from or to compensate for other exploitive or unscrupulous practices?*

- *Will affiliation with the person/agency compromise the agency's effective delivery of prevention services?*
- *Will affiliation with the person/agency involve the agency in controversy that will divert it from its primary purpose?*
- *Will affiliation with the person/agency weaken the moral and professional authority with which the prevention agency speaks within the community?*

In many cases, the question will be the CONDITIONS under which affiliation would be appropriate or the DEGREE of affiliation which would be appropriate. For example, a prevention program in the above vignette whose posters were primarily targeted at youth might find placement of their posters in an adult bookstore highly inappropriate; a prevention program whose posters dealt with AIDS awareness might find placement of their posters in adult bookstores quite appropriate.

Iatrogenic Effects

Many criticisms of drug education approaches over the past thirty years have suggested that some of these approaches may have stimulated, rather than prevented, drug experimentation. If an ethical premise of addiction treatment (borrowed from a sister profession) is "First do no harm," how can any potential iatrogenic effects of prevention programs be minimized? What standards could help prevent unintended, but untoward, effects of prevention interventions? The next several vignettes will help explore approaches to avoiding such unintended effects of prevention services.

♦♦ 179 ♦♦

You work in a youth-oriented prevention program serving a predominantly rural county that has experienced a dramatic rise in drug-related adolescent deaths during the last six months. Today you are speaking to an 8th grade class as a component of a comprehensive alcohol, tobacco and other drug abuse curriculum used at the middle school. You discover shortly into your presentation that 5-6 students in the class have had significant drug experiences. The nature of their questions and comments suggests that they are into extremely high-risk drug choices and high-risk methods and patterns of drug use. Although your task was to talk about drug abuse and self-esteem, this small subgroup of students are asking very specific questions about drug dosages, drug effects, and the dangers of certain drug combinations.

Discussion Questions

How would you respond to this situation?

Is providing such information—which could reduce drug-related casualties among the users—a legitimate "prevention" activity?

Is there any danger that providing this information within the context of the classroom could have unintended effects upon those students who have not experimented with drugs?

The situation above poses potential risks to all parties—the using students, the non-using students and the prevention worker. The drug-experimenting students are involved in drug choices, the use of drug combinations and drug dosages that could be debilitating or lethal. The prevention worker, if he or she provides detailed aspects of drug pharmacology to reduce the risks of toxic-lethal drug reactions, may inadvertently convey permission for their drug-using activity. If such information is withheld, the prevention worker may feel an accomplice in any subsequent drug-related injury or death of the involved students. If the worker provides the detailed information in the classroom, there could be unintended effects upon the non-drug-using students, e.g., stimulating curiosity about drugs, decreasing student fears about particular drugs. The prevention worker is also potentially vulnerable to challenges to his or her professional integrity through charges that he or she is "teaching kids how to use drugs." The prevention worker must find a way out of this quandary that resolves all of these potential vulnerabilities. Options include the following:

1) *refrain from responding to the needs of a few students in a manner that could have negative effects on the majority of students, e.g., not provide the information in the context of the class presentation; and*
2) *respond to the needs of the drug-experimenting students by*
   a) *meeting with them at a later time to discuss their information needs, e.g., after class*
   b) *referring the students to early intervention groups that may address their information needs, or*
   c) *referring the students to a student assistance program counselor or school counselor to provide an avenue for intervention into their drug experimentation via their desire for information.*

Social policy on illicit drugs in the United States has been to withhold information and technology (access to quality-controlled drug supplies, sterile syringes, etc.) that would reduce the risks associated with consumption of the drugs. The subsequent high risks associated with such use, it is believed, will serve as a deterrent to drug experimentation. Persons representing the extreme end of this policy would say that the provision of any information and assistance that increases the ability of the potential or actual drug consumer to use without these severe risks is promoting drug use and is unethical. At the other end of the continuum, one could posit that having information that can reduce the risks of injury or fatality and not providing such information is a breach in ethical responsibility. The conflict occurs when actions designed to achieve a public good might, through their rigid implementation, compromise the health of some individuals. Each prevention agency should define its own position on the ethics of providing or withholding drug information and explore ways in which the interests of the society and the interests of individuals can best be reconciled. What do you think this position should be?

♦♦ 180 ♦♦

You are responsible for coordinating a community-based drug prevention program with a primary focus of public information, drug education in the schools and the coordination of a number of adolescent alternatives projects. During the past year, a number of newly recovering adolescents have approached you offering to serve as prevention program volunteers. They are particularly interested in opportunities to speak to younger children and other adolescents about their life experiences. They feel their experiences can be used to help others avoid the problems they encountered and that the opportunity for such public witnessing will be an important support for their own ongoing recoveries.

Discussion Question

Describe any ethical issues potentially involved in this situation.

Whether working with recovering volunteers who are youths or adults, the prevention program has a responsibility to assure the integrity of persons publicly identified with the prevention message. The practice of placing alcohol/drug offenders with minimal or no sobriety time at podiums in elementary and secondary schools or in other highly visible prevention roles is viewed by many prevention professionals as highly questionable. One concern is that the image or charisma of the presenter and elements within his or her presentation may inadvertently glamorize or otherwise increase the appeal of drug experimentation. The person with minimal sobriety time is probably much more an expert on the drug experience than on the recovery experience. Another concern is that any subsequent arrest or relapse of this person weakens the reputation of the prevention agency and the integrity of the prevention message. There may be roles and activities within the prevention field for persons at early stages of addiction recovery whose potential relapse would not have such harmful effects to the effectiveness or reputation of the program. Prevention programs have a responsibility to protect their reputation and their capacity for continued service to the community.

Honesty

♦♦ 181 ♦♦

A biology teacher who is involved in teaching her portion of a K-12 drug education curriculum seeks out your advice as the local prevention specialist. She is concerned with the potential effect of honest answers to questions posed by freshman and sophomore students during discussions about various drugs and their effects. The teacher offers the following example to illustrate the point. If the teacher responds to student questions as to why cocaine is so popular or why it is so addictive with a discussion of cocaine's euphorigenic properties, won't this lead to increased curiosity and potential desire to experiment with this drug in spite of warnings of its addictiveness. The teacher expresses her concern that by emphasizing cocaine's pleasurable, and thus addictive properties, her statements could potentially incite adolescent drug experimentation.

Discussion Questions

Discuss the ethical principle of honesty as it relates to drug information dissemination.

What options are available when a straightforward presentation of factual information may increase rather than decrease drug experimentation?

Is it ever okay to lie, distort the truth or withhold the truth with the intent of preventing youthful drug experimentation?

There is much in the discussion of honesty and deception in the treatment context (Chapter Six) that is applicable to prevention activities. The value of honesty constitutes the ethical foundation upon which any healthy service relationship can be based. As such, any deviance from this stance must be ethically justified. The issues of honesty, deception, and discretion are important to address in the prevention context because of their potential effect on people's decision-making. The danger of dishonesty and deception is evident in early prevention programs that sought to utilize fear as a force to prevent drug experimentation among youth. These programs, designed with the most benevolent of intentions, progressed to the routine use of deception and lies in the effort to prevent drug experimentation. As often happens with such benign deception, there are unanticipated and untoward side-effects. The exaggerated and fabricated information used to scare youth from marihuana in the late 1960's all but destroyed the credibility of prevention workers when they attempted to inform youth about drugs of much greater risk and may have contributed to youth extending experimentation beyond marihuana. What followed was a commitment to the dissemination of factual information that would also be discovered in many cases to have unanticipated and undesired consequences. If unedited honesty is at one end of a continuum and outright, intentional lying is at the other end, the value of discretion represents the center. Discretion demands that the communicator understand the kind of developmental filter through which information will be received. It demands that the communicator understand the meanings which the listener is likely to attach to information. It demands that the communicator recognize the applicability of the concept of iatrogenic (intervention-caused harm) to prevention activities.

Social Action / Civil Disobedience

♦♦ 182 ♦♦

Shelly works in an urban prevention project that has worked intensely for more than two years to develop and implement culturally sensitive and competent prevention programming in a predominantly African American and Hispanic community. Today Shelly, along with two other community activists (a priest and an elementary school teacher), were arrested for criminal destruction of property for defacing billboards throughout the community that promoted alcohol and tobacco products. The "criminal" acts were committed by Shelly on her work time.

Discussion Questions

What should be the agency's response to Shelly's conduct? A memo of censure? A memo of commendation?

What ethical issues are raised by this situation—both the targeted promotion of legal drugs and the destruction of the media of such promotion?

Should Shelly be paid for the time (three hours of regularly scheduled work time) that she was involved in the above activity or for time lost while in jail, visiting her attorney, appearing in court?

What organizational values should guide our response to a worker involved in such activity?

The response to Shelly's activity would vary depending on the values of the organization and the extent to which social action and civil disobedience are a reflection of a violation of those values. As social action escalates in the prevention field, it will be increasingly important for prevention organizations to define if, and under what circumstances, civil disobedience will be viewed as a legitimate professional activity. As discussions about the use of civil disobedience increase, organizations may be able to more fully articulate if, when, and how prevention workers should be involved in such actions. Parallels to the civil rights movement may emerge in which there will be ethical issues raised for individuals and for organizations by either participation or lack of participation in acts of civil disobedience.

A cautionary legal note: committing a criminal act should never be considered within the scope of one's employment. This understanding should be clearly stated in your organizational Code of Ethics. If the employer condones the behavior, the organization may be liable for the damages.

Freedom of Access Versus Harmful Use of Information

◆◆ 183 ◆◆

You supervise a private not-for-profit drug prevention information clearinghouse which provides library and literature search services. You have an extensive collection of audiovisual materials, curricula, books, journals and reports that serve the clearing house's mission of providing support to alcohol, tobacco and other drug abuse prevention efforts in local communities. You have been the repository of the raw data from two alcohol and drug use surveys conducted within your state. These two studies, which document recent changes in attitudes and behaviors related to drinking, smoking and drug use, have received nationwide attention and many persons have come in to investigate findings in the raw data that were not published. For the past week and a half, two persons have been at the clearinghouse daily pouring over the study data. Today one of their notebooks was inadvertently returned with an assortment of research materials. When you open the notebook to discover its owner, you see a heading indicating work on a "Distilled Spirits Account." What then follows are notes scattered under two headings: "Who doesn't drink and why" and "Why people choose to drink beer and wine over distilled spirits." You then notice a business card stapled to the inside of the notebook—the card bearing the name of a national marketing and advertising firm. It appears that the two regular visitors have been using the latest research data to help prepare a new marketing campaign for the promotion of alcoholic products.

Discussion Questions

How would you respond to this situation?

What ethical issues are raised by the use of the clearinghouse for purposes diametrically opposed to its mission?

Discussion of this vignette with prevention workers quickly generates a divergence of opinion that roughly splits into two camps. The first of these camps is reflected in the following argument:

The ethical issues in this situation may be elucidated by contrasting the public library with the clearinghouse of a not-for-profit agency prevention agency. Both the library and the clearinghouse open their resources to the public as long as the guidelines of each are followed. One interesting difference has to do with the motivations of the consumers—how the consumers intend to use the information they receive. In the case of the library, there is no inquiry as to WHY the consumer wishes to check out a particular book—such an inquiry would be seen as intrusive and invasive. While the same principle is generally true of the clearinghouse, the clearinghouse differs from the library in one important respect. The clearinghouse offers information services specifically to enhance the prevention of alcohol, tobacco and other drug abuse. If the clearinghouse discovers persons who are obviously using the agency's information services to promote alcohol or drug consumption, then those persons' rights to access to those services could, and some would say should, be ethically revoked. This action would reflect the position that the agency's resources will not be used for purposes or activities incompatible with the agency's mission.

A second camp argues from a very different position.

> *Restrictions on freedom of access to information from public library and clearinghouse services is unthinkable and potentially violative of first amendment constitutional rights. The administrative definition of who can and cannot use reference information violates the value of autonomy. Even when some harm could result from access to this information, the restriction of access to information poses a greater evil than does the potential misuse of the information. Professional libraries and clearinghouse services tend to support this latter position, particularly those who see themselves bound by the Code of Ethics of the American Library Association. This code's adamant stand against censorship would make it difficult, if not impossible, to ethically justify selectively controlling access to library holdings based on the purposes for which such materials were to be used. This side is also supported by the fact that most libraries and clearinghouses who receive state or federal funds are contractually prohibited from denying the public access to their information. Even if such denial was legally or ethically justified, the selective denial of access is practically impossible when library and clearinghouse holdings are open to the public and/or available online.*

Restriction on Speech

♦♦ 184 ♦♦

You have applied and received a prevention services grant but have just been informed that there are contractual restrictions only allowing funds to be dispersed to agencies who take an adamant stand against the concept of "responsible drug use."

Discussion Question

Are there any ethical issues that could influence your consideration of the acceptance of these funds?

While the potential ethical issues that spill out of the "responsible use" controversy cannot be adequately summarized here, the principles of honesty and fidelity may prohibit the abdication of organizational values for transient gain. The ethical command of honesty demands congruence between word and action and that the values implicit in those words are not sacrificed for expediency or profit. If the prohibition against use of the concept of "responsible use" is congruent with an agency's historical philosophy, then there would be no contradictions in their acceptance of the grant award. If the agency's philosophy conflicts with this required position, then the agency would need to seriously consider refusing the grant.

Intrusive or Abusive Interventions

♦♦ 185 ♦♦

Following the drug-related deaths of two students, a newly formed parents' group presented a petition to the school board calling for mandatory random drug testing for all students that will be financed by local business and industry. The school board, in considering this proposal, has solicited your opinion as the local drug abuse prevention expert.

Discussion Questions

Separate from issues of practicality and effectiveness, what ethical issues, if any, do you see in mandatory testing of minors within a school system?

Are any of the ethical principles outlined in Chapter Two potentially violated through such testing?

There are a number of ethical issues that might be raised in the exploration of random testing of minors within the school environment. Proponents of such a proposal would have to address some of the following concerns:

Autonomy:	*Does the mandatory solicitation of body fluids from children and the supervision of "urine drops" constitute an unacceptable invasion of personal freedom and privacy?*
Justice:	*Would the procedural rights of students be rigorously protected through both the testing process and any subsequent disciplinary action?*
Nonmaleficence:	*Are there any sources of unforeseen and unintended harm that could occur through the implementation of such a program?*
Stewardship:	*Is the expenditure of funds to pay for laboratory testing of urine the best potential investment of community prevention resources?*

Proponents of testing programs would contend that the potential of testing to serve as a deterrent against drug experimentation outweighs any concerns raised by the above questions. What is your view?

A public school – like any other agency of government – must comply with the United States Constitution and with the constitution, statutes, regulations and court decisions of its state. There is currently no national statute governing drug testing of students. Various federal (and state) courts have ruled that drug testing is a "search" that may violate the federal and/or state constitution if the search is unreasonable.

In <u>Vernonia School District 47J v. Acton,</u> 115 S. Ct. 2386 (1995), the U.S. Supreme Court held that a public school district's random urinalysis drug testing of student athletes did not violate the students' federal or state constitutional right to be free from unreasonable searches, because the school district had an immediate, legitimate concern in preventing student athletes from using drugs. According to the Court, since student athletes do not have the same privacy expectation as adults, the invasion of the students' privacy interests was not significant. Some of the factors the Supreme Court considered to determine whether this school's policy was constitutional included: the circumstances in which testing was done, how the urine sample was collected, how accurate and fair the testing procedure was and what was done with the test results.

Drug testing certainly impacts a student's rights and associated legal accountability. Because the law is changing so quickly, any school considering instituting a program should consult an attorney familiar with the law in its state before taking any action. See Vignette #193 for additional search guidelines.

◆◆ 186 ◆◆

Nearly everyone is familiar with the "Scared Straight" program and the more recent advent of "Bootcamp" programs for drug-involved juvenile offenders. A principal in a middle school launched his own version of the "Scared Straight" approach which he affectionately referred to as "my prevention program." Students, who the principal determined to be at high risk for trouble (e.g., drugs, delinquency, and attitude), were removed from the school and taken on a tour of a nearby prison. The program had been specially planned by the principal. When the inmates asked at a planning meeting what their role was, the principal responded, "Scare them to death!" The students taken through this program were subjected to intense verbal abuse and intimidation. The first two groups of students who experienced this tour appeared to be terrified into transient meekness and compliance. Most of the parents responded positively to its observed effects. Immediately following the second tour, the parents of one of the participants complained that their son was emotionally anxious, had been having terrible recurrent nightmares, and had begun bed-wetting since his trip to the prison.

Discussion Question

Comment on the ethical issues raised by the principal's prevention program.

There are multiple risks associated with programs whose methods are invasive and potentially abusive. One involves the failure to get the informed consent of the parent or guardian for the participation of a minor. For a discussion on informed consent see Vignettes #4 and 71. Another issue is the effect of labeling. What effects would accompany the youth's selection to be a participant in the principal's prevention project? Would the participant's perception of himself or herself change as a result of his or her selection? Would any changes in how he or she was seen by his or her peers enhance rather than decrease social deviancy? Another risk is the potential untoward effects of the invasive or abusive experience. Even when such harshness of methods could be justified, there must be careful scrutiny in the selection process. The selection process should include screening devices to divert persons who might be potentially harmed by the experience. Where no such screening technology exists, serious consideration must be given as to whether the potential benefits of the program outweigh the program's potential risks. Even where the general effects of such programs are described positively, the potential for severe iatrogenic effects to a small number of students must be carefully weighed.

Early Intervention: Employee Assistance Programs (EAP) and Student Assistance Programs (SAP)

For SAP and EAP programs many legal issues can arise around:

- *General confidentiality of the record*
- *SAP disclosures to parents*
- *SAP disclosures to the school*
- *SAP disclosures to law enforcement*
- *Rights of minors*
- *Conflicts surrounding disclosure with the Family Educational Rights and Privacy Act (FERPA), 20 U.S.C. §1232(g)*

- *EAP disclosures to employers*
- *EAP disclosures to government regulatory authorities*
- *EAP self-referral restrictions*
- *Conflicts with state school codes governing records and reporting under 34 C.F.R. Part 99.*

For a thorough discussion on confidentiality issues for SAP and other school-based programs, consult the Legal Action Center's book entitled "Legal Issues for School-Based Programs." For employee assistance programs that perform drug testing, assessment and other referral services, you should consult the guidelines and regulations published by the U.S. Dept. of Transportation, Office of Drug and Alcohol Policy (202)366-3784 and 49 C.F.R. Part 383. Many of the rules governing disclosures under the confidentiality laws are addressed in Chapter 6. These are tricky areas, make sure your legal counsel is familiar with applicable federal as well as state confidentiality and records laws and regulations.

Integrity of Organizational Structure

◆◆ 187 ◆◆

An addiction treatment agency that offers EAP services contractually through a thinly-veiled sister corporation consistently and significantly underbids its EAP competitors. It does so based on the assumption that money lost through lower per capita fees paid by companies will be made up through increased treatment revenue generated through a pattern of preferential referral.

Discussion Questions

What ethical issues are involved in this practice?

What conflicts might arise for professionals working for this EAP?

There are ethical issues anytime the referral of an EAP client is based on anything other than the independent and objective assessment of a client's needs and where those needs can best be met. Conflicts of financial interest that can bias the assessment and referral process are a growing concern in the EAP field. Jim Wrich (1990) has painted a poignant picture of these potential conflicts by holding up the specter of a future in which half the EAP providers will be bought out by insurance and managed care industries in an effort to keep everyone out of treatment while the other half of the EAP providers will be bought out by treatment programs trying to admit everyone into treatment. The ethical mandate for the EAP counselor is to avoid both real and perceived conflicts of interest in the assessment and referral process.

If your EAP provides services to an employer covered under the U.S. Department of Transportation regulations, in most situations a substance abuse professional is prohibited from self-referring to its treatment and/or remedial education programs. See 49 C.F.R. Part 383 and more specifically 49 C.F.R. 382.605(e). Although the rules generally prohibit self-referral, some exceptions exist. You should also have a local attorney check your state laws as well as review the exemptions in the federal regulations. Additionally, some states have enacted health care legislation limiting referrals to entities in which a health care practitioner has a financial or investment interest.

Independence and Objectivity of Professional Judgment

♦♦ 188 ♦♦

Maya works for a freestanding employee assistance program that provides EAP services contractually to a wide variety of public and private sector organizations. Maya has just been contacted by a private treatment program that specializes in inpatient psychiatric and addiction treatment services for adult and adolescent clients. To acquaint Maya with their services, they are offering to pay all expenses to fly her in to visit their facilities for two days. Maya's sister, who she hasn't seen in over a year, lives 30 miles from the treatment facility site.

Discussion Questions

How should Maya respond to this offer?

How would accepting this trip (valued at $700) differ from accepting $700 in cash as a "gift" from this program?

The above vignette raises the question of appropriate boundary issues in the relationship between an assessment and referral service and the organizational resources to which it refers. The first concern in this situation is whether acceptance of the "free" trip will create a sense of obligation or duty to return the gift of the trip with client referrals. A second concern is whether or not the proximity of Maya's sister to the treatment agency and the desire to see her sister would unduly influence her decision to go or not go. Would this simply be mutual needs being met or would this be mutual exploitation: the program seeking to exploit the referral potential of the EAP counselor and the EAP counselor exploiting the offer of travel to visit her sister. There are ethical issues involving the twin commands of beneficence and nonmaleficence that must be addressed. Acceptance of the trip would be a breach of ethical conduct to the extent that it influenced and contaminated the objectivity of the EAP counselor in the client referral process. The same would be true of acceptance of money, gifts, free meals, or other goods or services provided by a service agency seeking the favor of the EAP counselor.

Definition of Client / Conflicts of Loyalty

♦♦ 189 ♦♦

You provide contractual EAP services to a local company with 3,000 employees. An employee of this company in seeking counseling services, describes as part of her current problems the unwanted sexual advances made by the Director of Human Resources. This employee is unaware of, and you are acutely aware of, the fact that this is the person within the company who awards the EAP contract and to whom the EAP contractor reports.

Discussion Questions

Would you inform this employee of the legal redress that may be available to her due to sustained sexual harassment and would you strongly encourage her to seek such redress?

Would you attempt to approach the Director of Human Resources and resolve the problem directly?

Would you become an advocate on behalf of this employee by supporting the submission of a formal complaint of harassment to the Vice President to whom the Director of Human Resources reports?

Who is your client in this situation?

How would you respond to this situation?

There is an enormous potential for conflicts of interests and conflicts of loyalty in this situation. The first responses of the EAP counselor should be a recognition of these potential conflicts, an acknowledgment of these conflicts to the client and an exploration of the most appropriate counseling resources within or outside the framework of the employee assistance program. Potential intervention steps could include:

- *advising the client that there are administrative and legal channels of redress*
- *advising the client that she could use emotional as well as legal counsel to explore her options and to proceed through a course of action*
- *advising the client of the relationship between the employee assistance program and the Director of Human Resources with assurances that her discussions will remain confidential (although if a sexual harassment lawsuit is filed against the company and/or the Director of Human Resources – it is highly unlikely that the client's discussions will remain confidential. There are legal procedures to compel disclosure. This of course depends on state law confidentiality protections and type of counseling provided. The type of counseling would dictate which confidentiality laws would apply on the state and federal levels.)*
- *advising the client that this relationship poses a conflict that could jeopardize the objectivity of the EAP counselor*
- *referring the client to an outside resource that could provide the needed emotional support and legal advice.*

Where no viable outside options for counseling exist, it would be advisable for the EAP counselor to seek external consultation to assure that the needs of the client are not being compromised by the financial interests and personal relationships of the employee assistance program personnel.

Environmental Stressors

♦♦ 190 ♦♦

You conduct assessment and referral services for a private EAP contractor. In the past six months you have assessed five employees who work within the same unit of the same company. All five were suffering from severe stress reactions generating not from stress in their personal lives, but from the stress experienced within the work environment of this unit. Although the stress reactions differed for the five employees, all reported the same stressors: staff shortages due to high turnover, excessive work demands, mandatory overtime, inadequate equipment, and an alcohol-impaired supervisor who is verbally abusive.

Discussion Questions

Do you have a responsibility to report these conditions?

Should you try to work through the company in order to change these conditions?

What ethical responsibility does an EAP professional have to his or her client(s) in this situation?

See analysis after next vignette.

♦♦ 191 ♦♦

EAP professionals are in unique roles to identify the incidence and prevalence of toxic working conditions within the companies for whom they work. What ethical responsibilities does the EAP professional have when he or she discovers:

- conditions or practices that pose a threat to worker safety or public safety
- discrimination based on age, sex, race, religion, or sexual orientation, or
- business practices that are a violation of law?

If the company is the "client" of the EAP contractor, is the EAP professionally bound to keep confidential knowledge about company practices obtained through the EAP role?

Let's explore four different potential points of view that would influence the EAP counselor's response to the above vignettes.

Position One: *The ultimate responsibility of the EAP counselor is to the needs of the individual employee being assessed. The source of stressors in the above situation is not important. What is important is the EAP counselor's ability to counsel and/or refer the above employees with the goal of decreasing the stress-related impairment to their personal health and job functioning. Getting caught up in politics of trying to change the work environment should be avoided because such efforts will serve as a diversion from the individual needs of the employees and will threaten the continued accessibility of EAP services to the employees of this company.*

Position Two: *The EAP counselor has a moral obligation to confront any organizational conditions that compromise the health of employees seeking services through the employee assistance program. Advocacy to alter toxic working conditions is an integral part of the EAP counselor role.*

Position Three: *The primary contractual obligation of the EAP counselor is to the company. While the needs of the individual client should be addressed to the greatest extent possible, the obligation of loyalty would not allow the EAP counselor to take any action which would harm the company. The EAP counselor is bound by confidentiality not to disclose information gained through EAP interviews in a manner that would do harm to the company or its representatives.*

Position Four: *The EAP counselor has a duty to uphold ethical and legal standards of professional conduct regardless of the needs or demands placed upon him or her by the individual EAP client or the company which contracts for EAP services. The ultimate loyalty of the EAP counselor should be to the profession. The EAP counselor cannot become an accomplice to illegal activity through his or her silence.*

The two vignettes involve potential conflicts of loyalty—loyalty to individual EAP clients and loyalty to the organization for which EAP services have been contracted. The four positions above represent the fixed points within which the EAP counselor must seek an appropriate course of action. It may be helpful, whenever possible, for the EAP counselor to see these as concurrent rather than competing loyalties. The counselor can then diplomatically seek areas of compromise in which the needs of employees seeking EAP services and the needs of the company can be mutually satisfied. General guidelines on the resolution of conflicts of loyalty include the following steps:

1. *Identify and clarify the nature of the loyalty conflicts.*
2. *Communicate the nature of the conflict to all parties involved.*
3. *Seek mutually agreeable solutions that can meet the needs of all involved parties.*
4. *When the parties interests are so incompatible as to make compromise impossible, seek clinical and legal consultation.*

In the first vignette, the EAP counselor could recommend that the individual employees develop more effective means of coping with the high stress work environment. At the same time, the EAP counselor could seek to positively effect the working conditions within this particular unit. The long-term interests of the employees and the interests of the company would both be met by the EAP counselor utilizing the chain of command—within the EAP and between the EAP and the company—to acknowledge the existence of specific conditions that compromise the health of employees. Such conditions will inevitably do harm to the company via employee turnover, increased absenteeism, stress-related health care costs, and poor employee morale.

In the second vignette, the EAP counselor would have to utilize the process of supervision to determine the best course of action—whether to take no action, whether to work within the company to get the illegal practices stopped, or to notify some external authority of the illegal activity. In making his or her decision, the EAP counselor will have to consider issues like the following:

- *Does the context in which the EAP counselor obtains information of the illegal activity fall within the normal confidentiality restrictions?*
- *Do the company's practices pose imminent or long-term harm to employees or the public?*
- *To what extent will the EAP counselor's failure to notify authorities of the illegal activity make him or her an accomplice to the action?*
- *Will the failure to act, or the act of disclosure, damage the reputation of the EAP counselor and the employee assistance program?*
- *How will disclosure affect employees' future accessibility to EAP services?*

See Chapter Eight for a discussion of threats to public safety encountered in the EAP role.

The situation described above may be one in which ethics and legal concerns may not be congruent. Depending on the nature of the allegations involved in the illegal conduct, the EAP counselor needs to be aware of causing or contributing to further legal problems for the client employee, the client company, him/herself and his/her organization. For example, in the second vignette, allegations of discrimination could result in a civil lawsuit initiated by the individual or the EEOC (Equal Employment Opportunity Commission) and allegations of unsafe work conditions could result in civil as well as criminal penalties and fines under OSHA (Occupational Safety and Health Administration) laws and regulations. An EAP counselor does not want to be the repository for information related to criminal violations, (e.g. price fixing, securities violations for insider trading, embezzlement, false statements to the government, or fraud and abuse). Otherwise, he or she could get dragged in as a witness or worse yet charged with obstruction of justice for failing to disclose information to the government. If there is a lawsuit, active government investigation or current prosecution, we advise the EAP counselor to do the following:

- *Only provide counseling within your expertise and training.*
- *Do not give legal advice or discuss legal issues.*
- *Do not elicit or discuss specific facts or incidents that may relate to an investigation.*
- *Do not counsel the clients with regard to specific circumstances relating to this investigation.*
- *Prior to discussing any issues with an employee, acknowledge that you are aware of the stressful situation due to the publicized or known allegations/violations.*
- *Assure the client that you are there to serve his/her needs for counseling and psychological assistance that may be required as a result of the increased stress.*
- *Inform the client for his/her protection and the protection of your agency that counselors do not discuss specific facts or incidents that may relate to this investigation or that relate to the business practices of the company that may or may not be inducing stress.*
- *Tell the client that your agency counselors are not prepared to give legal advice or discuss legal issues or counsel employees in any way that deals with specific circumstances of the investigation.*
- *Most importantly, inform the client that although conversations may be protected by state and federal confidentiality laws that apply to substance abuse and mental health treatment services, information can usually be obtained pursuant to an appropriate court order.*
- *Advise the client that the content of conversations may only be protected as a result of an attorney-client relationship and therefore, any concerns the client has that relate to the investigation should be discussed with his/her attorney.*

Early Intervention: Student Assistance Programs (SAP)
Confidentiality

◆◆ 192 ◆◆

You are a Student Assistance Program (SAP) counselor working contractually through your agency with a local middle school. Many students have met with you to discuss issues related to their drug usage have named a single supplier of their illicit drugs. The supplier is reported to be aggressively distributing drugs to middle and high school students. From the accounts of students, you also suspect that the dealer is trading drugs for sexual favors from some of the students.

Discussion Questions

What would you do, if anything, in response to this situation?

What ethical issues would dictate, or prevent, you taking action on this situation?

Can information be disclosed that was obtained from multiple interviews with different sources as long as the persons who made the disclosures are not identified? Would disclosure under these circumstances be a breach of confidentiality?

Many counselors in the above situation would find themselves torn between the normal strictures of confidentiality and the desire to stop the victimization of students via exploitive and predatory behavior. SAP counselors who have carefully weighed their responsibilities in this situation have drawn different conclusions. Some have taken the position that the risk of imminent harm is not specific enough to justify a breach of confidentiality and that any disclosure of information obtained in the counseling session without the client's permission is unethical. Other SAP counselors, aware of the risks associated with acting and the failure to act in the above circumstances, have sought some middle ground. Some have sought confirmation of the information with other students outside the context of counseling—information that could be shared without violating confidentiality. Some have sought permission from students to identify the supplier—without disclosing the identity of the students—to authorities who could investigate the situation.

In sorting through one's professional responsibilities in the above situation, the appropriateness of any proposed action could be assessed by the following questions:

1) Will the proposed course of action increase the vulnerability of one or more students to harm?

2) Will the proposed course of action undermine the current relationships between the SAP counselor and students who are involved in counseling?

3) *Will the proposed course of action potentially damage the reputation of the SAP counselor—decreasing the attractiveness of the Student Assistance Program to other students who might need the program's services in the future?*

4) *Does the proposed course of action intervene to prevent imminent harm where such harm is identifiable?*

5) *Is there a way to share information without disclosing any client identifying information?*

6) *Does your state have an intervenor immunity law that may legally protect your actions? Depending on your specific actions, such activities may be protected by state law; see for example, Illinois' Alcoholism and Drug Addiction Intervenor and Reporter Immunity Law, 745 ILCS 35/1.*

Disposition of Contraband

♦♦ 193 ♦♦

You are a SAP counselor at a high school working under a contract between a local drug abuse prevention agency and the school district. Sharon, a student who recently went through an inpatient addiction treatment program, enters your office to give you drugs that she just purchased. Sharon reports that she bought the drugs on impulse and knows she will use them if you don't take them.

Discussion Questions

Do you take possession of the drugs as requested? If so, what would you then do with them?

Would the confidentiality of the student be protected in the above situation in light of her illegal possession of drugs and the prohibition against possession of contraband on school property?

Is the fact that Sharon bought the drugs from someone on the school grounds a concern for the SAP counselor? Is it the counselor's job to seek the identity of those who sold the substance?

What policies exist regarding the receipt and disposal of drugs and other types of contraband?

There are three inter-related issues and interests woven through the above situation: the protection of the student, the protection of the SAP counselor, and the protection of the reputation of the school (and if applicable the external agency contractually providing the SAP counselor). To protect students, there needs to be mechanisms so that students can give drugs or other contraband (e.g., weapons) to staff. In the above case, for example, the ability to receive the drugs and provide immediate counseling may avert a relapse. At the same time, it is crucial that there be clear protocol established for the transfer and disposal of contraband once it is received. This protocol is most likely dictated by the school policies or possibly the state school code. On the federal level, there is a general statute relating to drug- and gun-free schools. Safe and Drug-Free Schools and Communities Act of 1994, 20 U.S.C. §7111.

The lack of or disregard of policies on contraband can lead to any number of potential problems. Other students could witness the presence of contraband in the SAP counselor's desk and rumors could fly about the SAP counselor's own drug use. In the midst of such rumors, a principal or local police could investigate and find illegal substances in the possession of the SAP counselor. The establishment of clear policies on the receipt, transfer and disposal of contraband can protect the personal, professional and institutional interests of everyone in incidents like the above. Protocol regarding confidentiality needs to be explicitly defined as part of the SAP planning process. In light of increased violence in the schools and corresponding concerns for student and school staff safety, the SAP program should also have specific protocols for addressing weapons.

If public schools experience high levels of violence and drug use, school officials may wish to consider adopting search policies that permit them under certain circumstances to screen students and search school property for weapons and drugs. Public school officials, like law enforcement officers, are State officers bound by the Fourth Amendment. Thus, school officials must understand the basic dictates of the Fourth Amendment--both to comply with the law and to implement an effective drug and weapons search policy. Before implementing a search policy, schools should consult the school attorney, the local district attorney, or the State attorney general. The general rule is school officials do not need a warrant or probable cause prior to conducting a search. The U.S. Supreme Court has held that schools have a substantial interest in maintaining security and order in the classroom and on school grounds. The Court has determined that this interest justifies a more flexible standard of reasonableness for student searches that are conducted by school officials as opposed to law enforcement officers. In order to conduct a search, school officials need only a "reasonable suspicion" that the search will turn up evidence that the student broke the law or the rules of the school. For example, the following have been held to be permissible searches:

- *searching a student's purse, after a teacher saw her smc* *and the student denied having smoked or being a smok*
- *searching a student's purse, after several other students s distributing firecrackers*
- *searching a student's pockets, based on a phone tip abou ᴊᵣom an anonymous source believed to have previously provided accurate information.*

Other guidelines for searches include:

- *A search of a student's jacket or book bag requires less suspicion than a physical pat-down or, at the extreme, a strip search. Courts consider strip searches to be highly intrusive of an individual student's privacy; thus, they should be premised only on probable cause.*
- *Courts are more likely to uphold searches conducted by school officials of lockers, secured desks, and other areas in which students store personal effects when certain steps are taken to reduce the reasonable expectation of privacy students may have in these areas.*
- *At the start of each academic year, school administrators should provide students with a written school policy of conducting random, unannounced searches throughout the year of student lockers, desks, and any other targeted areas within the school and specify that all such areas are "public," not "private."*

Outreach
Confidentiality/Duty to Disclose

♦♦ 194 ♦♦

Outreach workers are often exposed to and must work/live in very dichotomous worlds. In this marginal role, they sometimes see a hidden underworld of the community and become privy to a wide assortment of discomforting information. Andy works as a detached "street worker" out of a community-based prevention and early intervention program. In the past week, through the normal working of his information networks, he has heard numerous confessions of criminal activity, references to an impending fight between two gangs, reports of a prominent physician who has been purchasing enormous quantities of cocaine, and separate reports that a particular adolescent is talking about suicide.

ussion Question

Which ethical standards should guide what actions Andy takes in response to this information and to whom may Andy communicates such information?

not mapped

Ethical issues remain largely uncharted in the outreach worker's professional terrain. How does one operate in helping relationships that fall outside of the traditionally defined "counselor-client" relationship? What rules of confidentiality govern Andy's role in information dissemination, case-finding, informal referral for services with persons not formally defined as agency clients. In weighing what, if anything, he needs to do with the information above, Andy may need to consider some of the following ethical principles and questions:

- **Discretion:** *What information would a reasonable person in Andy's position keep confidential out of respect for the privacy of the person who shared the information? Should personal confidences that pose no threats to others be treated with the same strictness of confidentiality as the counselor-client relationship? (See Chapter 6 for guidance on who is a client protected by federal confidentiality regulations).*
- **Honesty and Fidelity:** *What expectations of confidentiality have been communicated or implied to those persons from whom the information was received? Was the information passed to Andy specifically for the purpose of some action being taken?*
- **Beneficence:** *What action could be taken to protect, support, or prevent harm to persons referenced in the information received? Does the story of the adolescent considering suicide warrant immediate disclosure and intervention? (Consult Chapter 8 for an in depth discussion on duty to warn and public safety issues).*
- **Nonmaleficence:** *What inadvertent consequences could proceed from the act of disclosure? What imminent harm is likely to occur if no disclosure is made or no action is taken? Does the potential threat to public safety of a cocaine-addicted physician demand disclosure and supervisory review of potential courses of action?*
- **Loyalty:** *Could Andy's and the agency's ability to continue service to this client population be harmed, via damage to reputation, by disclosure or failure to disclose.*
- **Self-interest:** *What actions might be necessary for Andy to take in order to protect his own vulnerability and liability after receiving the above information? Through what mechanisms are decisions to disclose or not*

to disclose, including the supervisory review process, documented?

Such issues are complex and raise conflicts over competing duties. Access to regular and rigorous supervision is essential for outreach workers. Charting an ethical course of action through supervisory consultation is a process of reaching best mutual judgment rather than a process of applying arbitrary rules or prescriptions.

Worker Vulnerability

♦♦ 195 ♦♦

You have just been funded to begin an innovative outreach program aimed at reducing HIV transmission among intravenous drug users. The project calls for a cadre of outreach workers to penetrate social networks of drug users and attempt to shift these individuals from high-risk to low-risk methods of drug ingestion via education and personal persuasion. Two of the finalists you are considering for an outreach worker position are recovering addicts with less than one year of recovery time.

Discussion Questions

What ethical issues are involved in sending addicts early in recovery into social networks of active drug users?

Would you hire these individuals? If so, how might you structure this job so as to reduce the personal risks of relapse?

What ethical responsibilities does the agency have to address "occupational safety and health" issues of outreach workers who will be paid to work daily in a predatory and increasingly violent subculture?

Placing addicted persons with minimal recovery time in professional roles that expose them to environments saturated with drug-enhancing sensory cues is a highly questionable practice. The stories of relapse which emerge from such experiments are prolific. Recovering persons may be high-risk for such environments regardless of the duration of their continuous sobriety. The program's ethical mandate is to refrain from placing any employee into situations likely to compromise their health and safety. Compliance with this mandate requires careful screening of job candidates and the development of significant support structures for the outreach worker. Screening of candidates might include a review of such factors as:

- *the vulnerability—naivete, curiosity, immaturity—for drug use through exposure to the culture of addiction for those candidates without adequate addiction/treatment recovery histories*
- *the duration and stability of the candidate's program of personal recovery for those who present with addiction/treatment/recovery histories (although you need to be careful establishing minimum sobriety requirements, see Vignette #140 in Chapter 7 addressing this issue)*
- *the candidate's familiarity with "street" culture, e.g., knowledge of culture of addiction, ability to accurately read verbal and non-verbal cues related to safety*
- *vulnerabilities of physical and emotional health that might be compromised in the outreach worker role*
- *the scope and intensity of the candidate's social replenishment network.*

Practices that can support the health and safety of outreach staff working within the culture of addiction would include the following:

- *utilizing two person outreach teams as opposed to individual assignments*
- *detailed training related to assessing and managing threats to physical safety*
- *permission to not enter or immediately leave any environment that poses a risk to the physical/psychological safety of the worker*
- *creating an emergency response protocol for a worker in trouble in the field*
- *mandatory supervisory debriefing on an almost a daily basis*
- *access to other outreach workers for personal and professional support*
- *strong encouragement and support for personal programs of recovery, e.g., not scheduling work assignments to conflict with self-help meetings*
- *utilization of staff meetings, training opportunities, professional meetings as a means of support and replenishment*
- *active support of the treatment of any persons who relapse while in an outreach role.*

Relationship Boundaries

♦♦ 196 ♦♦

Ricky is an outreach worker who has become well known in the gay community for his long history of service working in projects sponsored by the community AIDS foundation. For the past two years, Ricky has worked in AIDS education serving as a point of contact for information, service referral, crisis management and informal counseling. His office is the streets and bars and other gathering places within the gay community. He is a one-man campaign on the role of alcohol and drug use in the continued spread of HIV within the gay community. Ricky's worklife and lifestyle are almost inseparable. The world of his work and the world of his personal life share the same physical and social space. He claims membership in the same community as his clients.

Discussion Questions

When indigenous persons are recruited to work professionally within such communities, what distinguishes lovers, friends, and acquaintances from "clients?"

How could Ricky separate, for example, information received as a member of this community versus information he received in his work role?

What, if anything, would separate appropriate from inappropriate social or sexual relationships between Ricky and his clientele?

Outreach workers are in a particularly nebulous ethical quandary when they are highly visible members of the community they serve professionally. In such circumstances, the line between one's personal and private life becomes particularly difficult to define. An essential step in providing some degree of role clarity for these outreach workers would be for agency or project level management to answer the following questions:

- *Is the outreach worker-client (or whatever name we give those who are the consumers of the outreach services) relationship characterized by an inequity of power and/or emotional vulnerability that could result in harm or exploitation?*
- *Are there special duties and obligations inherent in the relationship between the outreach worker and his or her individual service constituents?*
- *Is the effectiveness of the service relationship between the outreach worker and client compromised by concurrent social, sexual, and financial relationships as would be the case in a counselor-client relationship?*
- *What boundaries of appropriateness will the outreach worker be held accountable to in his or her relationships with clients/constituents/*

consumers?

Compensation

◆◆ 197 ◆◆

A pilot project designed to work with chemically dependent women and their children is about to be replicated through all regions of the state following the very positive evaluation of the pilot service sites. The five-year evaluation report as well as everyone associated with the project attribute much of the program's success to an aggressive and innovative approach to in-home services provided by indigenous outreach workers. The outreach workers were known to have initiated and sustained client involvement in the treatment process through skill and tenaciousness. In spite of the praise of the outreach workers, a close scrutiny of the project budget reveals that the outreach workers were often paid as little as one third the salary of "professional" staff working on the project.

Discussion Question

Comment on any ethical issues inherent within such differences in compensation.

There is a concern that indigenous outreach workers within health and human service agencies—among whom women and people of color are highly represented—are exploited for their talents through unjust compensation. There are many projects whose success is attributed to the skills and passionate involvement of outreach workers. Yet their salaries are markedly less than other staff, there exists no supports for their continued education, and there are no structured career ladders or paths to provide for their future. In short, their importance is matched by their expendability. Under such circumstances, it is little wonder that an outreach worker cast aside in a funding cut or at the end of a grant has the sense of having being used. The ethical principle of justice calls for the distribution of rewards by merit. In the case of outreach workers, it may be time that the factors used to determine merit are reassessed. It is of particular concern that people whose life circumstances have precluded access to education and whose successful job performance involves knowledge and skills not achieved through traditional education, should have their value judged so arbitrarily. The principle of fairness calls for the careful review of systems of compensation and the extent to which such systems may have been unduly influenced by classism, sexism, and racism.

Training

Use of Agency Resources for Personal Gain

◆◆ 198 ◆◆

Jerome delivers addiction-related workshops and seminars throughout the United States as an employee of a training institute.

Discussion Questions

Comment on the following practices.

- Jerome accumulates a considerable number of free trips through frequent flyer programs sponsored by the airlines. Jerome uses these free trips for his own personal vacations without formal permission or negotiation with his employer.
- Due to his membership in certain frequent flyer programs, Jerome always tries to schedule flights with United or TWA so that he can get the benefit of frequent flyer miles. As a result of this practice, organizations contracting for training sometimes pay higher travel fees than are available.
- When Jerome drives to a training event in his home state, he is paid $30 per day for meals if he leaves before 6:00 a.m. and returns after 6:00 p.m. Jerome often leaves earlier than necessary just to receive the benefit of the meal reimbursements.

These are examples of how an employee can manipulate the work environment for his or her own financial advantage. Benefits such as free trips obtained through the expenditure of agency resources should accrue to the agency unless negotiated as a specific perk for those who travel excessively. The manipulation of work structures for financial gain unduly depletes agency resources, breaches the values of honesty, loyalty and stewardship in the employee-employer relationship, and can, as in the case of the above situation, breach the same values in the relationship between an agency and its external clients.

Self-disclosure

♦♦ 199 ♦♦

Betty, a recovering alcoholic who works for an addiction studies training institute, spends the majority of her time speaking to professional audiences about various dimensions related to the assessment and treatment of addiction.

Discussion Questions

Under what conditions would it be appropriate or inappropriate for Betty to self-disclose her status as a recovering person?

What factors should be considered in this decision?

If Betty is an active member of a 12 step program such as Alcoholics Anonymous, how can she speak to professional groups about AA without inadvertently violating AA's tradition of anonymity?

What standards should guide the professional trainer (recovering and non-recovering) to avoid the appearance that they represent or speak for a 12 Step Program?

There are direct parallels between the issue of counselor self-disclosure discussed in Chapter Six and the issue of trainer self-disclosure. The ethical question posed to a trainer working under a contractual obligation of service is simply this: whose needs are being met through the use of this self-disclosure—the trainer or those of the trainees? It is a question of whether the self-disclosure constitutes a technique of teaching or public confession—a learning tool for the trainee or a tool of catharsis for the trainer. The acknowledgment of a trainer's recovery status must be done carefully, if at all. Both recovering and non-recovering trainers need to explicitly define who they speak for and who they do not speak for. It is advisable for all persons in training roles to acknowledge that they speak about—NOT on behalf of—12 step recovery programs and that they will be speaking from knowledge based on professional, rather than personal, perspectives of these programs. Acknowledging affiliation with a particular recovery program may or may not—depending on the training context—be a breach of compliance with the anonymity tradition governing the group life of most 12 step programs. Self-disclosure of support group affiliation in a closed training context—outside the purview of press or other public media—might not be a violation of anonymity, but might still represent a violation of the trainer's pledge of service to the needs of the trainees. If the self-disclosure serves the trainer's needs rather than, and at the expense of, the trainees' needs, then it breaches the promise of service made to the trainees by the trainer. To the extent that self-disclosure is viewed by trainees as an exercise in narcissistic exhibitionism, the service relationship has been harmed by the act of self-disclosure, diminishing the trainer's capacity to serve.

Relationship Boundaries

♦♦ 200 ♦♦

Mark is a part-time counselor in an addiction treatment program who spends the remainder of his professional time working contractually as a trainer on addiction-related topics. Most of his training activities involve 3 to 5 day residential training experiences that bring together trainees from throughout his state. Over the past two years, Mark has developed a fairly consistent pattern of sexual involvement with trainees during these training retreats.

Discussion Questions

Do the ethical boundaries that preclude counselor-client sexual involvement extend to the trainer-trainee relationship?

If a fundamental difference in the therapist-client and trainer-trainee relationship is the duration of power inequity and the duration of vulnerability, could a trainer get involved with a trainee *after* a training event without being suspected of a breach in ethical conduct?

Would a trainer who was attracted to a trainee be ethically prohibited from pursuing that relationship after the training event was over? Where the prohibition against a therapist-client sexual relationship might last forever, might any prohibition against a trainer-trainee sexual relationship be relatively time-limited?

Discuss ethical issues and standards related to this situation.

While the inequity of power and the vulnerabilities within the trainer-trainee relationship differ in intensity and duration from those found in the therapist-client relationship, there is still the potential for unethical and exploitive conduct within the milieu of training. This potential may differ according to training format and trainee group composition. One could posit that a trainer who presents for one hour to 300 people has less power to exploit this medium than a trainer involved in a five-day, highly experiential training process with 20 participants. The latter could, at least, for the time-span of the training, closely approximate the inequity of power and emotional vulnerability of the therapist-client relationship. Mark's behavior in the above vignette would raise ethical issues to the extent that the following conditions existed:

- *trainees were subjected to unwanted sexual advances by the trainer violating the trainee's physical and psychological safety*
- *the training content and process resulted in a significant imbalance of power in the trainer-trainee relationship that diminished the free choice and powers of assertion of the trainee*
- *the trainer manipulated the emotional vulnerability of the trainee for the sexual gratification of the trainer, e.g., sexually approaching the trainee at a time his or her defenses were weakened*
- *the trainer utilized deceit or coercion in soliciting sexual favors, (e.g., framing the sexual relationship as part of the training experience, misrepresenting the nature of the relationship, or threatening removal of the trainee from the training group), if sexual favors were not granted.*

A pattern of predatory sexual behavior by a trainer within the training milieu breaches the fundamental contract of service that requires the trainer to structure the training process to meet the learning needs of trainees.

Marketing of Seminars

♦♦ 201 ♦♦

A brochure marketing a workshop on family counseling clearly outlines learning objectives and notes that the learning methodologies used in the workshop will include lecture and discussion of videotaped vignettes from family counseling sessions. During the workshop, the trainer alters the agenda and learning methodologies without negotiation with the trainees. Workshop participants find themselves suddenly "volunteered" to play key roles in psychodramatic recapitulations of their own families of origin.

Discussion Questions

What ethical issues are involved in this situation?

What guidelines should govern the use of highly experiential training methods?

A marketing brochure for a training event constitutes a promissory agreement between the trainer and his or her audience. Trainees chose to come to the workshop based on the learning objectives and teaching methods outlined in the brochure and reiterated at the beginning of the workshop. For a trainer to arbitrarily and significantly alter this content or the teaching methodologies without negotiation with the training audience is a breach of this promissory agreement. Principles of honesty and fidelity demand congruence between the workshop promoted and the workshop delivered.

Professional Impairment

♦♦ 202 ♦♦

You are conducting a workshop with more than 35 participants representing health and human service workers from a variety of agencies in your state. The workshop involves a number of small and large group discussions. By mid-morning, it is quite obvious that you have a participant who is highly impaired. The participant is experiencing flight of ideas, rambling incoherently, misinterpreting and personalizing other participant responses as highly threatening, and aggressively challenging comments by other participants and by you. By late morning, he retorts to the group, "well, if you aren't going to listen to my ideas, I'm just not going to share them; it's your loss" and remains silent. At the afternoon break, the participant leaves the workshop and doesn't return. The participant runs a private counseling practice that includes the assessment of DUI offenders.

Discussion Question

What duties and responsibilities do you have as the trainer in such a situation?

There are multiple interests that must be protected in the above vignette. The impaired participant must be managed to minimize his disruptiveness to the learning of the other participants. In short, the contractual agreement for learning must be kept with the participants. The trainer must also tend to the psychological safety of the impaired member who may be vulnerable to scapegoating by the group. Protection of the impaired trainee may involve supportive comments aimed at deactivating the trainee's defensiveness as well as actively diverting or dissipating group hostility targeted at the trainee. A more difficult issue is the potential threat to public safety resulting from the trainee's impairment within his professional practice. Given that this trainee works by himself in private practice, the trainer may be one of the few persons in a position to detect and intervene to address the impairment. If the trainer judges the trainee's impairment to pose a threat to his clients or to the public, the trainer is ethically bound to bring the potential of impairment to the attention of some investigative body. The trainer could potentially contact the state counselor certification agency, the state agency that licenses and monitors DUI evaluation services, or the presiding circuit judge within whose courts the impaired professional's DUI evaluations are received.

◆◆ 203 ◆◆

You coordinate an addiction counselor training program that involves two years of formal classroom training and a supervised field experience. One of your students, Leonard, a recovering alcoholic, who is 18 months into the training program and scheduled to begin his field supervision experience next month, comes in today and confesses that he has relapsed.

Discussion Questions

How would you respond to this situation?

What potential ethical issues are involved in Leonard's continued participation in the program?

There are multiple issues involved in this situation. There is the threat to Leonard's health due to the relapse and some implied duties of the training program to support and protect Leonard's health. There is a potential threat to clients posed by an impaired intern or worker within the field. Depending on Leonard's drinking-related behaviors, there may also be potential threats to public safety, e.g., drinking and driving. There is also a threat to the reputation of the program if it is known to enroll actively drinking alcoholics. An approach that would address all of the varied interests might involve the following steps:

- *Provide strong encouragement and support for Leonard to seek treatment or otherwise reactivate his recovery program.*
- *Assess any immediate threats to himself or others posed by Leonard's return to drinking, e.g., the intention to drive home from the office of the*

training program while intoxicated.

- *Provide Leonard a health-related leave of absence from the training program.*

- *Reassess the appropriateness of Leonard's career choice of addiction counseling after, and only when, he has re-established a stable program of sobriety.*

Use of Clients in Training

♦♦ 204 ♦♦

Thomas has developed a new clinical technique for working with adult survivors of sexual abuse who have had difficulty maintaining sobriety. Thomas has written several professional articles on this technique and has begun to get many speaking engagements to describe it. To illustrate this technique, Thomas has asked several of his current clients if they would be willing to participate in a live session to demonstrate the technique at a professional meeting.

Discussion Questions

What ethical issues are raised by this situation?

What universal values are at greatest risk of violation in this situation?

The inclusion of clients in training in a way that identifies them as clients must first meet the earlier discussed standards of confidentiality. The question is whether any request of a client to participate in such an arena is inherently so coercive as to defy the concept of informed consent. In other words, is the power differential between the counselor and a particular client so great as to render refusal an impossibility? The potential harm to the client and the client-counselor relationship would nearly always exclude use of clients in a training format. Where witnessing clinical work is essential for training, this must be done in a way as to reduce the potential harm to the client. For example, in order to use the videotapes of an actual client session, the client much first grant permission for their use. In addition, great caution must be taken in not abandoning the fiduciary obligation to the client and conducting sessions not with a focus on the needs of the client, but on the needs of potential trainees who are or will potentially witness the session. It is very difficult under such circumstances not to shift the focus of the session from what the client is feeling, thinking and doing to what the counselor is feeling, thinking and doing.

See Vignette #4 and 71 in Chapter 6 for an analysis of informed consent issues and confidentiality concerns when involving clients in training or other activities that could be considered exploitation of clients.

Consultation
Confidentiality

♦♦ 205 ♦♦

Sonya has served as an organizational consultant to a large number of addiction treatment agencies and private businesses. She is also a prolific writer and is often called upon to make speeches at professional conferences. Sonya has routinely integrated stories drawn from her consultation experiences into her articles and speeches. Although she refers to her consultation clients by name and summarizes her consultation methodologies and their outcomes with particular agencies, she has been very careful not to disclose information she believes would harm the agency in any manner. It has not occurred to Sonya that formal permission should be obtained from her organizational clients prior to such disclosure.

Discussion Questions

What rules of confidentiality should apply to this situation?

Do confidentiality expectations apply even where no discussion of confidentiality has occurred?

There is implied, and often contractually mandated, confidentiality governing the relationship between a consultant and his or her organizational clients. There are two basic ways that Sonya can ethically incorporate her consulting experiences into her articles and speeches. The first is to ask permission of her clients for such inclusion. The request should specify both the range of information to be disclosed and the precise audiences to which disclosure would be targeted. The second option is to delete the name and all information that would identify the organization from any story or anecdote. Where an organization or event is so unique as to defy masking of the organizational identity, then no disclosure can ethically occur without the permission of the organizational client.

Support of Toxic Organizational Conditions

♦♦ 206 ♦♦

Ricardo has a long and distinguished history as an organizational consultant to prevention and addiction treatment agencies and other health and human service organizations. His name is always on the preferred consultant list for anyone seeking outside assistance to help with organizational problems. Over the past five years, a large service agency has developed the following pattern of interaction with Ricardo. At a time of internal crisis (three such crises in the five years), the agency contacts Ricardo to come in and provide assistance for a variety of presenting problems, most of which have severely impacted staff morale. For each of the three times, Ricardo used a process of problem identification and strategy development that involved all agency staff and resulted in a detailed plan of action. In each case, the agency failed to follow through on the plan; in each case, staff involvement and hope was elevated and then dashed.

Discussion Questions

How should Ricardo respond to the next request for help from the agency during a time of crisis?

Are there ethical issues involved in a consultant's complicity in being used to bail an organization out of crisis that has no apparent intention of resolving fundamental problems of leadership, structure or process?

Ricardo must ask himself whether he is being used to avoid or to facilitate change. There is concern that Ricardo's services are being used to sustain, rather than eliminate, toxic organizational conditions. There is a concurrent concern that the repeated use of Ricardo's services in this manner could damage his professional reputation as an organizational consultant. Organizational consultants who find themselves in such a dilemma may consider a number of the following options:

- *confront the contracting agency with what appears to be a historical breach of good faith by not addressing problems identified within the consultation scope of work*
- *refuse to do further work with the contracting agency*
- *structure any future contracts in definable stages, with each successive stage of work being contingent upon clearly defined actions on the part of the contracting agency.*

Research

As you review and contemplate the ethical issues posed in the Vignettes 207 through 212, keep in mind the legal implications of acts or omissions in these case studies. Clinical research is an area of increased legal and regulatory scrutiny that will only continue to grow. The most common ethical/legal issue that arises is informed consent. The Nurenberg principles provide general ethical guidance on consent and the necessity that the consent be voluntary (The Belmont Report–Ethical Principles and Guidelines for the Protection of Human Subject for Research, OPRR Reports, Apr. 18, 1979.) Those principles define voluntary consent as the research subject's legal capacity to give consent; that the person should be able to exercise free power of choice, without the intervention of any element of force, fraud, deceit, duress, over-reaching, or other ulterior form of constraint or coercion; and should have sufficient knowledge and comprehension of the elements of the subject matter involved as to enable the subject to make an understanding and enlightened decision. That last element is informed consent. For human subjects' research, the issue of "informed consent" is defined by federal regulation. See 45 C.F.R. §116. State statutes and regulations may also have requirements for research informed consent, however, the federal regulations will supercede control unless the state regulations are more stringent.

The federal regulations governing informed consent require the following information to be provided to each research subject:

• a statement that the study involves research, an explanation of the purposes of the research and the expected duration of the subject's participation, a description of the procedures to be followed, and identification of any procedures that are experimental

• a description of any reasonably foreseeable risks or discomforts to the subject

• a description of any benefits to the subject or to others that may reasonably be expected from the research

• a disclosure of appropriate alternative procedures or courses of treatment, if any, that might be advantageous to the subject

• a statement describing the extent, if any, to which confidentiality of records identifying the subject will be maintained

• for research involving more than minimal risk, an explanation as to whether any compensation will be given and an explanation as to whether any medical treatments are available if injury occurs and, if so, what they consist of, or where further information may be obtained

- provision of a contact person for answers to pertinent questions about the research and research subjects' rights, and whom to contact in the event of a research-related injury to the subject
- a statement that participation is voluntary, refusal to participate will involve no penalty or loss of benefits to which the subject is otherwise entitled, and that the subject may discontinue participation at any time without penalty or loss of benefits to which the subject is otherwise entitled. 45 C.F.R. §46.117.

When appropriate, the following additional information is also required under the federal regulations to be provided to each subject:

- a statement that the particular treatment or procedure may involve risks to the subject (or to the embryo or fetus, if the subject is or may become pregnant) which are currently unforeseeable
- anticipated circumstances under which the subject's participation may be terminated by the investigator without regard to the subject's consent
- any additional costs to the subject that may result from participation in the research
- the consequences of a subject's decision to withdraw from the research and procedures for orderly termination of participation by the subject
- a statement that significant new findings developed during the course of the research which may relate to the subject's willingness to continue participation will be provided to the subject
- the approximate number of subjects involved in the study.

In addition to informed consent, other areas have heightened attention from federal law enforcement officials as well as the Office for Human Research Protection (OHRP). As a result, programs engaging in research need to be cognizant of (1) institutional review board (IRB) requirements; (2) IRB composition requirements; (3) procedural issues regarding expedited review of research; (4) other requirements in the regulations governing humans subjects protections; and (5) funding contract or grant requirements. Currently, the federal law enforcement agencies are examining numerous clinical research grants as part of the federal anti-fraud effort. Recent investigations resulted in the return of $20 million in grant funds for one university and the shutdown of all human subjects research at two other universities. (See Journal of Health Care Compliance, Vol. No. 6, page 15, November, 1999.)

If a program conducts clinical research funded by the government, it must also comply with the Public Health Service Misconduct in Science Regulations. 42 C.F.R. Part 50. These regulations impose a responsibility on research staff not only to prevent unethical behavior in research, but also to be alert to and deal effectively with instances in which unethical research behavior is suspected. The types of misconduct could include deliberate falsification of data, ranging from outright fabrication to purposeful plagiarism, misappropriation of others' ideas, or other practices that seriously deviate from practices accepted in the scientific community. The mechanisms for reporting, investigating and addressing unethical behavior in research depend on whether an organization has a corporate compliance officer, a research integrity committee, an IRB or a combination of the above would dictate. The regulations also prescribe certain annual reporting requirements as well as immediate notifications depending on the violations.

Sponsorship of Research

♦♦ 207 ♦♦

An addiction treatment program, after some years of pressure to report treatment outcome data to local and state funding sources, assigned a staff member to conduct a follow-up study of clients who had gone through treatment during the past five years. When the study was completed, the program widely circulated the results of the study, but did not identify who had sponsored the research or who had conducted it. The report only included that the treatment program had been evaluated and what the findings were.

Discussion Questions

Does failure to disclose who sponsored a particular study constitute a breach of professional ethics?

If an outside agent had wanted to fund the research but wished their sponsorship to remain secret, what ethical issues would be raised by such agreement of secrecy?

The ethical principle of honesty demands a full disclosure of contextual elements of research so that its scientific integrity can be assessed and assured. In this case, the researcher (staff member) may have a vested interest in the outcome of the research such that the conduct or interpretation of the research could be compromised. It is not the conduct of the research by internal staff that poses ethical problems, but maintaining the secrecy of the sponsor (in this case, self-sponsored) and the relationship between the sponsor and the research team (employer-employee). Such issues could be addressed by:

- *fully identifying the researchers and their credentials so others may make reasonable judgements about the qualifications of those conducting the research*
- *fully disclosing the nature of the sponsor-research team relationship*
- *providing a detailed presentation of the research methodology so that its integrity and rigor can be evaluated*
- *making raw data available to other researchers for independent evaluation.*

Research with Human Subjects

♦♦ 208 ♦♦

Bernard is a new outpatient therapist at an addiction treatment agency. Since his prior work had been in primary mental health, Bernard has been quite fascinated by various controversies surrounding the most appropriate addiction treatment interventions and the paucity of research available to answer such questions. Deciding that he can help answer some of his own questions with some informal research, Bernard decides to randomly assign his next forty clients to one of two very different counseling approaches and then follow the clients to see how the treatment outcomes differ for the two groups. Two months into this process, Bernard happens to mention to you (his supervisor) for the first time this informal research he is conducting.

Discussion Questions

How do you respond?

What ethical issues are raised by such informal research?

Bernard cannot escape the ethical mandates guiding research with human subjects simply by thinking of his research as "informal." To meet the normal protocol for research involving humans, Bernard would have to conduct such activities as:

- *develop a formal research plan that details the research design and an analysis of potential benefits and risks to participants involved in the research*
- *seek formal approval through the appropriate Institutional Review Board*
- *assure a process of informed consent for all persons participating in his study.*

Just a few of the ethical issues raised by Bernard's informal research would include the following:

- *The random assignment of clients to the two treatment approaches would violate the agreement that clients will be assigned to treatment activities based on an objective assessment of their individual needs.*
- *Withholding information from the clients that they are research subjects is a breach of honesty in the helping relationship.*
- *Failing to provide a process of informed consent through which the client is oriented to risks and benefits of the research and offered an opportunity to accept or refuse participation without coercion violates client autonomy.*

Confidentiality, Security and Disposition of Data

♦♦ 209 ♦♦

A follow-up study is being conducted of clients in which interviews are being tape recorded, transcribed and then analyzed. The resulting report will include excerpts from the client interviews to illustrate key findings.

Discussion Question

What procedures would you recommend related to the confidentiality, security, and eventual disposition of the tapes and transcripts?

A research protocol for this study should generally include a detailed description of the following:

- *the informed consent process that will be used with all clients participating in the study*
- *procedures for protecting the identity of the client (by not using the name in the audiotape or in the case of videotape, keeping the camera on the counselor)*
- *a specific client consent process for taping and transcribing interviews that will include informing the client of the eventual disposition of the tapes, (e.g. "All tapes and transcripts will be erased following the completion of the final research report") (This consent must be written and adhere to the requirements in 42 C.F.R. §2.31 – see analysis in Vignette #71 in Chapter 6).*

- *an orientation on confidentiality that will be used with all transcriptionists working with client tapes*
- *a plan for controlled access and storage of tapes and transcripts*
- *a plan for, and person designated in control of, destruction or long-term storage of tapes and transcripts in accordance with applicable research grant requirements, federal confidentiality security and research requirements (42 C.F.R. §2.16 and §2.52) as well as disposition of records in accordance with applicable record retention requirements.*

The purpose of such procedures is to assure the confidentiality of research participants and to assure that use of the data does not extend beyond the parameters of use that were agreed upon as conditions for participation.

Scientific Role Versus Clinical Role

♦♦ 210 ♦♦

A follow-up study of adolescents and their families following substance abuse treatment was conducted using addiction counselors as trained interviewers for the study. You have been hired and oriented as one of the interviewers. Each interview consists of a one-hour structured interview in which data is solicited on post-treatment client and family functioning. In about 75% of the cases, you are able to conduct a straightforward interview and solicit all of the needed information. In the other 25% of the interviews, clients get into painful self-disclosure about the problems they have encountered since they left treatment. Some have intimated thoughts of suicide and others have referenced their need to get back in treatment. Your instincts are to respond to these disclosures as a counselor rather than as a researcher. The time constraints won't allow for a full clinical response to these clients needs and still allow you to collect all of the data you have been hired to collect.

Discussion Questions

How would you resolve the above conflict?

How does the researcher collect scientific data from clients who present problems of great immediacy and intensity that need assistance?

This vignette involves conflicts of loyalty between the researcher's contractual obligations to collect data and his or her human and professionally enhanced obligation to respond to persons in pain or crisis. The PRIMARY responsibility of the researcher in this situation is to collect scientific data and to conduct the interview in a manner that assures the most complete and objective presentation of information from the client. At the same time, the clinical researcher cannot simply ignore persons in imminent crisis. Resolution of these conflicting responsibilities can be enhanced by actions such as the following:

- *Clearly define the purpose of the interview with the client and the role of the interviewer focusing on the distinction between information collection and problem resolution.*
- *Allow an adequate amount of time for the interview, recognizing that data collection involving very personal areas of life functioning is likely to be accompanied by strong emotion (clients should have adequate time to both report information and emotionally re-center themselves prior to exiting the interview).*
- *Arrange availability for direct and timely linkage for counseling services for those clients in crisis or who wish to seek additional help.*

Honesty in Reporting Findings

♦♦ 211 ♦♦

You are the principal investigator of the evaluation of a highly politicized service initiative within your state. The program was launched two years ago by the Attorney General to fuel his future candidacy for Governor. As a result of this political context, the program you are evaluating has received enormously positive press coverage. The state agency representatives that contracted for the evaluation research on the project have become quite concerned about the findings and tone of the evaluation report. As you complete the tabulation and analysis of the data, you are getting enormous pressure from multiple sources to frame the outcomes in the most positive terms. There are numerous references to how much future contractual work may be available if this particular report is well-received.

Discussion Question

What ethical issues are raised by the interpretation of data and recommendations in the above context?

The researcher has enormous control over the selection, presentation and interpretation of data. The primary ethical question in the above vignette is whether scientific integrity will be sacrificed for long-term financial gain. If the investigator capitulates to the political and financial pressure by positively framing interpretations and recommendations that are unsupported by the true findings of the research, a number of ethical breaches will occur and will further unfold from this action. These breaches include the following:

- *There will be a breach in honesty through the misrepresentation of the effect and value of the project.*
- *There will be a breach in professional fidelity to the principles of scientific research and to the promises inherent within the contract for the project.*
- *There will be a breach in the principle of professional competence: errors resulting not from lack of knowledge and skill, but from exploitive self-interest.*
- *There will be a potential breach in the principle of nonmaleficence if, as a result of the distorted findings in the research report, resources continue to be allocated to a project that may have no effect or potentially harmful effects.*
- *There will be a potential breach in the principle of stewardship if continued and potentially expanded funding of the evaluated project will deny resources to other service projects of potentially greater need and effectiveness.*
- *There may also be a violation of a research integrity policy, funding contract condition or federal regulation governing misconduct in science.*

In addition to the above, scrutiny of the research report by the scientific community may lead to a recognition and public exposure of the extent of distortion resulting in damage to the reputation of the researcher and the research community as a whole.

Responsibility for Use of New Knowledge

♦♦ 212 ♦♦

One of the exciting areas of addiction research is the search for biological markers that could identify high risk for addiction prior to exposure to alcohol and other drugs. Researchers predict a day in the not too distant future when an economical and reliable mass screening process could screen and identify grade school children at high-risk for adult alcoholism and other addictive diseases.

Discussion Questions

If the discovery of such biological markers and mass screening devices were available today, what ethical issues might be raised related to their misuse?

Is it the responsibility of the researcher to explore the potential misuse or misapplication of his or her discoveries?

Potential ethical issues raised by such discoveries could include the following:

- *What concerns do you have about releasing technology to identify high-risk persons for disease before there are breakthroughs in prevention and early treatment of the disease? How could a parent respond when told his or her son or daughter is high-risk for adult alcoholism?*
- *Are there potential negative consequences that could be associated with the status of high-risk for addiction? Could the labeling of such risk have iatrogenic effects? Could it alter the developmental trajectory of those so identified? Would labeling alter family and social relationships?*
- *Could the identification as high-risk for adult addictive disease be used against someone in harmful ways, e.g., mandatory testing for risk and potential denial of health and life insurance or denial of occupational opportunities?*

The ethical mandate to think through and prepare for the potential implications of one's discoveries exists and is inescapable. The burden of consequence and its moral weight cannot be avoided. Einstein always said in interviews that he deeply regretted the day he wrote a letter to President Roosevelt informing him of the German experiments to build nuclear weapons and encouraging a similar program of American research—research that when initiated would lead to the development of the hydrogen bomb, the devastation of Hiroshima and Nagasaki and the birth of nuclear proliferation.

Index

Bibliography

A.A. Guidelines for A.A. Members Employed in the Alcoholism Field. (ND). NY: General Service Office of Alcoholics Anonymous.

Advertising Code for Alcoholism Treatment Programs. (1982). In: *Principles and Practice.* Irvine, CA: National Association of Addiction Treatment Programs, Inc.

Anderson, B. and Blankman, B. (1986) Impaired Counselors: A National Survey. *The Counselor,* 4(5):18-19.

Barker, M. (1996). The Ethical Dilemma of the Two-Hatter. *The Counselor,* 14(3):15-16.

Barry, V. (1983). *Moral Issues in Business.* Belmont, CA: Wadsworth Publishing Company.

Bayles, M. (1989). *Professional Ethics.* Belmont, CA: Wadsworth Publishing Company.

Biggs, D. and Blocker, D. (1987). *Foundations of Ethical Counseling.* NY: Springer Publishing Company.

Bissel, L. and Royce, J. (1987). *Ethics for Addiction Professionals.* Center City, MN: Hazelden Foundation.

Blankman, B. and Anderson, B. (1986). Peer Assistance for Counselors. *The Counselor,* 4(6):8-9.

Bok, S. (1978). *Lying: Moral Choice in Public and Private Life.* NY: Pantheon Books.

Bowie. N. (1982). *Business Ethics.* Englewood-Cliffs, NJ: Prentice-Hall.

Briar, K.H.; Vinet, M. (1985). Ethical Questions Concerning an EAP: Who is the Client? (Company or individual?). In: S.H. Klarreich, J.L. Francek, and C.E. Moore, Eds., *Human Resources Management Handbook: Principles and Practice of Employee Assistance Programs.* NY, NY: Praeger Publishers, pp. 342-359.

Brooks, M.K. (1997). Ethical and Legal Aspects of Confidentiality. In: J.H. Lowinson, P. Ruiz, R.B. Millman and J.G. Langrod, Eds., *Substance Abuse: A Comprehensive Textbook.* Third Edition. Baltimore, MD: Williams and Wilkins, pp. 884-899.

Casebook on Ethical Standards of Psychologists. (1967). Washington, DC: American Psychological Association.

Chapman, C. (1997). Dual Relationships in Substance Abuse Treatment: Ethical Implications. *Alcoholism Treatment Quarterly,* 15(2):73-79.

Christopher, J. (1988). *How to Stay Sober: Recovery Without Religion,* Buffalo, NY: Prometheus Press.

Clinebell, H. (1956). *Understanding and Counseling the Alcoholic through Religion and Psychology.* NY: Abingdon Press.

Code of Ethics. (1979). Arlington, VA: National Association of Alcoholism and Drug Abuse Counselors.

Code of Ethics. (1985). Silver Springs, MD: National Association of Social Workers.

Conroe, R.M. and Schank, J.A. (1989). Sexual Intimacy in Clinical Supervision: Unmasking the Silence. In: Schoener, G. , Milgrom, J., Gonstorek, J, Luepker, E. and Conroe, R. *Psychotherapists' Sexual Involvement With Clients.* Minneapolis, MN: Walk-In Counseling Center.

Daghestani, A.N. (1997). Forensic and Ethical Issues in Addiction Psychiatry. In: N.S. Miller, Ed., *Principles and Practice of Addictions in Psychiatry,* Philadelphia, PA: W.B. Saunders Company, pp. 458-463.

Daghestani, A.N. (1997). Forensic and Ethical Issues. In: N.S. Miller, M.S. Gold, and D.E. Smith, Eds., *Manual of Therapeutics for Addictions.* NY, NY: Wiley-Liss, pp. 325-335.

Ethical Dilemmas in Workplace Counseling: A Casebook. (1996). Houston, TX: Houston Chapter of the Employee Assistance Professionals Association.

Ethical Principles of Psychologists. (1981). Washington, DC: American Psychological Association.

Fillmore, K.M.; Sigvardsson, S. (1988) "A Meeting of the Minds": A Challenge to Biomedical and Psychosocial Scientists on the Ethical Implications and Social Consequences of Scientific Findings in the Alcohol Field. *British Journal of Addiction,* 83(6):609-611.

Gensheimer, L.K.; Ayers, T.S.; Roosa, M.W. (1993). School-based Preventive Interventions for At-risk Populations: Practical and Ethical Issues. *Evaluation and Program Planning,* 16(2):159-167.

Glaser, F.B.; Warren, D.G. (1999). Legal and Ethical Issues. In: B.S. McCrady and E.E. Epstein, Eds., *Addictions: A Comprehensive Guidebook.* NY, NY: Oxford University Press, pp. 399-413.

Grodin, M.; Hingson,R.; Meyers, A. (1988). Ethical and Legal Issues in the Treatment of Alcoholism: Drunk Driving. In: H.N. Barnes, M.D. Aronson, and T.L. Delbanco (Eds.), *Alcoholism: A guide for the primary care physician. Frontiers of Primary Care Series.* NY, NY: Springer-Verlag, pp. 205-210.

Grisso, T. and Vierling, L. (1978). Minors Consent to Treatment: A Developmental Perspective. *Professional Psychology,* 9, (1):117.

Group for the Advancement of Psychiatry. (1990). *A Casebook in Psychiatric Ethics.* NY: Brunner /Mazel Publishers.

Guidelines for Psychologists Conducting Growth Groups. (1973). Washington DC: American Psychological Association.

Haas, L. and Malouf, J. (1989). *Keep Up the Good Work: A Practitioner's Guide To Mental Health Ethics.* Sarasota, FL: Professional Resource Exchange, Inc.

Heyward, C. (1993). *When Boundaries Betray Us.* NY: HarperCollins Publishers.

Hicks, S. and Hammond, E. (1990 Sept/Oct). Alcohol Industry Influence: Two Views. *Student Assistance Journal,* pp. 26-32, 47-49.

Imhof, J. (1991). Countertransference Issues in Alcoholism and Drug Addiction. *Psychiatric Annals,* 21(5):292-306.

Kasl, C. (1992). *Many Roads, One Journey.* NY: Harper Collins.

Kinney, J. (1983). Relapse Among Alcoholics Who are Alcoholism Counselors. *Journal of Studies on Alcohol,* 44(4):744-748.

Kirkpatrick, J. (1986). *Goodbye Hangovers, Hello Life.* NY: Ballantine Books.

Kirkpatrick, J. (1986). *Turnabout.* NY: Bantam Books.

Levine, M. (1972). *Psychiatry and Ethics.* NY: George Braziller.

Lisnow, F. (1989). Is Impairment a Current Issue Facing Alcoholism and Drug Abuse Counselors? *The Counselor,* 7(4):18-19,42.

London, P. (1986). *The Modes and Morals of Psychotherapy.* Washington: Hemisphere Publishing Corporation.

Lubben, P. (1987). Ethics. *The Counselor,* 5(5):12-16.

McCrady, B.S.; Bux, D.A. Jr. (1999). Ethical Issues in Informed Consent with Substance Abusers. *Journal of Consulting and Clinical Psychology,* 67(2):186-193.

McGovern, T., Wright, L., and Wright, N. (1990). National Understanding of the NAADAC Code of Ethics. *The Counselor,* 8(3):37-38.

McGovern, T. (1994). Being Good and Doing Good: An Ethical Reflection Around Alcoholism and Drug Abuse Counseling. *The Counselor,* 12(3):14-18.

McGovern, T. (1996). Ethics and Managed Care: An Interview with Tom McGovern. *The Counselor,* 14(3):25-26.

Manning, G. and Curtis, K. (1988). *Ethics at Work: Fire in a Dark World.* Cincinnati, OH: South-Western Publishing Company.

Masson, J.M. (1990). *Final Analysis: The Unmaking of a Psychoanalyst.* Reading, MA: Addison-Wesley Publishing Company, Inc.

Milgrom, J.H.. (1992). *Boundaries in Professional Relationships: A Training Manual.* Minneapolis, MN: Walk-In Counseling Center.

Moore, R. (1961). Reaction Formation as a Countertransference Phenomenon in the Treatment of Alcoholism. *Quarterly Journal of Studies on Alcohol,* 22:481-486.

Moyer, D. and Moyer, N. (1989). Relapse and the Counselor. *The Counselor,* 7(4):16-17.

NAADAC Ethical Standards of Alcoholism and Drug Abuse Counselors: Specific Principles. (1994). *The Counselor,* 12(3):22-24.

NAPPA: Know What to Look for When Controversial Sources Offer Money. (1995-Jan). *The Addiction Letter,* pp. 4-5.

Paying the Piper: The Effect of Industry Funding on Alcohol Prevention Priorities. (1996). Center for Science in the Public Interest, pp. 1-9. (Http://www.cspinet.org/booze/ppstudy.html)

Perez, P.J. (1993). Navigating Ethical Dilemmas at the Disclosure off Fetal Alcohol Exposure: A Family Therapist's Search for Effective Treatment. *Journal of Family Psychotherapy,* 4(4):53-68.

Petrila, J. (1998). *Ethical Issues for Behavioral Health Care Practitioners and Organizations in a Managed Care Environment.* Substance Abuse and Mental Health Services Administration. DHHS Publication No. 98-3241.

Powell, D. (1992). Ethical and Legal Concerns in Supervision. *The Counselor,* 10(4):24-27.

Schoener, G. (1989). Sexual Involvement of Therapists with Clients After Therapy Ends: Some Observations. In: Schoener, G. , Milgrom, J., Gonstorek, J, Luepker, E. and Conroe, R. (1989). *Psychotherapists' Sexual Involvement With Clients.* Minneapolis, MN: Walk-In Counseling Center.

Selzer, M. (1957). Hostility as a Barrier to Therapy in Alcoholism. *Psychiatric Quarterly,* 31:301-305.

Sherry, P. (1991). Ethical Issues in the Conduct of Supervision. *The Counseling Psychologist,* 19(4):566-584.

St. Germaine, J. (1996). Dual Relationships and Certified Alcohol and Drug Counselors: A National Study of Ethical Beliefs and Behaviors. *Alcoholism Treatment Quarterly,* 14(2):29-44.

Stein, R. (1990). *Ethical Issues in Counseling.* Buffalo, NY: Prometheus Books.

Szasz, T. (1971-Nov). The Ethics of Addiction. *The American Journal of Psychiatry,* 128:5, pp33-37.

Temerlin, M. and Temerlin, J. (1982). Psychotherapy Cults: An Iatrogenic Perversion. *Psychotherapy: Theory Research and Practice,* 19(2): 131-141.

Thibodeaux, M. and Powell, J. (1985-Spring). Exploitation: Ethical Problems of Organizational Power. *SAM Advanced Management Journal,* pp. 42-44.

Thompson, A. (1990). *Guide to Ethical Practice in Psychotherapy.* NY: John Wiley & Sons, Inc.

VandeCreek, L. and Knapp, S. (1989). *Tarasoff and Beyond: Legal and Clinical Considerations in the Treatment of Life-Endangering Patients.* Sarasota, FL: Professional Resource Exchange, Inc.

Wagner, C. (1981). Confidentiality and the School Counselor. *Personnel and Guidance Journal*, 59(5).

Wallack, L. (1984). Practical Issues, Ethical Concerns and Future Directions in the Prevention of Alcohol-related Problems. *Journal of Primary Prevention*, 4(4):199-224.

Wein, C. (1989). Certification Standards and the Impaired Counselor. *The Counselor,* 7(4):9 .

Weinstein, B.A.; Raber, M.J. (1998). Ethical Assessment of Structured Intervention with Chemically Dependent Clients. *Employee Assistance Quarterly*, 13(3):19-31.

White, W. and Tolnai, B. (1997). *The Ethics of Affiliation: The Relationship between Alcohol, Tobacco and Other Drug Prevention Agenbcies and the Alcohol, Tobacco and Pharmaceutical Industries.* Chicago, IL: Prevention First, Inc.

White, W. (1997). *The Incestuous Workplace: Stress and Distress in the Organizational Family.* Center City, MN: Hazelden.

White, W. (1996). *Pathways from the Culture of Addiction to the Culture of Recovery.* Center City, MN: Hazelden.

White, W. (1999). *Slaying the Dragon: The History of Addiction Treatment and Recovery in America.* Bloomington, IL: Lighthouse Training Institute.

White, W. (1990). The Ethics of Competition, Keynote Address, 21st Annual Chemical Dependency Fall Conference, October 25, 1990. Bloomington, MN.

White, W. (1992). A Systems Perspective on Sexual Harassment and Sexual Exploitation. *Proceedings: Sex and Power Issues in the Workplace*, March 20-21, 1992. Bellevue, WA.

Williams, E. et.al., (1990). Counselor Wellness and Impaired Practice: Survey Results of the Kansas Alcoholism and Drug Addiction Counselors Association. *The Counselor,* (1):9, 39-40.

Wrich, J. (1990 Jul/Aug). Ethics and EAP Practice. *EAP Digest,* pp. 36-40, 60-61.

Wright, N. and McGovern, T. (1988). Ethics for the Alcoholism and Drug Abuse Counselor. *The Counselor,* 6(3):17-19.